The Healing Doll Way

A Guided Process Creating Art Dolls for
Self-Discovery, Awareness, and Transformation

The Healing Doll Way

A Guided Process Creating Art Dolls for
Self-Discovery, Awareness, and Transformation

Barb Kobe

ISBN 978-0-9862618-0-0

LCCN: 2020907040

Editors: Angela Wiechmann and Kristopher Kobe

Proofreader: Cindy Read

Designer: Kristopher Kobe

Photography: Barb Kobe and students from her classes

Unless otherwise stated, all photos in this book are credited to the featured artist.

Printed in the United States of America

First Printing: 2018

Second Printing: 2020

24 23 22 21 20   6 5 4 3 2

Barb Kobe

Minneapolis, MN

www.barbkobe.com

www.healingdollway.com

BEAVER'S
POND
PRESS

Beaver's Pond Press, Inc.

7108 Ohms Lane

Edina, MN 55439-2129

(952) 829-8818

www.BeaversPondPress.com

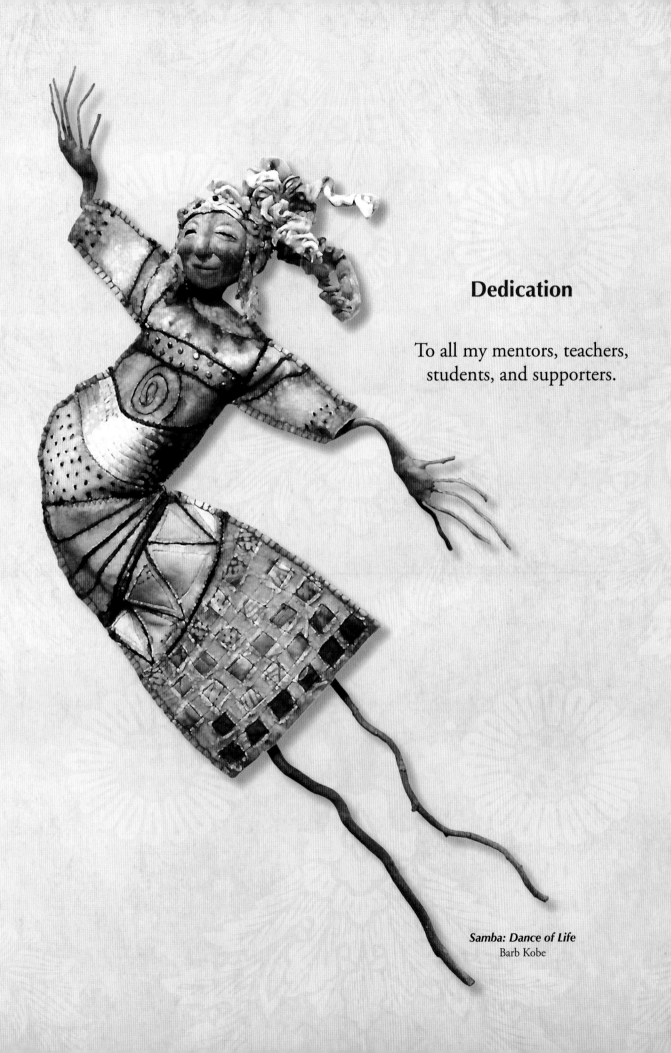

Dedication

To all my mentors, teachers, students, and supporters.

Samba: Dance of Life
Barb Kobe

Acknowledgements

Kathy Wise (creative psychotherapist) for nuturing and supporting me from the conception of the Endagered Feelings Animals through my process of creating, sharing, learning, and growing with my healing and dollmaking

Elinor Peace Bailey for being the midwife to the birth of my dollmaker self and for being an ongoing example of how to live a creative life

Brenna Busse for her ongoing inspiration and enthusiasm for art and healing dolls

Maureen Carlson for being my muse, friend, and mentor

Members of Stonesoup Dollmakers group

Kay Porterfield for her friendship, encouragement, and courage to push me out of my box and put my voice into this book

Pamela Hastings for her guiding light and friendship

Joan Ungar and the members of the Minnesota Art Therapy Association for acknowledgment and support

Carole Gesme for her friendship, for her support, and for saying, "I'll wait until you believe you are an artist"

Jean Illsley Clarke for her teaching and training in group dynamics and multiple ways of learning and growing, and for her ongoing encouragement to step into my knowing and trust my intuition

Marney Makridakis (Artelland coach, teacher, mentor) who embraced and nurtured my creative soul, welcomed me to her tribe, and continues to remind me that healing and transformative artmaking can be fun to make and powerful to experience

Marcy Nelson Garrison for her friendship, coaching, encouragement, and creative nudges

Bill Kobe for forty-plus years of support and love

Kris Kobe for his patience as I learn the process of writing and designing a book, and for his editing, humor, and creative genius

Jane Kobe for her ongoing support of me as I take my dream out into the world

Contents

PLEASE NOTE

The Healing Doll Way contains an intentional, creative, and expressive arts process of making three-dimensional figures called healing dolls. Making these healing dolls may assist in the healing of a physical ailment or disease, in the expression and release of uncomfortable feelings, and in finding balance and becoming more self-aware. When you make art to heal yourself, it can help release negative thoughts and fears that can block your body's ability to heal itself physically, emotionally, and spiritually. It can also help you maximize your bodymind's ability to work harmoniously and in concert with any form of prescribed treatment.

Please keep in mind that this process is in no way meant to be a substitute for conventional medical or emotional treatment. If you are working with a medical professional, please let them know you are participating in this process.

These creative activities incorporate artistic materials and approaches. Please do not judge your dolls based on their artistic qualities. They are meant as vehicles of individual expression, of how the creative energy moves through you.

In the appendix, you will find a list of healing-arts professionals who have taken my Medicine Dolls, Transformative Art of Healing Dolls, and Healing Doll Way online classes. I also included a list of helpful professionals and national organizations that sponsor and promote healing art.

Foreword

by Lani A. Gerity, PhD, DA, ATR

Barbara Kobe has created an extremely beautiful and inspiring book for any artist, art therapist, or art educator working with dolls, puppets, transformation, and/or "healing." When I think back on my own work as an art therapist in the area of body image and recovery from early childhood trauma, everything would have been so much easier if this book had been in my art room. I can imagine the people I worked with poring over it, studying the beautiful images of these mythic characters (Guardian, Scapegoat, Loving Kindness, Talisman, and Inner Healer). The varieties of dolls and personal stories in each chapter of this book are so helpful, so encouraging. Barbara and the individuals who have taken her workshops have created a treasure trove for us.

I should say a bit about my work so you can imagine what a wonderful tool this book is for anyone working through trauma. I was working in a New York City day-treatment center as an art therapist with adults who were traumatized as children. Working with these individuals, I witnessed artwork depicting separation, dissociation, and aggression toward the self. I had an idea: if we could work with the human form in a kind a consistent basis, maybe this aggression toward the self could be diminished and body image issues could be improved. Always willing to experiment, I suggested to a drama therapist that we colead a puppet-making group (so named to create an inclusive environment for those who might be squeamish about making and playing with dolls).

As I watched participants in the puppet-making group, I noticed the creative process was indeed being used to repair disturbed body images, to bring together dissociated parts of the self, and to provide the artists with a sense of history and meaning. I saw amazing transformations: papier-mâché and cloth becoming magical, animated little creatures; a dreary room becoming a wonderful land of possibility; and alienated people transforming into warm, generous human beings.

In a 1995 discussion on the wounded storyteller, Arthur Frank described a process of "colonization," in which a patient hands over his or her body and life narrative to someone else. The individuals I was working with had, as children, been forced into a form of colonization by their abusers. As they matured, they had very little experience in decolonizing themselves, so their childhood colonization was repeated in relationships with peers, family, and psychiatric "experts." However, through making puppets, they could reclaim their agency and construct new narratives from the wreckage of their childhood trauma. Being the "puppet lady" somehow exempted me from the role of psychiatric expert. I was more of a kind person with lots of art supplies.

With no set framework, the puppets and stories developed organically. The resulting tribe and history was fondly referred to as Puppetland over the twelve years I ran the group. These puppets seemed to (like magic) pull empathy from the hardest hearts with the greatest of ease, making Puppetland an amazing healing group. At that time and even after research for a dissertation and a book on the topic, I continued to be baffled by the power of these small creatures.

In creating the puppets and their narratives in a group, changes would be documented, witnessed, and remembered in the group's oral history. Often the original story of trauma and pain could be retold in a more distanced way through the life and struggle of the puppet. This distancing allowed the artist renewed access to create hopes, dreams, and new possibilities, and to conceive of life as a spiritual journey rather than a chaotic series of disasters. These hopes and dreams could become tangible as parts of the puppets, such as clothing, hair, or expressions.

For the group leaders and the participants, the stories they shared seemed to effect change in a mysterious way. Sometimes the group members would put their puppets down and talk about the subversive qualities of the process, that they could feel things shift and change within themselves but were having a hard time identifying the changes. Also, the group narrative itself would evolve as it was handed down to newcomers sitting around the metaphorical campfire. This kind of listening fostered much healing and growth.

On one of these occasions, a particularly beloved intern was leaving. The intern prepared a story about a wise old woman in the forest who provided wisdom and comfort. The wise old woman had gifted her little beads for the puppets, to guide them on their journeys. Although we were losing the intern and her puppet, there was this reparative gift, this archetypal Wise Old Woman (so much like Barb Kobe's Guardian) who had come to life in story. It was clear that the group would benefit from adding this nurturing and caring elder to their community in tangible puppet form. Once the Wise Old Woman puppet was constructed, the group brought her to life. Each member had a chance to hold her or work on her, to discover who she was. We learned that she had simple gifts for each of us, that she was 104 years old, and that she lived in an underground hogan or kiva. She also had knowledge of the earth —its herbs and seasons and life in general. All the aspects of this puppet were warm and generous. From the Wise Old Woman's emergence, I learned about the importance of generosity.

As I look back, remembering various puppets and puppeteers, I can see that we had indeed created analogues of every one of Barb's characters. Although we didn't have the map then that you have now, we were doing the same work. The characters parallel to Barb's Guardian, Loving Kindness, Talisman, and Inner Healer guided the artists and supported them internally, even when they were not in the group. The characters parallel to Barb's Scapegoat gave the artists a way to look at what they considered negative aspects of themselves and even laugh and joke about them a little.

As I read this lovely book, I was compelled to pull out some cardstock and brads to create some fast versions of these characters. And yes indeed, it is still as compelling, healing, and magical as it ever was in Puppetland. If I could give you advice from my experience with this book and my memories of Puppetland, I would encourage you to have an adventurous heart; to take the opportunity this book provides to create the Guardian, Scapegoat, Loving Kindness, Talisman, and Inner Healer dolls; and to think about creating quest narratives for them. See where the adventure leads you and the people you work with.

End note: I first wrote about Puppetland and its inhabitants in the book, *Creativity and the Dissociative Patient: Puppets, Narrative and Art in the Treatment of Survivors of Childhood Trauma.*

Doll Vessel
Barb Kobe

Introduction

An art doll is a personalized, original work of art that a dollmaker uses for self-expression, to mark an experience, to release or contain emotion, or for play, power, or performance. Each doll becomes a tangible reminder of what the dollmaker learned and felt while making the doll. The doll and the dollmaking can be a community-building experience and a reminder of the artist's self-worth, humanness, and connection to life.

This is a book about an artmaking process I created in 1999 using art dolls for healing and transformation. I designed this process while researching and writing a final paper for my last college class at Metropolitan State University in Saint Paul, Minnesota. I titled it *Medicine Dolls—How to Make Healing Dolls for Yourself: An Exploration into the Healing Power of Dollmaking*. My teacher returned my paper unmarked and said, "I think this is brilliant, and you should publish it." I took his suggestion to heart. Two years later, I offered the class at a retreat setting in Jordan, Minnesota. I was amazed at the dolls the participants made, and I was encouraged to continue exploring what happens when women make healing and transformative art dolls.

I taught this kind of transformative dollmaking at Edina Art Center in Edina, Minnesota, for many years. I also offered an online learning experience called the Medicine Doll Project (later changed to just "Medicine Dolls"), an opportunity to learn about healing dolls and how to make them. I invited several friends and anyone else who might be interested to participate. Since 2004, I have offered many more online classes with over five hundred participants.

And now this book details the guided dollmaking process I first used in the Medicine Doll retreat and later within the online classes. Throughout the book are pictures and stories of my healing dolls as well as those of the participants.

This is also a workbook that involves the process of making five art dolls: **Guardian, Scapegoat, Loving Kindness, Talisman, and Inner Healer.**

Holding Compassion for Herself
Barb Kobe

In part 1, I share my personal journey as a healing artist and discuss what it means to make a healing doll. Part 2 focuses on what to know and do before the dollmaking. Part 3 guides you through the creative process of making the five dolls. The appendix and my Pinterest boards offer a variety of creative doll making resources.

My continuing quest is to find innovative artmaking ways to create change in myself and others—from a state of pain, numbness, and disease to one of well-being, continuous growth, and healing. This led me to the creative art therapies that focus on the physical, mental, emotional, and spiritual aspects of healing. My degree in psychology, my studies in human development and group dynamics, and my training in Neuro-Linguistic Programming and hypnosis have all informed me about the mind-body connection and convinced me that our minds and beliefs powerfully influence our ability to heal. With dollmaking, I create healing icons that shift my perceptions and beliefs, produce change, and make a difference in how I engage with and move through my life. It has served as a catalyst that induced my healing processes. These dolls have awakened long-lost stories and created change and transformation in my life.

My ultimate goal is that you entertain the possibility that making healing and transformative dolls for yourself can create positive change and help you deal with pain, struggle, uncomfortable feelings, or life challenges. This process can be an opportunity for you to learn more about yourself, grow in your wisdom, connect with your intuition, and transform an aspect of yourself and your life.

In Touch with Her Intuition
Barb Kobe

Ways to Move through the Process

Healing Doll Muse — Creative Action

I highly suggest that you create a Healing Doll Way journal: you can write about your process, include the stories that come from your dolls, and even glue in pictures of them. The doll above is called *Playing with Her Imagination*. She sits on a chair that is a doll as well. She will be your Healing Doll Muse, providing guidance throughout this process. When you see her on a page, she invites you to take Creative Actions: play, write, mind-map, draw, make doll, etc.

Designing Your Original Healing Dolls

When I started making art dolls, I knew how to sew and manipulate fabric; and as an experienced graphic artist, I knew how to paint and draw—basically, I already had some skills that I could use to make dolls. After doing the research paper on dollmaking and healing, and after seeing art dolls in gallery shows, I knew I wanted to make my own.

At first, I admired dollmakers who used fabric, then I discovered others who were using a variety of materials. I practiced and played with the materials and the process of making art dolls. Along the way—through the showing and selling of my dolls, as well as much work and study—I realized that my dollmaking was healing for me. That's when I decided to start making dolls specifically as part of a healing process, starting with my own.

Using Patterns

I do not provide specific patterns for healing dolls made as part of the Healing Doll Way process, and yet original, one-of-a-kind healing dolls have been created in my classes for over fifteen years. These dolls are made from a variety of materials, limited only by the imagination, curiosity, energy, and persistence of their creators as they practice an awareness of human qualities and features both inside and outside of themselves. There are so many great resources to assist you in making your healing dolls. My favorite resource for this is Susanna Oroyan's book *Anatomy of a Doll: The Fabric Sculptor's Handbook*. There are other resources listed on page 232.

Elinor Peace Bailey says a pattern is a tool; it just shows you what will happen if you follow the directions—it can save you some work. A good pattern opens doors (instead of closing them). In the beginning, I flipflopped between using patterns—primarily those of Elinor as well as Pamela Hastings—and playing with body forms made from sticks and roots.

In *Dollmaking as a Transformative Process*, Pamela Hastings says the following about making original healing dolls:

- Your doll will express your reality and life story.

- The doll you make is not you; it is a vehicle for making the invisible visible, and therefore can be easy to change.

- In the safe environment of dollmaking, you can take your feelings out to play, have the power to accept and acknowledge them, and go on with your life in greater freedom.

- You can continue to haul emotional baggage around with you for the rest of your life, or you can salute it and put it to rest, even transform the anger for change, the sadness into a full range of feeling, and the despair into hope for small possibilities.

- Approach your dollmaking materials with no preconceived notions about what will come out. Limit your material choices to avoid distraction.

- The aim is not to make "great art." The conscious effort of making a "beautiful" or "artistic" piece can interfere with allowing yourself to play and perform feats for your amazement and amusement.

* The above list was adapted/paraphrased with Pamela's permission.

The Importance of Character — Dealing with Depth, Emotion, and Power

While the design of the dolls is important, what is even more important is the character, personality, and emotional expression. These emotional healing dolls invite you to think about aspects of the human condition and draw attention to the feelings the dolls express. The more you think about the design, construction, and depth of a piece, the more likely you will have an evocative or provocative reaction capable of opening your eyes to possibilities and creating change.

Making healing dolls is using your creative energy. If you believe you are not creative, this is a big opportunity for you to rethink that belief. There are two parts to everyone's creativity: one is your creative ability, and the other is your creative power. Both of these are true whether you currently believe it or not.

Creative power is having the capability and will to manifest a creative idea. Creative ability is possessing the knowledge and understanding to direct the flow of your creative power (or energy) to manifest what you want. In 2018 I created an e-book called *Inner Selfies*, which offers ways to learn about your creative powers by making Inner Selfie paper dolls. This e-book is available to you at no cost if you have purchased *The Healing Doll Way*. You can access it if you are a member of the Healing Doll Way Book Club private group on Facebook, or by emailing me at bkobe@healingdollway.com.

How Long Will It Take to Complete the Process? (Make All Dolls)

There is no way for me to know how long it will take you to complete the process. In the past, I have offered the class in three-, six-, and twelve-month formats. Some people were able to get absolutely every doll done, but most did not. It depends on a lot of variables, especially what is happening in your life as you move through the process. If you are interested in making your healing dolls with support from me and a group, you can sign up for the year-long Healing Doll Way online class. Visit www.healingdollway.com for details.

Moving Through the Process

Here are several ways I imagine you could move through the process:

- Start at the beginning, read each page, do all the Healing Doll Muse activities, and make all the dolls in three-dimensional form.

- Do the same as above, only make paper dolls instead.

- Read the introduction, skip everything else, and go directly into making the five dolls.

- Jump right into the process and make dolls in the order presented, or in any order that works best for you.

- Move through the process your way and do all the art, dolls, and journaling in your visual journal—using paint, markers, and collage.

- Move through the process your way and use the same pattern, or material (like sticks), for each doll, but change colors, facial expressions, and embellishments.

- Move through the process and post stories and pictures on the Healing Doll Way Book Club private Facebook group.

- Move through the process with an art buddy.

- Move through the process and create a dance, story, song, or rap (or any other creative-arts modalities) inspired by images that come to you for each of the archetypes.

- Collage images that represent the five archetypes and any other images that come to you while moving through the process, then create a card deck using the images you come up with.

Part 1:
Healing Art

"What matters most is experiencing your feelings and gaining insights."
Lucia Capacchione

Me with my wild woman puppet, Ruby Roja, and other dolls

Endangered Feelings Animals with the Fulls (first design)

16

How I Became a Healing Artist

Dolls have always been a part of my life. Each Christmas I would receive a doll as a gift from my parents along with handmade doll clothes from my grandmother. I played with my collection of dolls, dressing and re-dressing them and then putting them on display in my room. I had bride dolls, fashion dolls, one of the first Barbie dolls, and baby dolls that drank water and wet their diapers.

I grew up in a creative family: my grandmother was a seamstress, my mother did needle arts, and my father built things out of wood. I loved the visual arts. I painted murals for school plays, musical productions, and dances. After one year in college focusing on art, I entered the work world and spent over twenty years in the fields of engineering drafting, graphic arts, advertising, and print and multi-media production. During this time, I taught myself to sew and made my own clothes.

My career as a professional graphic artist changed with the birth of my children in the early 1980s. I spent my time creating art with my son and daughter, encouraging them to express themselves. But at the same time, I would say, "I'm not an artist," and I never took ownership of my creative life.

My journey of embracing my creative life began when people saw my creative potential and encouraged me to take risks. This involved taking small creative steps, then being gently mentored and nudged to take more. Each creative step sparked my curiosity and led me to want to know more about creativity and myself. I noticed that when I did art with my children, I gave them permission to be creative, to take risks (color outside of the lines, use unusual color combinations, or add three more things to a drawing), and to find out "what happens if . . ." I was beginning to give myself the same permissions.

In 1989, I created a set of characters to teach my children about emotional communication. They were called the Endangered Feelings Animals: Angerilla, Crynoceros, Trifearatops, and Happypotomus. Later the designs took the form of puppets. I also created other little soft-sculpture dolls called Numbfull and the Fulls: Tearfull, Fearfull, Ragefull, Joyfull, Stressfull, Powerfull, Shamefull, and Peacefull.

My mother's first and only childhood doll

Mom made this Betsy McCall doll for me from a pattern

One of my baby dolls had a knob on top of her head that I could rotate to change the doll's expression. Who knew this would foreshadow a thread of my creative work as an adult?

Numbfull and the Fulls
Tearfull, Shamefull, Numbfull, Stressfull, Powerfull,
Joyfull, Ragefull, Fearfull, Peacefull

I used my puppets to talk to my children about their feelings. I noticed that a doll or puppet was a useful, nonthreatening tool to aid in teaching about feelings and emotional communication, to transform beliefs, and to affirm the expression of feelings. I showed the puppets to a group of friends who were art therapists, social workers, and teachers. Their enthusiasm for the characters and for my message was encouraging.

One of the social workers, who worked in Minneapolis elementary schools, created a list of contacts for me so I could share the puppets with groups of schoolchildren in their classrooms. I had never done anything like that before and accepted the invitation as a creative risk, to see what would happen. The children loved the characters and shared feeling stories from their own lives. I remember one third-grade girl standing up in the middle of the presentation and saying, "You mean we're supposed to have feelings?"

I realized making art
changed my emotional state. And if it worked for me, it might create the same response in others.

A year after the puppets' conception, I started getting purchase requests from teachers, social workers, and therapists. I had the original patterns for the prototypes, so I began taking orders, sewing sets, and selling them. As I sewed each of these soft sculptures, I noticed I was working through my feelings—anger issues when making Angerilla, grief and sadness with Crynoceros, fear with Trifearatops, and joy and happiness with Happypotomus. As I created these feeling faces, my face and body muscles shifted into the same expressions.

I was invited to show the feeling puppets at a meeting of the Minnesota Art Therapy Association. After my presentation, the characters and I were welcomed into the small community of art therapists. I began to attend meetings and volunteered to use my graphic arts skills to produce their newsletter and website.

I also attended a Healing Your Inner Child workshop by art therapist Lucia Capacchione. She introduced a creative process in which participants wrote and drew using both of their hands. I loved the process of asking questions with my dominant hand, then getting answers from an inner part of myself by writing or drawing with my nondominant hand. I began to use this dialog technique with my feeling characters, journaling in their "voices" using my nondominant hand. I felt I belonged to this community of art therapists and started reading books about art therapy as wells as making strategies and processes with myself.

As I used Angerilla, Crynoceros, Trifearatops, and Happypotomus with groups of children in schools, I noticed a similarity between having a conversation with myself using my nondominant handwriting and using puppets as spokespeople for my feelings. I would speak as a puppet, giving the feeling a voice, and the children would have a conversation with the puppet. I was surprised and delighted by the stories the children told and amazed by the number of children—and adults—who seemed to have never talked about their feelings.

I used Numbfull and the Fulls to talk about stuffing feelings. I would walk into a classroom with the little Fulls stuffed underneath my shirt. As I pulled each one out, I would talk about that specific feeling and what it looked like, sounded like, even smelled liked. I would then ask what would happen if someone tried to stuff the feeling away. I felt as if I were in some sort of emotional learning laboratory; each visit to a classroom added more to my internal database of emotions and feelings.

I was beginning to see evidence that art—in the form of nonthreatening three-dimensional objects such as puppets—could be used as an instrument for learning, transformation, change, and growth. I believe these characters were my first healing dolls.

A drawing made with
my nondominant hand

"Every person who comes and goes makes his or her unique contribution. When therapists joined the process, they invested it with their own psychology. Jungians made it Jungian; Buddhists made it Buddhist; artists, poets, ritualists, and storytellers have all offered their gifts."

Cassandra Light
Way of the Doll

Shaman Dancer
Barb Kobe

Connecting to Spirit
Barb Kobe
(Made from an Elinor Peace Bailey pattern)

Earth Elemental Root Doll
Barb Kobe

Nature of Belonging
Brenna Busse

Along this journey, I had a variety of other experiences that convinced me of the healing power of visual metaphor. I learned about metaphors in Neuro-Linguistic Programming and hypnosis training. I taught classes at professional seminars, workshops, elementary schools, and community centers. The subjects included parenting, self-esteem, emotional intelligence, and creativity using art and visual metaphor. I continued my study of psychology and art therapy, which uses the visual language of artistic expression to communicate a person's stories and beliefs, helping them to transform and heal.

My focus on dollmaking began with the discovery of the book *Mother Plays with Dolls* by Elinor Peace Bailey. Elinor's book, which I read in one evening, filled a creative void brought about by mass-producing set after set of feeling characters. I knew my creations were making a difference in children's lives. But at the same time, producing them was draining me of vital energy.

Elinor's discussion of a psychological theory called transactional analysis was familiar to me. I had studied it, taught it in parenting classes, and used what I learned with myself and my family. She wrote:

> *I have used the doll as a tool to free my personality. Dolls have enormous potential for amusing their makers and, in the process, for offering insight. Something so benign can take the danger out of imagining. Playing with dolls is a safe way to explore change and make discoveries; and play, after all, is the very center of the creative act.*

I wrote a letter to Elinor expressing my gratitude for her book and her inspiration. She called me. When I asked her what I should do about my exhaustion with making the puppets, she said, "If you're tired of doing them, stop. Something else will open up."

Nature had a big influence on my dollmaking.
Each fall, I would harvest different kinds of roots, wash them, and hang them up to dry on the clothesline. I incorporated these roots as body parts, many times with the roots coming out of the head.

Not long after this, I visited a gallery showing of dolls by Brenna Busse of Minneapolis. On the wall next to each was a story of the doll's meaning. Brenna's dolls and their images and stories spoke to me. I felt as if I were back in my childhood Catholic church, visiting the stations of the cross. My heart opened up, and the stories woke up a lost creative part of me. I walked away from the gallery saying, "I could make these kinds of dolls. I could do this. No—I *can* do this!" I began by imitating Brenna's style, making clay faces, wrapping the body with fabric, and embellishing with beads, sticks, seed pods, shells, feathers, and stones. Later I would stray from Brenna's style and start developing my own.

Wisdom of the Grandmothers was my first big doll. I used my interest in Native American culture for inspiration. She had a simple cloth body form. Her face was made from polymer clay, and her body was wrapped in torn fabrics. I loved the process of making her—making the face, tearing the fabric, putting colors together, and embellishing her with symbols. I was connecting with my creative self, and I wanted to create more.

Six months after my conversation with Elinor, I received two invitations: The first was from Maureen Carlson, a recognized expert in polymer clay and doll-making who lives in the Twin Cities area. She invited me to be part of a new doll group she was starting, which later became known as Stonesoup Dollmakers. Second, the Urban Dollmakers in Minneapolis–Saint Paul invited me to submit slides for a doll show they were putting together. I joined the doll group, and they accepted my dolls into the show. I was starting to feel confident about my work and was developing my own style.

Nature had a big influence on my dollmaking. While walking through my back-yard garden, I came across a strawberry root. I gently pulled it from the earth and washed it off. I put a small polymer-clay face on it, wrapped it in a variety of colorful fibers, used some lamb's wool for hair, and attached a bell. She was complete. The root theme was my inspiration for the next three years. Each fall, I would harvest different kinds of roots, wash them, and hang them up to dry on the clothesline. I incorporated these roots as body parts, many times with the roots coming out of the head.

Around the same time, Clarissa Pinkola Estés's *Women Who Run with the Wolves* was published. I loved reading the stories and her Jungian analysis. I was delighted when I read,

> *Dolls are one of the symbolic treasures of the instinctual nature. For centuries, humans have felt that dolls emanate both a holiness and mana—an awesome and compelling presence which acts upon persons, changing them spiritually. Dolls are believed to be infused with life by their makers. They are used as markers of authority and talismans to remind one of one's own power.*

I read the Vasalisa story. It is about the relationship between a young girl named Vasalisa and a small doll she receives at her mother's deathbed. She keeps the doll in her pocket, and the doll's voice guides and helps her as she encounters challenging adventures in her world. The doll is a symbol of protective love from her mother and becomes the voice of Vasalisa's intuition. The story grew more and more meaningful as I came to believe that my art, my dollmaking, would help me connect to my intuition, my power, my wisdom, and myself.

Estés says the Vasalisa story represents a woman letting go of the "good little girl" and discovering her wild side or authentic self. I was particularly fascinated

Wisdom of the Grandmothers
Barb Kobe

"Basically, dolls are complex fetishes. The maker is intentionalizing spirit and meaning into the doll."

Cassandra Light
Way of the Doll

Strawberry Root Doll
Barb Kobe

21

Baba Yaga
Barb Kobe

Spider Woman
Barb Kobe

by a character in the story called Baba Yaga. She was mean and nasty—she invited me to explore those parts of myself stuffed away in a dark corner of my mind and imagination. Baba Yaga has her roots in the stories and culture of the Slavic countries of Eastern Europe. The word *baba* is a form of "grandmother" in Russian and is a term of respect for elder women in general. Baba Yaga can be a good symbol to study when experiencing darkness, depression, or spiritual emptiness. My fascination with her was an invitation to look into the dark mirror of my soul and seek an understanding of the energies coming through me as I created my dolls.

My dollmaking helped me work through emotional issues of pain, loss, shame, and grief. At the same time, I was learning about women's developmental stages. There was an awakening happening within me. I was becoming conscious of the disempowering messages that educational institutions, family, culture, and the media use to define what it means to be a woman. I was forty-eight years old, and my daughter was an adolescent, yet it seemed both of us were struggling with the same power issues and questions: Who am I now? How do I separate being the mother/daughter and being myself? How do I separate from my mother/daughter and still be loved? How can I stand in my own creative power? While reawakening lost parts of myself through my dolls, I came across a number of authors, art therapists, and other influential people whose written work supported what I was beginning to believe about my work. They include Julia Cameron's *Artist's Way*, Pat Allen's *Art Is a Way of Knowing*, Barbara Ganim's *Art and Healing*, Dawna Markova's *No Enemies Within*, Sandra G. Shuman's *Source Imagery*, and Karla McLaren's *Language of Emotions*.

Each doll I created expanded my emotional literacy and communication skills with myself and others. I was getting comfortable talking about feelings and making dolls that expressed my emotions—except anger and fear. If I made a doll face that showed those feelings, I would destroy it, only to have it appear again in another attempt. I wondered what was going on with me. To tell the truth, I wondered what was *wrong* with me.

I first encountered the concept of shadow in a psychology class in college. Psychologist Carl Jung said our shadow is the person we would rather not be. I wanted to know more. I learned from Debbie Ford's book *The Dark Side of the Light Chasers*:

> *Our shadow, formed long ago, contains all the parts of ourselves that we have tried to hide or deny, the parts we believe are not acceptable to our family, friends, and most importantly, ourselves. It is made up of everything that annoys, horrifies or disgusts us about other people or about ourselves. It holds all that we try to hide from those we love and all that we don't want other people to think about us or find out about us.*

I wondered if this was what was showing up in the faces I created.

Each doll I created expanded my emotional
literacy and communication skills with myself and others. I was getting comfortable talking about my feelings and making dolls that expressed my emotions—except anger and fear.

I attended a workshop presented by William Miller, author of *Your Golden Shadow*. He talked about the shadow as the part of ourselves associated with all that is negative in us and that we try to avoid. He pointed out that a shadow aspect may also contain positive parts of ourselves he calls "gold." He said, "We are powerless to deal with it (the shadow) until we make it conscious." He continued, "Our task is to reconcile the opposites that we discover—to somehow bring the persona trait and its opposite shadow trait together into a new entity." This was what my dollmaking was doing for me. My creative work was changing my self-perception and helping me deal with conflicts and problems in new ways. Each new doll—even the scary and angry ones—opened me up to new possibilities and helped me become more whole, allowing me to find greater fulfillment in my life.

No Enemies Within by Dawna Markova is one of my all-time favorite books. It is about turning shadow aspects into allies. Markova says,

> *Each of us is the ultimate healer of her condition. We can use creative tools to uncover the map to our paths. Every soul is born with something to give, something to experience and something to learn. There is a creative force at the very center of each of our beings—a flow of energy, pushing, stretching, and demanding to be transformed into the world. No matter what challenge we face, be it of body, heart, or soul, the first stage of healing is withdrawal into ourselves.*

> *We have to learn to switch our allegiance, from being loyal to outside people, situations and toxic substances, to becoming loyally committed to finding the things that nurture the sacredness in us, silencing the tired, old voices in our heads that moan about how selfish and inappropriate we are being. The truth needs to be given voice and image and movement.*

I had set a goal of finishing my Bachelor of Arts degree at age fifty. I had two electives remaining, so I decided to take a writing class. The assignment was to choose a subject I was interested in, research it, and write an academic paper. I chose the topic of dollmaking from a perspective of personal growth and healing. My thesis was titled "The act of making a doll can take the dollmaker through a process of creative imagination, healing, and growth."

Shame on Me
Barb Kobe

"The dolls you create begin to express your authentic self, full of creativity, enthusiasm, and vitality. Through the creative work you become a whole person with a range and depth of feelings. You come to trust your intuition and cultivate an inner life shaped by awareness."

Unknown Source

Golden Shadow
Barb Kobe

23

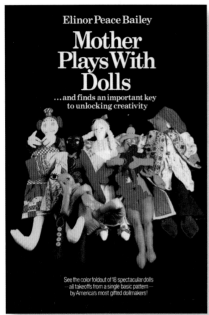

"So the doll, that errant bit of childhood whimsy, the ultimate sandbox, can be the symbol, the place to return to. Gathered in her little-girl dreams a woman can find the strength to imagine."

Elinor Peace Bailey

I began my research for the paper by searching for female artists who were using dollmaking for healing and transformation. I had read Elinor Peace Bailey's *Mother Plays With Dolls*, met her through a couple of workshops put on by the Stonesoup Dollmakers group, and felt inspired by her encouragement to move forward with my dream. I found articles about her in such magazines as *Contemporary Doll*, *Soft Dolls & Animals*, and *Doll Life*. She also had a newsletter for her national cloth doll organization, the Association of People Who Play with Dolls. I was encouraged by reading about Elinor in the February 1993 issue of *Doll Life*:

> *The importance of the doll is the process of making the doll. They are useless when finished. Because they have no special use, their makers can be totally free in a creative sense, experimenting with fabric, technique, line, form, color, and expressing their ideas in a tangible form. Some of the ideas are emotions that the maker is trying to work through. Sometimes it's a death or illness or larger concepts of God and universe. People have used dolls for these purposes. It's their very inconsequential nature that makes them consequential. Dolls have allowed people to take an uncontainable idea or an idea that stretches beyond their ability to hold it and put it into something diminutive that they can cope with.*

With Elinor leading the way and serving as one of my mentors, I started to seek out the dollmakers whom she "played with." I followed the creative bread crumbs—I researched every dollmaker that I read about in Elinor's newsletter as well as those I read about in magazines, books, and professional journals.

Susanna Oroyan came to a Stonesoup Dollmakers workshop and introduced her book *Anatomy of a Doll*. Susanna was an inspiration to meet, and she too encouraged me to follow my heart. Her book showed many ways to make an original, one-of-a-kind (OOAK) doll. Although I didn't see anything like my dolls in her books, I saw almost every way to design and make original dolls, along with many how-to illustrations and photographs of her and other dollmakers' dolls. I continued to seek out other dollmakers, and I felt as if I belonged to this tribe of creative women. I was learning the tools to use to teach other women.

Dollmaking was becoming a healing medicine
for my body, mind, and soul. The thought of taking it out of my life was inconceivable. Making dolls gave me a home, a path, a purpose.

Cassandra Light is the founder of the Way of the Doll School in California, as well as an artist and art therapist who creates dolls and masks for use in performance art. (She no longer offers classes.) I read about her dolls (which she calls "archetypes") and her book *Way of the Doll: The Art and Craft of Personal Trans-*

Doll I made from one of
Susanna Oroyan's patterns

formation in the November/December 1989 issue of *Yoga Journal*. Up to that point, she was the only person I had encountered who was teaching a year-long dollmaking process for transformation and healing.

I inhaled every word Cassandra wrote about dollmaking and transformation and studied her process of inviting participants to engage in a yearlong creative circle as they made a doll. I was gathering the threads of my theory that dollmaking can be transformative and healing. I read:

> *Way of the Doll is the ultimate guide for self-discovery and evaluation. In its purest artistic form it is an avenue to reveal your most hidden talents and ultimate joys. There is sorrow and growth in the course that seems to last a lifetime, but only interjects at points of pure light in the soul. It is a lifetime of revelation molded in mixed media and color . . . it will never allow you to fall back, but to bless yourself a thousand times and move onward into the next phase of growth.*
>
> *These dolls are like seeds in that they contain all the processes—rational, imaginative, conscious, and unconscious—that later evolve into separate parts: art, science, pragmatism, and spirituality, but are in the beginning united in what, for children, is the basic experience of play.*

These words resonated with me. I had had so many of the emotions and experiences that Cassandra talked about. I could relate to the archetypes her students were creating. Even though I never met Cassandra in person, I felt her work informed mine and mentored me forward.

While looking at the pictures of dolls in Susanna Oroyan's books, I would pause at the dolls of one dollmaker more than others—Pamela Hastings. Her dolls were more abstract than most I was seeing, more outwardly emotional and courageous. I felt as if she had her finger on the pulse of healing and dollmaking. She was in the process of writing a book on the subject and was looking for stories and pictures. I contacted her.

We had a great conversation about dollmaking, transformation, and healing, and we discovered that we and our dolls had a lot in common. She lived on the East Coast of the United States and said she was planning a visit to her mother in Waterloo, Iowa. I was planning on visiting my mother in Davenport, Iowa, at the same time. We arranged to meet in person in Waterloo. We have been friends since then—yet another mentor and cheerleader.

Pamela sees her art and dollmaking as part of a journey of self-discovery. She believes that when people make dolls, they make an image that represents their own interpretation of reality. She says:

"Our dolls are shaped by the verbal 'clay' of these primal telling and retellings . . . every doll is a symbolic poem of the soul."
Cassandra Light
Way of the Doll

Nightmare (left) and
Celebrating Strengths (right)
Pamela Hastings

The Queen of May and Her Familiar
Pamela Hastings

When this is made visible through a doll, we can then choose whether or not this doll represents the particular reality we want to support with our lives and energy. The doll becomes a functional tool, to help us see our own lives and goals more clearly. The doll that you make is not you. It is a vehicle for making the invisible visible, and therefore easier to change, especially within a safe dollmaking environment.

"The journey inward called the spirit of soul and the deep mind, is healing. Healing comes to us from within, our own healing resources are freed to allow our immune system to operate optimally, and that is always how we heal."

Barbara Ganim
Art & Healing

Breasts: Triumph of Love over Change
Pamela Hastings

"When we create our experience of reality in a concrete form, through a doll or other symbolic work the finished product is not necessarily a work of art, but a functional tool to help us see our own lives and goals more clearly. The doll you create is NOT YOU. It is a vehicle for making the invisible visible and therefore easier to change. At times scary, ugly, or unpleasant images and words may come pouring from your hands. This is a Good Thing, and not a sign that you should be immediately institutionalized. We all contain a whole Pandora's Box of Gremlins, but in the safe environment of doll making we can take the little suckers out to play."

Pamela Hastings
Dollmaking as a Transformative Process

Having created the Endangered Feelings Animals and Numbfull and the Fulls, I knew that creating three-dimensional puppets and dolls could help me and others befriend feelings. In Pamela's book *Doll Making as a Transformative Process*, she mirrored back my knowing of the subject of dollmaking and befriending feelings.

As Pamela explained, we can "take dolls out to play, and then we have the power to accept and acknowledge them, and go on with our lives in greater freedom." She suggested that we could haul around our feelings like baggage, or salute them for the service they have performed, or convert their energy into change, possibility, transformation, growth, and healing.

I felt heard, witnessed, simply from reading about Pamela's experience with her dollmaking. With Pamela as another mentor, supporting and encouraging me to develop my concept and work, I was almost ready to write my paper.

We can haul around our feelings
like baggage, or we can salute them for the service they have performed by converting their energy into change, possibility, transformation, growth, and healing.

I titled my paper "The Dollmaking Circle: A Process of Personal Growth and Healing." In my research, I looked for an existing unending circular process upon which to base a design for a circular dollmaking process. I found the Native American medicine wheel to be the closest to what I was searching for. I liked that it used symbols from nature and that there were four distinct directions, or focal points. I believed this process invited and encouraged dollmakers to explore their range of perception through the dolls they made and, in doing so, reach a deeper level of understanding of themselves.

During a Friday night Stonesoup Dollmakers meeting, I shared my paper with Maureen. She liked it. She invited me to teach the dollmaking circle process at her new creativity center in Jordan, Minnesota. Within a month, I offered a class at Maureen's center and was surprised that it filled up. I began teaching what I believed was possible, that dollmaking could create change and growth in the dollmaker.

As I taught and facilitated the curriculum, I watched my students make their dolls. I did not give them patterns; they created dolls totally from their imaginations using a variety of art materials I provided. I noticed they were getting in touch with healing issues such as grief, loneliness, anger, and fear during the creative process. I started wondering about the connections between psychology, neurology, and immunology. I wanted to bring about better understand of the interplay of the mind, body, and emotions—or, collectively, the *bodymind*—and explore that realm using guided imagery.

In my research, I learned that doll-type figures have been used in healing rituals throughout much of human history. Medicine men and women created doll figures of human and animal forms because they believed these figures held symbolic meaning and influence with the great mysteries of life. These dolls were fetishes and totems that served important purposes in ritual and play. They became contact points to the inner person and the unknown. These first doll-makers believed their lifelike creations represented a connection to, and the ability to control, life force. I theorized that maybe my dolls were similar to these early healing dolls in that making dolls gave me a conscious or subconscious connection to healing energies.

Turtle
Barb Kobe

With this in mind, I decided to explore this possibility of connecting to my healing energies. I started making a doll focusing on healing an imbalance in my digestive tract. I cut some branches from a curly willow and contorted them into an interesting body shape. I wrapped the shape with batting to create bulk, then wrapped the body with purple fabric. I looked at the organs of the digestive system in an anatomy book. I made organ shapes out of solid-colored fabric and appliquéd them to the corresponding positions on the doll's body. I then sewed on orange beads, following the lines of the meridians—the body's energy pathways. On the back of the body, I put a symbol for the spine, knowing all nerves in the body connect there. I made the doll's face out of Crayola Model Magic and placed a veil over it, symbolizing "going within." I added multicolored hair, representing a connection with the mind.

These dolls were fetishes and totems
that served important purposes in ritual and play.
They became contact points to the inner
person and the unknown.

I held her at arm's length, looked at her, and asked, "Are you done?" I heard an immediate answer from a voice I had never really paid attention to before: "No, she's not. You have to wrap a yellow snake around her." I thought this was odd, but I followed the directive. I formed a yellow snake by wrapping clothesline with yellow fabric and using beads for the tail and head (picture on page 29).

As the Garden Grows
Barb Kobe

27

Moving Toward the Light
Barb Kobe

The Saint:
Bringing Back Parts of Herself
Barb Kobe

Again, I thought it was odd that I was led to put this yellow snake on this doll. I dug out my copy of Jeanne Achterberg's *Imagery in Healing*. I intuitively turned to the page that said that "a yellow snake represents women's healing power." As far as I was concerned, this supported my theory: when we are ill with a physical or mental problem, or when we need to grow, we can start to heal ourselves with art—by opening up to our inner voices of challenge and change and letting their messages emerge.

The yellow snake was my message: *trust your body to guide you*. The doll stood as a reminder to take care of my body and choose healthy and nourishing food. I have kept this doll. She hangs on my wall as a metaphor of how I digest life and how my intuition is a powerful guide in my creative process.

It didn't take too long for the house to fill up with dolls. My husband felt as if he were being watched. He suggested moving some of the "girls" out by having a show. I organized a show at a local art gallery and invited a friend to show her art quilts with my dolls. Some of the people who attended the opening talked to me about the meaning the dolls held for them. I knew the dolls meant something to me, but the possibility of them appealing to others surprised me. I sold all but a few of the dolls and was soon getting commissions for new dolls. Other people wanted to know how to make the dolls and if I were offering any classes.

Dollmaking was becoming a healing medicine for my body, mind, and soul. The thought of taking it out of my life was inconceivable. Making dolls gave me a home, a path, and a purpose. I knew that as I created my dolls, I was healing.

At first, I was excited by the response to my work, but then I got scared. I contacted Elinor Peace Bailey again. This time, I asked if she had any thoughts about how I might handle this unexpected attention. She said,

> *I hear your hunger to push your ideas and find limits. That is the stream from which you will find spiritual nourishment, never cease to do that. Do not let your present success own you and keep you where you are. Get a real job before you do that. Second, if you teach, teach with everything you have, and hold back nothing, or do not teach at all. If you are continually in search*

of new and fresh ideas, there is nothing to fear in the classroom. Your students can imitate your style but they cannot be you. That is your job, and it is dynamic, not static. As for marketing your work, make sure that you know all any rep might know about HOW and TO WHOM and HOW MUCH. That way you need never be dependent on someone else to do what you will always do best and with the greatest passion.

My inner work of healing, which came through my doll-making, became my outer work of teaching dollmaking and creating commissioned dolls. Each person I taught and each doll I created led me to learn more about myself. My healing path had taken me out of the safety of my studio and into the unknown of the community.

A woman contacted me to make a doll for her niece, who was graduating from high school. She was part of a large family of multigenerational women who assembled at a family cabin to celebrate their teen members' transitioning from adolescence to adulthood. They created a ritual that included special food, candles, and taking turns saying well-wishes and prayers for the girl moving on. She wanted a doll to be part of the ritual. I had studied women's development in college and knew the value of ritual in women's lives. In some small way, I felt honored to be asked to participate in this giving ceremony. For several years, I was asked to make such a doll for the next daughter, niece, or granddaughter.

Grounded
Barb Kobe

Digesting My Life
Barb Kobe

29

Garden Icon
Barb Kobe

Trust and Let Go
Barb Kobe

Creating commissioned dolls was a new experience. As a child, I was repeatedly told I was overly sensitive. I remember getting my feelings hurt easily and wanting to hide away in the safety of my room, which was full of dolls, crayons, and coloring books. My dollmaking had helped me get in touch with this early sensitivity, and I was becoming more sensitive and intuitive with each doll I created. This was especially so when making a healing doll for someone else.

For the first few commissioned dolls, I asked each person for minimal information, such as who the doll was for and what it would symbolize. But as I made each doll, I would intuit so much of the recipient's story that I would get overwhelmed. I had to find a way to focus on the core issue the doll represented. I became aware that my way of understanding another's issue was to feel what the other person was feeling and, through that feeling, create a visual metaphor. The people ordering the dolls were surprised when I unconsciously used symbols that connected with some aspect of their lives: ruby slippers on a doll for a woman who collected them or a mirror for someone reflecting on a deep aspect of herself.

Each person I taught and each doll I created led me to learn more about myself. My healing path had taken me out of the safety of my studio and into the unknown of the community.

I began to feel stressed from making dolls for others. It was as though I were being unconsciously empathic to the point of self-destruction. I needed to set limits and boundaries for myself. I developed a list of ten questions (The Ten Questions, page 222), which have changed slightly over the years, to create a structure for the design process as well as a boundary to protect myself from being overly empathic. With feedback from the questions, I could use my creative energies more efficiently and refine my focus.

I believed that when I created a healing doll, I entered into a collaborative agreement between the person wanting healing and myself as a healing artist. When I made contact with the person the doll was for—whether in person, by telephone, in writing, or psychically—I received intuitive inspiration and became part of a supportive group focusing on that individual's healing process.

While making healing dolls for others, I realized I was becoming more aware of my own physical and emotional healing issues. I decided that if I were to continue doing this type of work, it would be important to take good care of my body, mind, and spirit. I started getting regular bodywork, worked through some old issues with a family therapist, and made my own healing dolls. As with all healing work, one thing led to another. My art was leading me to a personal healing issue that would challenge what I believed about my work.

In 1999, shortly after receiving my Bachelor of Arts degree in psychology, I began to experience pain in my left hip. At first, the pain was sporadic enough to ignore. But over a year's time, it gradually worsened. I reluctantly went to see an orthopedist. The diagnosis was early arthritis and a hip joint abnormality. Total left hip replacement was recommended. Without surgery, I could look forward to multiple daily medications and a cane.

My first response was one of denial. I did not want to think this was possible. In my denial, I refused the surgery, thinking I could control the problem using alternative therapies. My husband was a chiropractor at the time, and I had a strong belief in the chiropractic approach of stimulating the body's self-healing abilities. I started to get chiropractic adjustments and incorporated acupuncture, massage therapy, and, of course, my own art for additional relief. My dollmaking was my sanity. It took my focus away from the pain and put it on my dolls. In fact, when I was making dolls, I did not experience pain.

However, my pain persisted whenever I moved. When my leg began to give out in late September, I consulted a hip specialist in Minneapolis. He concurred with the original diagnosis and recommended hip replacement surgery. I had tried my alternative approaches for a year, but the pain was affecting my quality of life. I reluctantly scheduled the operation for December 2000.

A few days after scheduling my surgery, and still apprehensive about it, I attended a Halloween dollmaking party. I fashioned a twenty-inch-long figure out of sticks and painted them green. I wrapped her in crimson fabric, stitched copper beads onto the fabric, topped the head with a halo of dillweed, and added a crown of deep-red raffia hair. Then I fastened a small bunch of lavender, which some consider a healing herb, over the doll's heart.

"One has the options of regarding images as infectious and diseased, or living ensouled entities worthy of tender care and respect."

Bruce L. Moon
Art and Soul

Celebrating Her Growth
Barb Kobe

31

When the figure was complete, I held it up and noticed its left hip jutted out. Almost immediately, I felt relief flood over me, and the anguish over my own hip faded away. The doll was "talking" to me through her body. It was a wake-up call, a sign from my intuition—and my hip—that I needed to make a decision so I could get my life back and move on. It was as if my hip were saying to me, "You have a choice. Now is the time to choose."

The physical pain was still there, but by the time I came home from the party, I was feeling relieved and confident about the decision to have the surgery—so much so that I moved the surgery up a month.

My surgery was very successful, and six weeks of rehabilitation followed. During my recovery, I made twenty small valentine dolls that helped me focus on healing and moving forward with my life. I believe my healing process from the hip pain began the day I made the red-haired doll with the protruding hip, and making the twenty little dolls during my recovery helped speed my healing process along.

In July 2002, the story of my healing process was published in a *Natural Health* magazine article called "Create a Healthy You." Art therapist Shaun McNiff was asked to give his opinion on my story. He said, "That doll making helped her deal with her physical pain is not as far-fetched as it sounds. The relationship between art and healing has been around forever."

Leaders in the art and healing field were quoted in the article, saying that making dolls could be healing for a variety of reasons, that the mere act of working on a creative project brings about healing. Others said creativity improves health by providing spiritual comfort and relieving stress. Most creativity experts agree that using the arts to express oneself releases emotions that aid physical healing. In the same article, McNiff said, "Creativity does something that words can't do, and people report that it's powerful."

Hip-Healing Doll
Barb Kobe

Estrella
Barb Kobe

The act of making a doll can take you through a process of
imagination, healing, and growth. You do not need to be an expert at
dollmaking—or artmaking, for that matter—to encounter the power of this kind
of healing work. I believe the dollmaking process invites and encourages the doll
creator to explore a range of perceptions and emotions—and, in doing so,
reach a deeper level of self-understanding.

33

Artist Statement

I am an artist who makes one-of-a-kind art dolls and healing dolls. My creative process in dollmaking has helped me develop confidence in myself and in my art. I have used my dollmaking to nurture my creative self and work through issues from the past and into the present. I have released stuffed and numb feelings and used my dolls to create containers that allowed me to hold them, express them, and make them my friends. The dolls I've created serve as symbols of my life lessons, and they have impacted and inspired those who have viewed them. This art, along with those who have mentored me along the way, has changed my life and put me on a path of creative personal growth and empowerment.

Holding Her Medicine Shield
Barb Kobe

See Yourself as a Healing Artist

Consider that you are, or can become, a healing artist. Healing artists, by definition, are people who use the creative process of art to heal themselves, others, and the earth. Making a healing doll can serve as a catalyst that induces the healing process, awakens long-lost stories, and creates a transformation. Doll-making and dolls can serve as healing tools.

Throughout the ages, humans have crafted figures in their own images. In the forms of fetishes, totems, and effigies, these symbolic dolls played important roles in religious rituals. As artist John Marriott states, the dolls served as "conduits for supernatural intervention and as contact points to the inner and the unknown worlds." He also notes, "Even the crudest representation of a body, such as a stick and a rag, is believed adequate to exert supernatural influence."

Dolls have also historically been used to heal or prevent illness. Sir James George Frazer, author of *The Golden Bough*, speaks of the benevolent use of homeopathic magic to heal or prevent sickness. He says, "Dolls, puppets, and representational objects are repositories of feelings or phenomena that the individual wants to get 'outside' of themselves—disease, negative feelings, and hostility toward others." This comes from a simple universal principle of homeopathy that states "like produces like." In other words, when a dollmaker creates a doll, the actions on the doll influence the thoughts, feelings, and sensations in the dollmaker's body and mind. Stories tell of dolls being made to make barren women fertile, assist in childbirth, and help parents of adoptive children "birth" their new children into their families.

Effigies, which are forms of dolls, were created to represent illnesses or people who were ill. An effigy would be used in a healing ritual to remove the illness and take it away from the sick person. This would be followed by burning, enshrining, or burying the doll. Often, such a vehicle that carries an illness away is called a scapegoat.

The ancient Scots made simple cloth dolls called poppets and filled them with various herbs to aid in healing, banishing curses, or protection against dark forces. Usually a blessing or incantation was said over the doll before it was given to the individual. In other cultures throughout history, medicine men and women, shamans, and healers made medicine dolls for healing rituals. I believe ancient healers made these dolls as part of their spiritual practices to assist others in healing. They may have prescribed their patients to make dolls and then perform rituals with it in order to activate the medicine.

Tree Mother Shrine Doll
Barb Kobe

Flora and Her Gathering Basket
Barb Kobe

As children, many of us played with dolls and stuffed animals, using them to unleash our imaginations. Doll playing opened us up to imaginary characters, worlds, and possibilities. Dolls and doll-like playthings helped us cope with life's challenges stay connected to our creative and emotional selves. Dolls encouraged—perhaps required—touching. Through touch, we understood them and made them our emotional companions. During adolescence, unfortunately, these creative, imaginative friends became untouchable objects and emotional relics. Often these childhood playthings—our sources of pleasure, fun, and fantasy—became forgotten, buried along with talents, yearnings, dreams, and intuitive wisdom.

Engaging in the creative process
and making art and healing dolls can help you heal at the physical, emotional, mental, and spiritual levels.

You can start to heal yourself with artmaking by opening up to your inner voices, listening to them, and allowing their messages to emerge. Pain or uncomfortable symptoms are, in fact, messages and markers—indicators of something that needs your attention. If you think of these symptoms only as a nuisance and try to mask them as soon as possible, you may miss out on valuable information. Usually, symptoms let you know something needs to be done differently.

The arts affect every cell in the body to create a healing state that changes the following: the immune system and blood flow to all the organs; perceptions, including attitude, emotional state, and pain perception; feelings of hope and abilities to cope with difficulties; and outlook and way of being in the world.

Expressive art is a powerful healing process; however, it is in no way meant to be a substitute for conventional medical treatment. Please seek professional mental health and/or medical support if you are dealing with deep issues and serious health conditions. The creative healing process can help you release stress-producing emotions and can work in partnership with any form of prescribed treatment.

Earth Spirit Energy Rising
Barb Kobe

Air Bowl
Barb Kobe

As you prepare for and enter into the creative process of dollmaking, experiment with the concepts I present in this book. I invite you to play with the idea that dollmaking can affect you in powerful ways. You may experience the following:

- You may have fun and experience joy.

- You may restore some balance in your life. Creating dolls may reveal areas out of balance but also present advice about the best way to restore order and harmony.

- You may change some aspect of your life, and the transformation will be simultaneously creative and destructive. In every creative act, there tends to be a loss of "what was." So if and when you are willing to experience change, hold no thought of return.

- You may shift your focus away from mental and physical pain. The creative exercise of dollmaking is a way to visualize a problem.

- You may notice that the deeper your relationship or your connection to the pain or problem, the more there is a possibility and/or potential to diminish that pain, heal yourself, or get better.

- You may step outside ordinary consciousness and discover a connection between you—the healer within—and a universal healing force.

- You may see the doll as a symbol of an event in your life and attach powerful feelings of that event to the doll.

- You may experience memories of negative events. But by creating an image and moving through those negative feelings, you may reclaim your past and your power and move forward in peaceful ways.

- You may encounter inner voices and discover a community of lost, neglected selves, which you will reclaim. But these parts will have their own resources and agendas and will take on a life of their own. Expect to feel uneasy and confused in this ambiguity—this is part of the creative process. It will be important to have a supportive person bear witness and be there if you need assistance.

- You may connect with a loving aspect of yourself, creating a reunion with a lost companion. This might show up as an image of a mother, angel, spirit guide, or friend.

- You may see the doll as a sign of your healing, a visible representation of your transformation.

- As it appears in front of you, your doll will look almost as if someone else had made it. Its beauty and wonder will be almost beyond you, and its message will be more than you could have known. Yet you will see it and bear witness to its message of growth, change, and transformation.

Holding Her Blessings
Barb Kobe

Creative Action

Make a list of dolls, stuffed animals, or any other doll-like characters you played with in your childhood.

What did you do with them?

What did they mean to you?

When did you start making dolls (if you did)?

If you have pictures of them, make copies and put them into your journal.

What drew you to this book and/or process?

Writing in your journal, tell the Healing Doll Muse your story using "she" (or your preferred pronoun) instead of "I" or your name. For example: "She was living her life day by day when something happened to wake her up. That something was _____."

Ode to Mother Superior
(Journal pages)
Barb Kobe

Ode to Mother Lake Superior
(Final doll)
Barb Kobe

A Discussion of Terms and Beliefs

When working with any method of creative healing, it is important to be aware of and understand what you know and believe about healing.

Consider these definitions of terms associated with healing. See whether you agree, disagree, or feel something in between. After reading, write your own definition of healing in your journal. (See part 2 for more information about journaling.)

Healing: The Noun

An innate, natural process in which the body repairs itself. Healing is not the absence of disease. It means "wholeness." But what does that mean? Philip Shepherd speaks eloquently to this in his book *New Self, New World*. He says it is "the wholeness of a body at peace with itself and in harmony with the world around it," and it brings with it the energies of "occasions of grace, spontaneity, ease, humility, and clarity."

Healing is not curing. In traditional medical science, curing is what a medical doctor intends to happen through external intervention and treatment in an effort to trigger your healing response. Typically, medical science's philosophy is based on dealing with the symptoms of a problem, not getting to the root cause.

Healing: The Verb

Taking action to move yourself through a transformative process toward a greater sense of wholeness, acceptance, and self-love. It is also taking action to reach out to professional healing services and communities. This can include making a connection to what you believe to be a higher power. Healing actions restore an inner order and balance that, in turn, fosters emotional strength, peace of mind, acceptance, and an understanding of personal truth. Healing actions integrate physical, emotional, mental, and spiritual energies—from illness to wellness, from dysfunction to integration, from breakdown to wholeness. All healing, whether by traditional or nontraditional means, occurs within you, working in cooperation with nature and, perhaps, the assistance of others.

Healing actions are meant to strip away layers of physical and emotional numbness and bring movement to what has become stuck, helping us respond to messages from the bodymind, reclaim the riches of the feeling world, and find our deepest level of integrity.

Healer

Someone believed capable of healing people who are ill or are experiencing pain, discomfort, or general "dis-ease." In some cultures, this person is called a shaman.

Inner Healer

Your body's natural ability to heal itself. You can notice how this self-healing mechanism has the innate ability to heal cuts, bruises, or sprains. You can partner with this inner healer and engage with it through creative, restorative processes. When you make art, it activates your inner healer, which changes your experience with your body, mind, and spirit.

Health and Wellness

A general condition of your body and mind when free from pain, illness, or injury. You normally don't notice feeling healthy, but if you do, you might often say, "I feel good!" When you feel healthy, you might feel fluid, flexible, and pain-free. Feeling healthy connects you to an optimal physical, mental, emotional, and spiritual goal you might define as "feeling good" or wellness.

Medicine

A substance, action (therapy), or practice given to an individual in order to prevent or treat illness and restore health and wellness. The word *medicine* is derived from the Latin *ars medicina*, meaning "the art of healing."

Mind-Body Medicine

A practice integrating modern scientific medicine, psychology, nutrition, exercise or movement, mindfulness, alternative therapies, and belief—and I will add creativity—to enhance the natural healing capacities of the body and mind. Mind-body medicine teaches individuals how to maintain or regain health by taking control of their lives and using their own healing power to reduce stress and other negative behaviors and thoughts. This approach to healing will be an underlying foundation of making healing dolls in this creative process.

Illness and Disease

I believe in the mind-body approach to describing illness and disease. Illness is, in part, a process of progressive desensitization—a loss of contact with our vital energies. It can be uncomfortable, yet it can drive you toward self-awareness and understanding of your life process. Pain and illness can be teachers; they can guide you toward resources and remind you of life's significance. Disease is being "out of ease," a condition of energy imbalance or disorder. If disease affects one level, eventually all levels will be out of ease.

Homeostasis

The principle of adjustment; the cyclical pattern of birth, growth, maturation, decay, death, and rebirth. It is the dance of life. It is ever-changing equilibrium—a dynamic pattern of feedback and regulation.

Mindfulness

Purposely bringing one's complete attention to the present experience on a moment-to-moment basis. Mindfulness means paying attention in a nonjudgmental, nonelaborative way. It is a present-centered awareness in which each thought, feeling, or sensation in the intentional field is acknowledged and accepted as it is. I believe mindfulness plays greatly in the process of making healing dolls or any other creative activity.

Transformation

A process that involves a profound and major change in a person, place, or thing, creating a shift in a new direction. When you go through a transformation, you experience a shift of consciousness that may allow you to see your life in a new way.

Complementary and Alternative Medicine (CAM)

A healing practice that differs from traditional medicine in historical origins, theories, diagnostic techniques, and therapeutic practices. CAM practices and ideas are self-defined by their users as preventing or treating illness or promoting health or well-being. Each CAM has its own relationship to the mainstream. Art therapy, expressive arts therapy, dance and music therapy, acupuncture, yoga, essential oils, and more are examples of these kinds of healing modalities. CAM may also include faith healing (e.g., claims that prayer, divine intervention, or the ministrations of an individual healer can cure illness). In the appendix, you will find descriptions of the specific theories of CAM healing used in this book.

Placebo

A medicine or treatment with no science-based medicinal value. It is presented as having healing properties to a person who is sick, in pain, or suffering. It is traditionally given by someone considered an expert within an environment that is perceived as a place where the person may improve, get well, or heal.

Placebo Effect/Placebo Response

When someone who was given a placebo experiences some type of benefit. The person's expectations, beliefs, and faith in the treatment play an important role in the placebo effect. The more people expect the "medicine" or treatment to work, the more likely they are to exhibit a placebo response. Psychiatrist Jerome Frank compared the placebo effect with the treatment offered in nontraditional, alternative practices. He believed there are certain shared elements explaining the efficacy of the various approaches:

- The patient's confidence in the therapist's ability and desire to help

- A socially sanctioned healing locale, especially where the patient can behave in ways that would not be acceptable elsewhere

- A "myth" or basic conceptual paradigm to explain the patient's symptoms

- A task to perform that involves the patient's activity

Amulet

A passive symbol for protection; a charm that is given power to protect from harm or illness.

Fetish

A natural object or an art object to which the possessor gives certain powers. It is usually human or animal in form and most often used in a ritual.

Talisman

An object charged for the purpose of protection or bringing something to the bearer.

Scapegoat

A person or thing blamed for some action, condition, or mistake, even though the person or thing may have had nothing or little to do with the situation.

Creative Action

Your Definitions and the Healing Doll Process

How do you define healing? How do you believe healing can occur? The answers to these questions will be woven into your healing dolls. Your intentions, beliefs, and actions will drive your dolls' creation. You are in charge of the choices you make toward your own healing, and your healing dolls will symbolize the choices you have made and will make.

It will be important to gather a healing team that offers all the resources available from their particular specialties. Your healing team might include friends, family, both traditional and nontraditional medical professionals, or anyone else you choose. Ultimately, healing is a personal—internal and external—process. You have many innate resources within you. Making healing dolls integrates artmaking and creative expression with embodiment, intuition, and imagination. It activates the soul in the healing process. You have the personal power to bring your body, mind, and spirit into balance and harmony, to heal yourself.

The work of spiritual teacher Jeff Foster (lifewithoutacenter.com) on healing resonated with me, so I adapted it to support my dollmaking process:

A true healing doll does not heal you; the doll simply reflects back to you your innate capacity to heal yourself. When you look at her, she will remind you of an aspect of your healing process.

A true healing teacher does not teach you; she does not see you as inherently separate from her. She simply reflects back your own inner knowing and reminds you of the vastness of your being. She is a mirror, a signpost, a guide.

Love is the space in which all this is possible. Love heals. And we learn best in a loving field, with no threat of failure, no punishment.

Journal

Write your definition of healing.

Spend some time writing your healing story.

What healing resources have you used or are using?

Part 2:

Discovery

"I have used the doll as a tool to free my personality. Because dolls are so wonderfully without consequences, they have enormous potential for amusing their makers and, in the process, for offering insight. Something so benign can take the danger out of imagining. Playing with dolls is a safe way to explore change and make discoveries; and play, after all, is the very center of the creative act."

Elinor Peace Bailey
Mother Plays with Dolls

Dreamer in the Flow
(Fabric collage using doll image)
Barb Kobe

Dollmaking Basics

In part 3, you will see I do not offer specific patterns for making the healing dolls in this process. If you've made art dolls but not healing dolls before, or if you've never made any kind of doll before, you may be wondering where to begin.

That's why part 2 is called "Discovery." Here you will build confidence and skills to help prepare you for the work ahead in part 3. This section features doll-making basics so you can experiment before beginning the healing doll process. This section will also inform and inspire you on the key topics I consider when making healing dolls. This includes metaphors, symbols, archetypes, embodiment, and more.

No matter how much experience you've had with dollmaking, now is the time for discovery. Once you feel more confident with your skills and knowledge, you will be more prepared for the healing doll process in part 3.

I can almost hear you saying, "Well, how can I move through this process if I have little or no dollmaking experience?" The answer is to build your doll-making intelligence, to copy others, to use patterns, and to practice. This will boost your dollmaking vocabulary, provide a library of techniques, and build your creative muscles.

When you make any doll from a pattern or by following another dollmaker's instructions, you are acquiring skills. When following others' instructions, you will notice how they move through a dollmaking process: what materials they use, how they begin and end, how they approach the face and body parts, and how they costume and embellish. At first, your dolls may look like the teacher's or the pattern. Trust me—before long, your dolls will have their own look, feel, and meaning because they have moved through your creative heart, mind, and muscles.

Once you have explored other dollmakers' work and gathered information, it'll be time to put your new ideas and skills to use, and play. Clear a space for a studio or a place to create. Gather materials. Feel free to use doll patterns, finding ones that match your imagined image. A few easy patterns are included in the appendix.

Don't worry that your healing dolls won't be "yours" if you start with patterns. Your symbols and color choices will allow your own energy to work through the doll. Your imagination has the ability to turn anything into a doll. Don't beat yourself up if the outcome isn't what you expect. Each doll will incorporate a part of your story. You'll also find ways to play with pictures of your dolls in your journal, which I highly recommend.

Note: You can also move through this process by creating paper dolls or drawing images in your creative art journal. However, I believe that working on and

Dreamer
Barb Kobe

"Clay is a mirror for the unconscious because it's an amorphous, feely material. The clay will receive our emotions and intuitions because it feels what you feel."
Cassandra Light
Way of the Doll

Girl's First Moon
Barb Kobe

**Connected to the Sky,
Grounded to the Earth**
Barb Kobe

"Speak to your work. Accept that the first thoughts which come into your mind in response to your questions are your work responding to you. "

Dr. Ira Progoff

Bringing Up Energy
Barb Kobe

holding a three-dimensional doll with your own hands has a way of directly connecting with your bodymind and inner healer.

I highly recommend Susanna Oroyan's book *Anatomy of a Doll*. It is both a workbook to help you develop ideas as well as a reference book that gives you details about how to make a multitude of different kinds of dolls—from simple to complex. It is full of pictures, pattern shapes, and drawings of technical details, all of which will help you design your healing dolls. Her book explains how to achieve certain effects and helps answer the "what happens if . . ." questions. Susanna says:

> *Dollmaking is a multi-media construction project. It really doesn't make a difference which type of dollmaker you are, or want to be. Nor does it make any difference which particular technique you choose. The main considerations when making a doll are to understand the desired effect or impression you want to make, then to be willing to play with variations of your idea and explore any directions that are suggested.*

See the appendix for a list of other suggested resources. They can help orient you with other dollmakers' dolls as well as provide pictures, patterns, and directions for your reference. There are a ton of Pins on Pinterest about how to make art dolls. You could start by visiting my Pinterest page.

General Note: You will see I use feminine pronouns to refer to the dolls; this is based on the preponderance of women in my classes and the tendency of their dolls to take female forms. This is not meant to exclude male—or other—doll forms, nor their creators, no matter how they identify. Actually, it took me a while before I could call a doll "she." I would see my dolls as female but noticed that others would say "he" when talking about them. This felt wrong and somehow disconnected from the story and energy of the doll. I could go into depths about patriarchy, the feminist agenda, or women's rights, but basically, I noticed that when I called a doll "she," I felt more connected to the doll and my strengths, beliefs, and story as a woman. Regardless of the pronouns I use here, I encourage you to identify your dolls in whatever way you feel best.

Autobiography Doll

Jeff Julseth, Minneapolis, Minnesota

Dollmaking has always been a creative problem-solving process for me. I was more interested in design and technique until the summer of 2003, when Barb Kobe challenged me to create a "self-doll."

I sketched the doll pattern and began the process with a melancholy mind. During the three months of deep creating, the doll mentally drained me, and I felt withdrawn and destitute. Still, I had no intentions to stop the transformation of this doll. I realized that this doll was only a chapter of my life, and there was a need to continue an autobiographical doll series.

Life is full of clues. A friend commented that I always played the same CD when I picked him up for lunch. I had to confess, "Annie Lennox's 'Little Bird' must be my favorite song." The lyrics are about despair and affirmation to start anew. (See right column.)

Symbols:

- The body contains twigs, roots, and feathers, sewn into the material—the foundation of a nest, cocoon

- Earth tones: hidden feelings underneath the surface, dirt/fertilizer for growth

- Hidden wings under the arms: unknown potentials

- The absence of feet: inability to journey

- Heavy doll (8 lbs.): being weighted to the ground

- Low-brim hat: shame and inability to look at oneself, melancholy

- Profile looking to the right: doll's head turns to the three sequential dolls of transformation

- Antique keys (30+): the ability to gain and open up unlimited knowledge

- Door lock placed on tablet: doll is hiding behind my fears

- Door lock: the biggest mystery is unlocking ourselves

The back of the doll is collaged in the same manner as an altered book. There are journaled words and images of myself hidden from the viewer when hanging on the wall. I have included the first lyric, "I feel so low," on the back of the doll. The remaining three lyrics will be placed on each sequential doll. The final autobiography doll will read, "We reap what we sow" and will be represented with the fall harvest season of my transformation, with wings ready to take flight.

Thank you, Barb Kobe, for inspiring me. I hope sharing this experience will inspire others to create.

"Little Bird"

But my my, I feel so low
My my, where do I go?
My my, what do I know?
My my, we reap what we sow
They always said that you knew best
But this little bird's fallen out of that
*   nest now*
I've got a feeling that it might have
*   been blessed*
So I've just got to put these wings to test

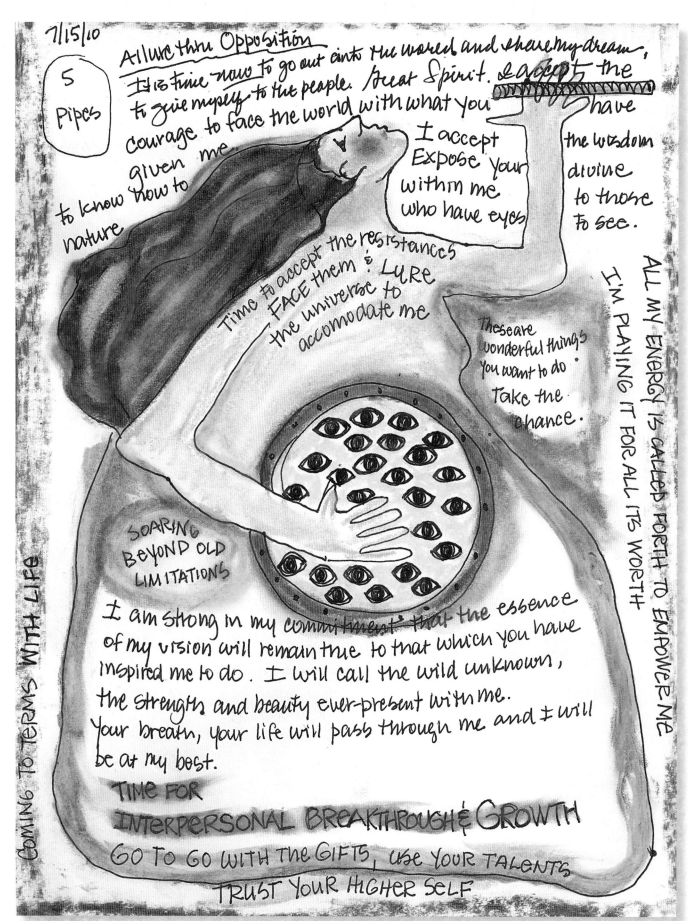

Eye of the Drum
Barb Kobe

Your Witness: A Believing Mirror

It is important to have people in our lives who can witness our creative processes. As you make your healing dolls, you may feel the work is getting too intense to move on. This is when it is helpful to have a nonjudgmental person—a witness, or as Julia Cameron calls it in *Artist's Way*, a believing mirror—look at your dolls and listen to the story of your process. Art therapist Pat Allen says you want this person to have "compassionate disinterest." This person can serve as a mentor, someone willing to offer protection, guidance, insight, and creative input. A mentor will help you stay focused.

Your witness can be an individual or a group, such as your fellow participants in a healing doll class or other creative workshop. Members of a group can help one another by witnessing, accepting, and celebrating the doll images that come through.

When looking for your witness or mentor, look for someone who will do the following:

- Give you positive attention

- Let you feel your feelings and not criticize, interrupt, or psychoanalyze

- Not take over the conversation by talking about him- or herself

- Not make you feel wrong, guilty, or bad about what you are creating

- Encourage you to take creative risks

- Honor you and your creative process

The Witness
Barb Kobe

"To find out who we really are, we need mirrors—not mirrors on the wall, but humans who can reflect back to us what we are or what we can be, not who we think we are or who we think we should be. To see yourself mirrored in another and to take back your disowned self."

Paul Brenner
Buddha in the Waiting Room

Creative Action

If you have a photo of your witness, put it in your journal. If you like, put a creative frame around the image.

Write about your witness or witnesses in your journal.

Include any agreements you have made with your believing mirror, counselor, coach, or creative friend, including what you will do if you get stuck or need help or support.

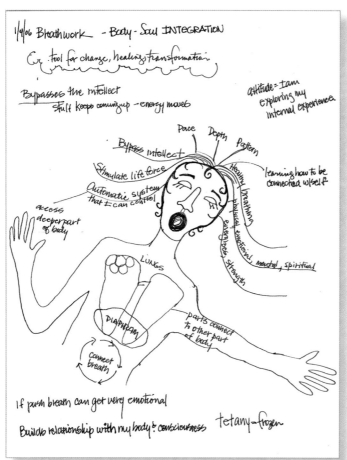

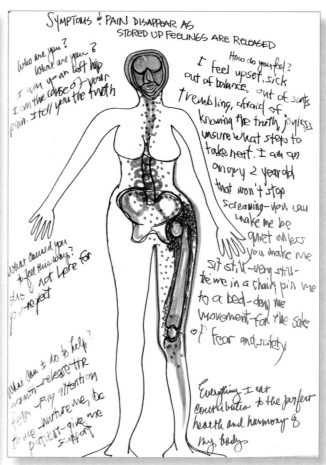

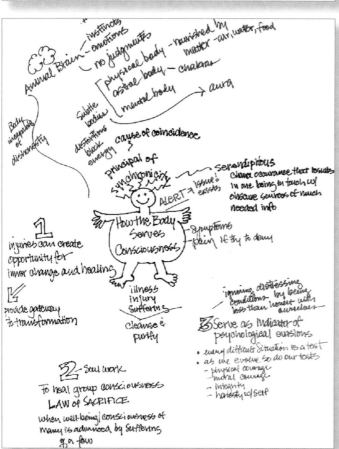

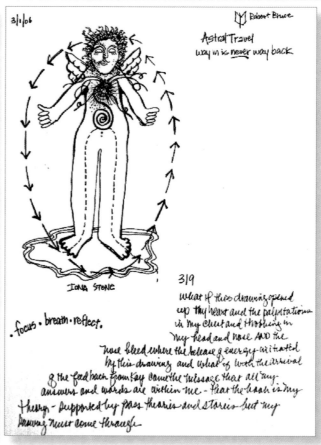

Examples of healing doll mapping

Journaling and Other Creative Tools

While you could move through the healing doll process by only making the dolls, you can deepen your healing if you also record your thoughts, feelings, and stories using words and images in a journal.

The unconscious mind needs time for musing and creating as well as time for structure. Dollmaking serves as the time to create, and journaling offers you time for structure. Journaling can balance the dollmaking process by defining the boundaries of your experience. It will also help you keep focused on each doll in the process. When you see "Journal" throughout this book, it is an indicator to visit your journal and use the creative tools of mind-mapping, writing with your nondominant hand, and more to make your entries. Let's discuss these creative processing tools in more detail.

Mind-mapping: Mind-mapping is one of the simplest—yet most powerful—tools you can have in your creativity toolbox. It is a nonlinear way of organizing information, and it allows you to capture the natural flow of your ideas. Do an internet search to find examples. I use mind-mapping to work through a problem, think about an idea, and help me remember a subject I'm reading about.

Writing with Your Nondominant Hand: This will be one of the most important tools for journaling through the healing doll process. Basically, it is a dialoguing technique using both of your hands to write or draw in your journal. Visit Lucia Capacchione's website at www.luciac.com. Play with some of the exercises on the "Creative Journal Exercises and Activities" page or check out her many books on the subject.

Meditative Walks: Go for a walk—especially in nature—with a question in mind. During the walk, imagine you are experiencing a dream. All that appears during the walk is a symbol that has a message that can be incorporated into your doll. See "Nature Walk Ritual" on page 229 in the appendix for detailed guidelines.

Collage: I make collages as inspiration when I feel blocked. Use this tool to get unblocked or deal with stress. Make a collage of your intention, or make one for the cover for your journal. Create a paper doll, then collage her body with images and/or words. Take photos of your dolls and collage them into your journal pages.

Storytelling: Every doll will represent a story you have to tell. Name each doll and let its story unfold. When you tell your dolls' stories, you will get in touch with the messages they have for you. Write your stories in your journal and collage your dolls around it.

Examples of collage and visual journaling

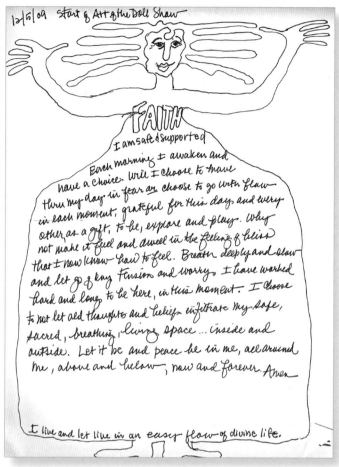

Examples of collage and visual journaling

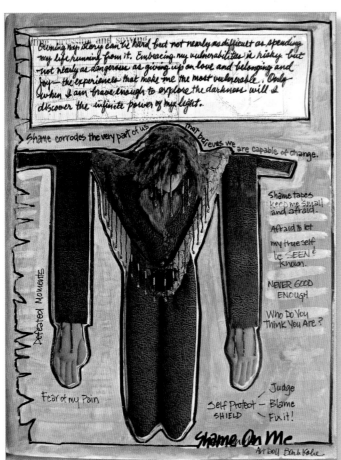

Examples of collage and visual journaling

Angel Fabric Collage
Barb Kobe

Symbols

Dollmaking offers you an opportunity to actively prepare a space for visual symbols and metaphors to emerge. The symbols, metaphors, and stories of your dolls will allow you to touch profound feelings without being threatened. These human-form images we call "art" or "healing dolls" will partner with you to take on the qualities you seek in order to feel healed or whole in spirit, body, and mind.

The word *symbol* comes from the Greek *symbolon*, meaning "token of identity." Each of us chooses visual symbols—images and objects—to place in our living environments. We are all drawn to certain colors, shapes, forms, patterns, and textures. We consciously or unconsciously use them in our home decor and the clothes we wear. So when you take a symbolic image from your life and put it on or in a doll, it can increase your understanding of yourself and your personal myth and stories.

Ultimately, you will apply your own symbols and meaning to your dolls. In the beginning, however, use resources at the bookstore, library, or online to teach you the language of symbols. These resources can help you understand your symbols or look for symbols that have meaning for you. For example, Louise Hay's book *Heal Your Body* details the symbolic meaning of body symptoms. You may also wish to research healing colors, herbs, and aromatherapy. Remember to use any resources about symbols as guides rather than the "truth."

Another helpful exercise is to study images of the human body. Think about what the body parts symbolize. Imagine making a doll's hands larger than expected to symbolize taking power back or being powerful. Imagine a doll with large feet to represent being grounded, or large lips to give voice to something. Also look at a picture of the internal organs. Notice the shapes you could use on a doll dealing with disorders involving breathing, digestion, or circulation, to name a few

You will also be amazed by the beautiful design elements that lie within the body. For example, look in an anatomy book at an image of a T cell, one of the immune system's principal means of defense. Now imagine using the cell image in a beaded design on a doll that represents dealing with disease. Dollmaker and teacher Cassandra Light has her students make charms to represent the chakras, or nodes of healing energy on the body. They then place the charms on their dolls in positions that seem right to them.

After exploring symbols in research, make a list of the symbols you notice around you. Take special note of the ones repeated in your home or office. For example, are you drawn to spirals—do you draw them when doodling, wear them in jewelry or clothing, notice them in artwork? Consider where your symbols come from. Are they from your imagination or your intuition, or are they universal symbols? Consider their color, shape, design, and meaning in your life.

Angel Taking Flight
Barb Kobe

Medicine Woman with Shield
Barb Kobe

Coming Home to Myself
Barb Kobe
A symbol of my inner self wrapped in a cloak of affirmations. The house represents a container for my outer self. Doll with open cloak is below.

If you aren't sure about a symbol's meaning, give it some time. In many cases, the depth of meaning does not come immediately. For instance, you may use a symbol on a doll without fully understanding why. At some point while creating the doll, or maybe sometime after the creation, your own meaning of the symbol will come forward. I often use dialoguing with my nondominant hand to discover the stories I am telling myself through my dolls. Sometimes the story of my dolls comes first, with my setting an intention; other times the story and meaning come after she is made. The meaning comes through insight when I least expect it.

In the Spring 2013 issue of *The Polymer Arts* magazine, dollmaker and art therapist Christine K. Harris wrote a very useful article called "Working with Personal Symbolism." She shares techniques for developing personal symbols that I summarize here:

1. Find Patterns: Look for repeating patterns of behavior, life events, situations, and relationships. What keeps showing up? What meaning can you make of this? What symbols might you use to "display" these patterns? What people, places, or things are you attracted to, curious about, and want to know more about? Are there animals, themes, colors, characters, or places that draw your attention and enlighten your imagination? Include what you like and dislike.

2. Borrow with Awareness: Many artists use symbols from other cultures. The spiral, circle, or square, for example, can be seen across cultures. Use these symbols in unique and personal ways that add meaning or specialness to the work.

3. Collect Meaningful Things: Gather images that you find you are drawn to. Gather words and phrases that speak to you and your story. Gather meaningful, historical memorabilia. These are usually things from your past, such as jewelry, fabric, toys, beads, and buttons.

4. Sketch and Write in a Journal: Capture dreams (great resources for personal symbols), record important events, express your feelings (my favorite), analyze emerging patterns, and discover connections. Take pictures of your finished dolls, print out the photos, and paste them into your journal, then write a story around them.

Visit www.whats-your-sign.com. It is a great internet resource for symbols.

"The best way to develop your symbolism into something person-ally meaningful and rich is to use symbolic objects and images in your art, even before you are completely sure what they mean. Go with what feels right and think about it later. As you reflect on your creations and the imagery you have used, you'll come to deeper realizations that you can explore in your next piece. It's a journey that can lead to art that communicates in a real and human way."

Christine K. Harris
Dollmaker and Art Therapist

"When you have spent an important part of your life playing Let's Pretend, it's often easy to see symbolism where none exists."

Gene Tierney

"The symbols and glyphs are my own iconography, yet they seem saturated with meaning, as if they have been handed down for generations. We are all individuals, yet we are all connected."

Barbara Ganim
Art and Healing

Going Within
Barb Kobe

Creative Action

Draw a symbol you love, then dialogue with it using your nondominant hand. Writing with your dominant hand represents your voice, and your nondominant hand responds as the symbol.

Create your own symbols. Scribble, doodle, and make inkblots, then look for symbolic shapes within them. Play with making up your own symbols and applyings meaning to them.

Walking Meditation: Choose a question present in your mind. Write it down in a small notebook you take with you on a nature walk. Spend about thirty minutes on the walk. Imagine you are walking through a dream world, keeping your question in the back of your mind. Come back to home base and journal the experience. Write down or draw everything you saw, heard, and experienced that could be a symbol in response to the question. Dialogue with these symbols using your dominant and nondominant hand (see "Nature Walk Ritual" in the appendix).

Blessing the Seeds of Growth

Barb Kobe

This is a doll I started at Maureen Carlson's Friday Night Open Studios. I stayed the night in one of her retreat rooms, had a massage that night, and made dolls on the following Saturday.

The inspiration for this doll came from bodywork that Friday. As my feet were being massaged, I began to have the sensation that I was beginning labor. The feeling intensified to the point that I had to change positions. It did not really subside until an hour later, after I got dressed and headed back to the center.

That night, I thought about the sensations. I started to form a body from wire, wrapping it with quilt batting. I attached hands and a head, then went to bed.

The embellishment of the doll included writing affirmations and sewing them onto her sacrum area. They include:

- Life is unfolding as I desire.

- I honor my body and feel good about my sexuality.

- I am moving toward a time when I am totally happy and fulfilled.

- Life offers me everything I need for the journey.

- I embrace change.

- I express my desires to myself and others.

- I accept my male and female sides.

- Who I am is good enough.

After breakfast the next day, I went for a walk along Sand Creek, next to the center. As I sat next to the creek in meditation, I looked to my right and found a broken open gourd filled with seeds . . . as if it were giving birth, resting at the bottom of a tree. This seemed the perfect symbol to rest in the dolls lap.

I placed the "seed pod" in her arms near her solar plexus—her power center. To me, her face expresses a bit of suffering, as the birth process often begins with pain. Yet there is compassion as she looks up to connect with a power greater than herself, as if she were asking for grace and strength to be with the growth process.

Putting on her "skin" took several months, as I twisted fabric, then wrapped and stitched it onto her body. This took time—time I need to be with the messages and to nurture the wisdom of my body that she represented. Once completed, I covered a stone with hand-dyed felt and sat her upon it. I trusted that the earth symbol would keep her grounded.

MEme

Constance Makela, Minnesota

I first took a tour of Barb Kobe's home studio. I was awed by the amazing array of healing and medicine dolls she has created. I wanted to make a healing doll for myself.

The first class set the stage for the doll. As the three of us discussed our responses to Barb's healing-related questionnaire, we each kneaded and manipulated a lump of air-dry clay in our hands. My lump developed into a misshaped face with its nose out of joint, pouting lips, and a generally grumpy demeanor. It was exactly the way I feel on the inside as I deal with the pain of rheumatoid arthritis. From there, I moved on to construction of a body. Initially, I only knew I wanted my doll to be large. Barb helped me make an armature. As I wrapped the armature with cotton batting and T-shirt knit, I thought about how to express my healing needs visually.

This photo shows *MEme* with her Burden Bag (on her back) and her Native American hand drum, sitting on her perch atop a high bookcase in my family room/studio area.

My first impulse was to weave a scaled replica of the Finnish birch-bark backpacks of my heritage. I called it my Burden Bag and began placing representative things into it, things that were burdens to me. The healing doll could symbolically carry my burdens, lifting them from me. My next inclination was to make clay feet. I wanted them to be bare and blue; my feet are cold, especially at night. Embedded gemstones and seed beads indicate pain points. Black toenails represent neuropathy.

As I sewed and stuffed the hands, I thought about how I'd represent the pain there. I started sewing fuchsia-colored seed beads in a circular manner onto the joint of the right-hand index finger, where I often experience intense arthritic pain. A floral design grew from that point. Ultimately, floral-like beaded designs covered most of both hands.

As the doll developed she became an amalgam of my life's experiences. I gave her the name *MEme*. Every part of *MEme* is significant to me. The costume, the symbols, and the beading all represent something special to me—all look joyful. I realized, among other things, that I was expressing thankfulness for being able to create art, because not long ago, that was physically challenging to do.

The healing doll class was a wonderful opportunity to learn while being surrounded and nurtured by Barb's strong creative energy and that of the other two participants. Everything I've involved myself in over the past few years relates to healing energy. I know I'm being directed in this way for a reason.

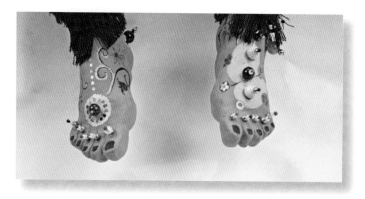

I Am Water
Barb Kobe

Metaphors

Along with symbols, metaphors are also important elements of the healing doll process. "Metaphor is the lifeblood of all art," says dancer Twyla Tharp. As metaphors, your dolls will help you take what looks strange or feels uncomfortable and transform it into something that looks familiar. I love how my healing dolls have helped me find new ways to connect to both my remembered and forgotten memories of facts, fictions, and feelings. As Twyla says, "You remember much more than you think you do, in ways you haven't considered." Metaphors show the relationship between your outer experiences and inner feelings. A metaphor makes intuitive sense and serves as a guide in your dollmaking design process.

Metaphors can also help you understand the meaning of your dolls. Have you ever seen a matryoshka doll, also known as a Russian nesting doll? It is a set of wooden dolls of decreasing size that fit one inside another. The dolls are often used as a metaphor for the recognizable relationship of objects inside similar objects. For instance, the nesting dolls may serve as a metaphor for an individual's different ages and stages.

You speak the language of emotion every day using metaphor. Consider how these emotional metaphors may be used on a healing doll:

- Having the blues
- In a black hole
- In a purple rage
- Green with envy
- Tied in knots
- Blowing off steam
- Frozen in fear
- Butterflies in stomach

Metaphors can speak to physical aspects as well. Expressive art therapist Barbara Ganim says, "Numerous studies in mind-body medicine have revealed that the type of illness or disease a person develops is often a metaphorical reflection of what is going on emotionally in that person's life." Likewise, in *Women's Bodies, Women's Wisdom*, Dr. Christiane Northrup says heart disease is frequently thought of as a metaphor for the fear of opening one's heart to love. Blocked arteries can be a metaphor for the inability to allow the joy of life to flow freely.

Wisdom of the Pain
(Drawing)
Barb Kobe

"I have found over the years than intention is strengthened by the creation of a visual object that acts as a symbol of the intention. I created a powerful healing doll that I had intended to leave at the shrine, placing my hair, stones and other objects in her body. As I prepared to take the journey, I worked with the doll, through prayer and meditation, to strengthen my intention to heal."

Katelyn Mariah
Empowered Health and Wellness

Contraction Drawing
Barb Kobe

A metaphor can even describe you. *Janitor of Emotions* is a doll I created while trying to balance my needs with what I call "their needs"—the needs of my children, husband, parents, extended family, and art. I began with a drawing of a janitor. It was a metaphor for the energy it took for me to feel other people's feelings and think I somehow had control over them. After I drew the image, I wrote:

> *I am a caretaker of feelings*
>
> *A janitor of emotions*
>
> > *Cleaning up messes . . .*
> >
> > *Dirty depressions*
> >
> > *Sloppy sadness*
> >
> > *Frozen fears*
> >
> > *Anxieties, angers*
> >
> > *Whatever you need cleaned up, call me.*

I then wrote:

> *I no longer have room to take on another feeling. I am overloaded to the point of exhaustion. I feel tense—tightness in my neck and shoulders. My eyes throb from seeing others' pain. I sleep only to awaken to more exhaustion. My body aches to breathe clear air only for me. I release the weight of others' emotions so that I may experience my own anew.*

I used this drawing and writing to inspire the doll. *Janitor of Emotions* created an opportunity to tell a story about an aspect of my life. I felt a release after I made the doll, an honoring of a stuck place I now knew and could change.

Janitor of Emotions: Taking Care of Others' Feelings
(Drawing and final doll)
Barb Kobe

Telling the Story of Your Doll

Your immune and nervous system are influenced by your emotions, images, and thoughts. These all intermix with your imagination, especially through the arts, to enhance your healing response. I often use dialoguing with my nondominant hand to discover the stories I am telling myself through my dreams and dolls.

Narrative psychology is the science of storytelling and healing. In his book *Poetic Medicine*, John Fox says that "there is a three-fold healing potential of image making:

- Power of an image to evoke a creative response

- The capacity of images to serve as containers of feeling

- The capacity of images to inspire a voice for feeling."

Janitor of Emotions became a transformative visual metaphor for how I was feeling. Drawing what I felt helped me connect with my emotional self, and creating the doll gave me an opportunity to express those feeling and tell a story about an aspect of my life.

Each time you work on a healing doll, it stirs up the possibility for healing or feeling more spiritually whole, regardless of your current psychological or physiological health. The metaphors in your healing dolls can put you in touch with profound emotions in a nonthreatening, creative way with the potential to change your life.

Many of the symbols mentioned in this book are ubiquitous, while others you choose may have more personal meaning. Either way, the symbols incorporated into your healing dolls flesh out their stories and their meaning to you. As you go about living, your dolls can be visual reminders of positive qualities you strive to possess, or of negative qualities you want to leave behind or learn to live with.

In her e-book *What to Do When Your Body Hurts*, Pat Samples writes,

> *Sometimes pain is best understood through metaphor. Ask yourself what this pain reminds you of. What is it like? Probe further once you get an answer by asking what that reminds you of. Keep exploring until a memory or metaphor arises that rings true. Consider what this memory or metaphor may be asking of you. Develop it into a story and see what opportunity or insight emerges.*

"Interacting with dolls has a tremendous healing effect on my clients because it enables them to re-experience and heal their trauma in a deep physical, emotional and psychological way. When they found the hidden doll, that represented a lost part of themselves, they cradled it to their chests and kissed it. In reality, when they did this, they were loving themselves."

Elena Avila
Woman Who Glows in the Dark

This prayer pocket doll first came as an image in my visual journal, then I made the paper doll below.

Releasing Prayers to Spirit
Barb Kobe

This is an example of a visualized, or imaged, story from one of my art journals. Can you imagine how any image like these could be used to inspire a healing doll?

Creative Action

Draw, paint, or doodle an image that represents a feeling, pain, or problem in your life. Once completed, dialogue with the image using your nondominant hand. This is how I came up with the poem and words for *Janitor of Emotions*. Seek and discover the story the image is trying to tell you.

Ask these questions by writing with your dominant hand, and answer them by writing with your nondominant hand:

- Who or what are you?
- How do you feel?
- What causes you to feel this way?
- What do you need from me?
- What do you have to tell or teach me?
- What story do you want to tell me?
- What characters from a fairy tale are you like?

Your answer from your nondominant hand represent the image.

Michelle's Scapegoat: *Justice*

Michelle Wolf, Hastings, Minnesota

I am justice and I am blindfolded, not blind. I see no truth, no fairness, no vindication. The justice system has failed. I turn my sight inward and see strength, dignity, and healing. I have no mother. I am the mother. My body and soul are pierced with the arrows of violence, molestation, and lies. I carry my own arrows. Arrows of calm, caring, and truth. This long, excruciating battle has sent me to my knees.

Yet I am not beaten. I kneel on the collective soul of female energy from women who have supported me in my fight. I carry much baggage. Baggage from past abuses. I carry a jar of tears and a container of screams. I carry the souls of three little girls. The ones I could not save. I carry my inner child in a small square box, tightly closed. I dare not open it. I am the mother. I carry the staff of never-ending strength, handmade by Lynne just for me. I am special. I carry my arrows in a pack filled with peace. Peace given to me by the energy I feel from all the people who truly care. My horns grew from hitting my head on anything hard. My tail from always needing to protect my back. I have learned well. I have the power. I am the mother. There may be no justice for the innocent this time, but there is still cosmic justice to be had. I will teach my daughters that the true winners are those who can heal themselves.

Gaia Contemplating Her Earth Self
Barb Kobe

Archetypes

The five healing dolls made in this healing doll process—Guardian, Scapegoat, Loving Kindness, Talisman, and Inner Healer—are archetypes. Archetypes are characters, images, and themes that embody universal meanings and basic human experiences. They keep the same characteristics regardless of plot or time period. An archetype evokes deep emotions. Some examples of archetypes include the Mother, the Father, Mother Nature, the Angel, the Goddess, the Clown, and the Child. Friends, family, and even strangers will play out these archetype roles in your life.

You will recognize archetypes in your dolls through their appearance, facial expressions, hair, body sizes, costumes—everything involved in making a doll. Knowing about archetypes will add to your toolbox of meaningful symbols and images that will, more likely than not, show up in the healing dolls you create.

Author Caroline Myss says that "archetypes are universal patterns of behavior" and "part of our personal mythology," beginning before we were born. In her book *Sacred Contracts*, she writes about the ten archetypal patterns that reflect the primary power issues defining women today, including their underlying struggles with personal empowerment: the Advocate, the Artist/Creative, the Athlete, the Caregiver, the Fashionista, the Intellectual, the Queen/Executive, the Rebel, the Spiritual Seeker, and the Visionary. Did certain images, people, or stories come to mind as you read through that list? Would you be able to draw these archetypes or at least find pictures of them in magazines, in books, or on the internet?

Storykeeper
Barb Kobe

In *The Four-Fold Way*, Dr. Angeles Arrien writes about the four archetypes inside us. Each archetype teaches a way of expressing, then opening our hearts to bring ourselves into alignment, or our center. Each archetype is connected to a "universal salve" of healing: dancing, singing, storytelling, and silence. The Warrior makes things happen—rather than just reacts to what happens—in her life and uses the rattle to call in dancing. The Visionary uses her ability to speak truth without blame or judgment and uses the bell to bring in singing. The Healer archetype focuses on what has heart and meaning and uses the drum to call in storytelling. The Teacher stays open to outcome, rather than attach herself to it. She uses sticks or bones to bring in silence, calm, and wisdom. Do these descriptions give you any ideas for your own dolls?

In *Way of the Doll*, Cassandra Light talks about her year-long classes, in which she noticed her students' dolls would fall into five different realms: the Human, the Personality, the Feminine, the Masculine, and the Quintessence. Within each of these realms are certain archetypes. For example, the Human realm includes figures of the Mother, the Father, the Child, the Elder, and even Pets. The book is filled with pictures of the realms in doll form.

Shaman and Her Drum
Barb Kobe

Merlin – Sacred Bear
Barb Kobe

Elinor Peace Bailey uses a simple dictionary definition for archetypes: "patterns or models from which all things of the same kind are copied or based." In her book *The Doll as a Messenger—the Body's Language*, she invites readers to select a messenger from the archetypes. She says it's important to find the right messenger for your message. And I might add that it's important to find the right visual symbol of the story you are telling through your dollmaking. Elinor offers categories of archetypes: storytellers; gatherers (peddlers, shell seekers, bag ladies, etc.); family figures; professional types (doctors, lawyers, etc.); clowns; wise women (prophets, wizards, crones, etc.); and fantasy or mythical figures.

My personal favorite archetypes are from the Hero's/Heroine's Journey: the Hero or Heroine, the Threshold Guardian, the Mentor, the Guardian, the Shadow, the Ally, the Trickster, the Shape-Shifter, and the Herald.

Once you finish one of your healing dolls, look at her and notice if there is an archetype within her that may want to start up a conversation with you. If you show your doll to a safe witness, chances are the universal energy and meaning of the archetype will speak to the witness, even if you had no intention of this while making of the doll.

"In the archetypal stories, we find the path from ailments to healing, from separation to union, from foolishness to wisdom. We find the stories that underpin our experiences and make our lives richer and more meaningful, more soulful, more connected to others. Sometimes, we can follow the thread of an archetypal story to find our way out of the dark passages of our lives.

"The making of Wisdom Dolls is connecting with this archetypal realm. We start with simple materials—calico, thread, paint, and as we work, we quieten and listen to the inner prompting to choose this shape, or color, or this decoration, or this. That doesn't mean we have to work in silence—the conversations we have as we make can be fantastic. We choose sometimes by intuition, sometimes by clear association and conceptual thought. In the end, we have made a Wisdom Doll, and then we tell the story of the Doll, and in the telling, we get to hear it ourselves. We hear our own insights, our delight or our grief, our authenticity. And we go home with that Doll and live with her (or him), and if we chose, we can continue this dialogue with what we have made, and explore where that might take us in conversation with ourselves."

Merilee Bennett
merileebennett.com

Native Guide
Barb Kobe

Everything I Touch Grows
(Guardian archetype paper doll)
Barb Kobe

Creative Action

Research archetypes using the internet or other resources. Author and medical intuitive Carolyn Myss has an extensive list of archetypes with descriptions in her book *Sacred Contracts*. You can view the list and descriptions, along with her other free resources, at www.myss.com/free-resources/.

What archetypes have appeared or are appearing now in your life? Make a list of five to ten archetypes that describe a part of your personality or identity. Write about them in your journal and add drawings or other images. Watch for these and other archetypes as you move through the *Healing Doll Way* process.

Make a paper doll of your favorite archetypes.

Mermaid
Barb Kobe

Anthropomorphic Dolls

Anthropomorphism, or personification, is giving human form or other characteristics to anything other than a human being, including animals. In dollmaking, anthropomorphic dolls have some part of them that look human. An example would be creating a bird or animal doll with a human face or other human traits. Another example is attributing human emotions or motives to forces of nature, such as my doll *Blue Moon River Woman* (page 73). When you see one of these dolls, they may have a human torso and be costumed as if human, but their face, hands, and feet may be those of an animal. The easy way to wrap your mind around these kinds of dolls is to think about how an animal with a human face could express emotion. Think of a protective mother bear or a sacred healing tree icon.

Folklore, rituals, ancient stories, and myths worldwide all involve animals as part of a sacred experience, a special relationship we have with the world. Animals' behaviors and traits, regardless of culture and location, teach us by example. They allow us to see how our lives can be lived more simply and with purity of thought and emotion. They invite our imagination and intuition, rather than our intellect and rational mind.

Animal healing dolls, whether real or mythical, are often called totems or power animals. While you move through this process, an animal image may come forward for you as a totem, mythical kin, spirit healer, guide, wise healer, or talisman. You may discover that an animal figure or a doll with animal qualities fits perfectly as a Guardian, Scapegoat, Talisman, or any other healing doll.

Animals can be symbols of our relationships with ourselves and with life. Each creature possesses its own power and presents opportunities to work on different lessons. In classes, I would keep the book *Animal Speak,* by Ted Andrews, nearby as a resource to deepen participants' understanding of why a particular animal's image would appear in the healing doll process.

For most of us, animals hold, or once held, a special place in our lives. Perhaps you had a stuffed animal or favorite animal character from a movie or book in your childhood. Maybe you had a family pet that held a special kind of loving energy for you.

In *Bear Shaman* (right), Carol used parts of a stuffed bear character. She opened up the seams and used the ears on the hat and the paws as feet and part of her power shawl.

Old Turtle Mother
Alma Williams

Bear Shaman
Carol Tombers

71

A Little Birdie Told Her a Fishy Story
Barb Kobe

Creative Action

Did you have any favorite stuffed animals or special pets growing up? Did you dress them up? Write about them in your journal. If you have or can find pictures of them, put them in your journal as well. Write down the qualities you admire and/or value in yourself or others.

Research "power animals" and "spirit animals" on the internet, adding specific animals you're interested in. Write down all the qualities you feel you and this animal have in common and that you value in yourself. Consider how you would costume the animal part of you. Check out images of anthropomorphic dolls on Pinterest or via other visual resources. If a story or poem comes to mind when you think of you and your animal self, write it in your journal.

Blue Moon River Woman

Barb Kobe

This doll was inspired by "The Story of the River and the Clouds" by Vietnamese Buddhist monk and peace activist Thich Nhat Hanh; the story appears in his book *No Death, No Fear: Comforting Wisdom for Life*. The following is an adaptation:

Once upon a time there was a beautiful river finding her way among the hills, forests, and meadows. She had begun as a joyful spring, dancing and singing as she streamed down from the top of the mountain, and she was still very young when she arrived in the lowlands, where she slowed down a bit. She was thinking about going into the ocean.

As she grew up, she learned to look beautiful, winding gracefully along the hills and the meadows. One day she noticed the clouds reflected within herself, clouds with all sorts of colors and forms. For days, she did nothing but chase after clouds, one after another. She wanted to possess a cloud, to have one for herself. But clouds float and travel in the sky, and they were always changing form. As she continued to chase clouds, her pleasure and joy dwindled, eventually turning into despair, anger, and even hatred . . . chasing . . . always chasing.

One day, a strong wind came and blew away all the clouds in the sky, leaving it completely empty. The river thought that life was no longer worth living, because there were no longer any clouds to chase after. She wanted to die, to cease to exist. She asked, "If there are no clouds, how can I live at all?" But how can a river take her own life? That night, the river contemplated her journey.

She had been running after something outside of herself for so, so long that she had lost touch with who she was. She heard herself crying for the first time—the sounds of water crashing against the banks of the river. She was able to hear her own voice and discovered something quite important. She realized that what she had been looking for was already inside her. The clouds are nothing but water. They are born from water and will return to water. She realized that she herself was water.

The next morning, she noticed something she had never seen before—the beautiful blue sky. Before, she had only been interested in clouds. She realized that the large blue sky had been in her heart from the beginning; this immense insight brought her peace and happiness. And she saw that as long as she had the vast and beautiful sky, her place in the world would never be lost again.

That evening something wonderful happened. When she opened her heart completely to the evening sky, she received the image of the full moon. It was a blue moon, beautiful and round, reflecting like a jewel within her. She had never imagined she could receive such a beautiful image. She joined hands with the clouds and the moon, and they all walked slowly to the ocean—together.

74

Emotions and Feelings

Making healing dolls will bring out feelings—often ones you think you've hidden or stuffed. When I show one of my dolls that symbolizes a deep healing process about anger, sadness, or fear, the person viewing it will often say it's too scary or ugly. Often I hear, "Is that a voodoo doll?" or "Why would you make such an ugly doll?" Despite these first responses, most people are still drawn to dolls made from the creators' deep emotional regions. They want to hear the stories and meanings of the dolls.

> ## Most people are still drawn to dolls made
> ### from the creators' deep emotional regions. They want to hear the stories and meanings of the dolls.

Your feelings are messengers delivering essential information about what's going on inside you. Feelings are meant to be felt, understood, explored, and then released. The more you try to hide from or ignore a feeling, the more persistent it can become. Most of us have learned to push down and bury our feelings, not knowing the language of emotions or ways to express them. Many women have especially learned the message that an expression of anger is unpleasant, unfeminine, and unattractive. Most men have learned it is not okay to cry because it would express weakness. Left buried, these wounds fester and grow. Stuffing pain and emotions doesn't make them go away; it just pushes their negative energy into your physical body, which could lead to illness or disease. In *Art and Healing*, Barbara Ganim says,

> Emotions and feelings are conveyed through the body on the waves of our electromagnetic energy field. What many call the good feelings like happiness, joy, peace are pleasant and create a state of relaxation allowing a flow of unblocked energy to move through your body. The other unpleasant feelings like anger, sadness and guilt activate a stress response which creates blocks of energy in the body. Blocked energy causes physical pain that could eventually result in deterioration along with immune system dysfunction. This could lead to illness and disease setting in.

Ganim recommends starting with these three simple exercises:

Exercise One: Get in touch with your pain and emotions—"you can't heal if you can't feel."

Exercise Two: Once you're feeling that pain or emotion, try to connect it to your past to uncover where that pattern of pain began.

Exercise Three: Embark on a healing ritual that will help you surrender that pain and anger once and for all.

Grief Expressed
Geralyn Sorensen

"Feelings are a necessity. It's your survival. It's your soul life. It's your truth. And without them, your art, your life, your writing will be generic—anybody's voice. With it, your work will be authentic, powerful—your voice."

Nancy Slonim Aronie
Writing from the Heart

Angry Paper Doll
Patty Gardiner

75

Feeling Faces
Barb Kobe

"Watch what emerges/evolves in your doll. The creations are tracks left along the path of progress, not YOU. If what you see is disturbing, remember that the whole range of human feelings is part of us, at least part of our legacy as humans."

Pamela Hastings
Doll Making as a Transformative Process

Llorona (Weeping Woman)
Valerie Cook

Dollmaking can be that healing ritual. It can help release these stuffed feelings. This is one of the most important parts of this process. Stuffed or blocked feelings come through and appear in your dolls, even if that is not your intention. Angry and ugly faces almost always appear when participants in my classes are learning to make faces from clay. I have seen many a beginner make a face and decide she doesn't like it because it looks angry or sad. She smashes the clay and starts again, but the same face reappears. Because we're used to blocking such feelings, this can create a block in the creative process as well.

In her book *The Dark Side of the Light Chasers*, life coach Debbie Ford said we can all find what is holding us back in life: "To go deeper, you have to be radically honest with yourself. All of your emotions are there to guide you." I encourage my students to accept what is coming through them and to work through the energy of the feeling by naming it, telling its story, and dialoguing with it. When a student makes an angry or ugly face, paints it, and applies it to a doll, the energy of that emotion moves through her and creates a shift.

In this healing doll process, you will make a doll about pain—the Scapegoat. Creating a doll that expresses your feelings about pain can help you get in touch with the emotion(s) that created the pain. It allows you to see the colors and shapes that describe the feelings in your body. Making the doll may not resolve the issue, but expressing how something feels in your body can change or shift your perception of the situation. It can offer insight and allow you to experience a sense of relief, even if you cannot change the pain. Art therapist Ilse Gilliland describes this as a "personal symbolic process where the artwork is the therapeutic tool that brings the artist in touch with herself, centralizing the energy and the mind into a clearer more focused awareness, as well as validates the feelings and emotions as responses to life."

I say as long as you're working with heart energy and approaching the process with personal integrity and honesty, you can trust your intuitive, creative self and allow it to guide you.

A key element of exploring your feelings through dollmaking is creating the doll's face. Our faces express our feelings to the world. In every one of my classes, students first hesitate then struggle with making faces. The face is important to the overall meaning of the doll. It is the first thing people look at, and the first question dollmakers usually get asked is, "Where did you get the face?" Therefore, if you're going to make a healing doll, I suggest you make the face yourself rather than use a mold. Or if you use a mold, I recommend you then change the face to express a feeling.

Making the doll's face can in and of itself change the depth and direction of the process for you. Or perhaps the overall symbol of the doll—regardless of the face—is what will raise consciousness and produce a change. I say as long as you're working with heart energy and approaching the process with personal integrity and honesty, you can trust your intuitive, creative self and allow it to guide you.

Sometimes when you make the face, it will look like your own. I think this is important to acknowledge and accept, as these are *your* healing dolls. So let it happen. You can always add to your technical skills in dollmaking—it's a lifelong process. At this point, make the doll image and see what happens. In other words, do not let the face-making part of the process stop you from making the dolls.

Student's series of feeling paper dolls

Feelings and the Body

Feelings are first recognized in the face, but they don't stop there. A healing doll expresses your feelings, your message, and your story through its form, its figure, and its body.

When I teach, I ask the dollmakers to first set a healing intention by answering the question, "What will you feel when you look at your completed healing doll? What will be her feeling story?" Once they identify this feeling, I ask them to position their bodies in a way that expresses that feeling, as if they were the completed doll. Then we look at the body language. What is the position of the head, neck, shoulders, arms, hands, torso, legs, and feet? For example, do your hands reach up toward the sky, or are they tightly wrapped around your waist? What would a doll sharing an angry or sad story look like? What size will her head, shoulders, belly, hips, hands, and feet be? Will some of these body parts need to be proportionally larger or smaller to emphasize the feeling, message, or story?

In *The Doll as a Messenger*, Elinor Peace Bailey details stages of human experience or consciousness: innocence; awakening; shame; anger; sexual objectification; reconciliation; empowerment; and crone, truth teller, or wise guide. Each of these human experiences contains messages that can be expressed visually by combining aspects of archetypes and feelings. What images came up for you when reading these? Was there just a face? A body part? A whole body?

When you create healing dolls, they become containers for your emotions and remind you of the relationship you have with your emotional body. These dolls can be a way to see your story. Making a healing doll gives you permission to move through a process to create change in your body, mind, and spirit.

"The more we resist, deny, or run away from a feeling, the harder it is likely to hit us when we finally do face it. If we learn to accept all emotions as natural signals, we can also learn that they can be accepted and expressed constructively. Yet, too many of us feel the need to hide our feelings."

Gabrielle Rico
Pain and Possibility

Embracing Her Wound **(Paper Doll)**
Barb Kobe

"The function of the soul's voice is to keep us informed through our feelings and emotions, to impart wisdom that will help us fulfill our destiny."

Barbara Ganim and Susan Fox
Visual Journaling

77

Numbing and Stuffing Feelings

When I first designed and created the small feeling characters the Fulls (Rage-full, Tearfull, Fearfull, and Joyfull), I showed them to a group of children who gathered together in a Children Are People group. Children Are People offers programming to at-risk youth in kindergarten through high school. As the program describes, "Participants receive caring attention from positive role models who help them focus on possibilities, not limitations—paving the way for positive futures." When I asked the group of children what they thought of my feeling characters, several of them said, "These are great, but one is missing!" "What could that be?" I asked. One of the children said, "Numbfull!" When I asked for an explanation, another child said, "We don't talk about feelings at our house. When we have them, we are told not to have them, or we're punished if we show them. So we stuff them until we feel numb!"

Numbfull
Barb Kobe

After this insight from these wise children, I went to work creating this new character. The Fulls stuff themselves down and live in Numbfull when they don't feel accepted or safe enough to be experienced or expressed. It's a simple metaphor for how we try to bury, block, deny, and repress our feelings. We think this gets rid of these feelings, only to discover that we have merely stored them. It takes physical energy to keep these stored feelings hidden away.

Stressfull
Barb Kobe

I think a creative act can shift something,

will wiggle loose some blocked energy that will lead you to take action toward your next healing. When I make a healing doll or put images and words in into my visual journal in artful ways, I am wiggling healing possibilities loose. I see these creative actions as inviting my intuition to play with my life events and see them as invitations to a healing journey.

Numbfull is gray for a reason: When we stuff our feelings or try to hide them, we lose our color—we look and feel like a gray, cloudy day. Numbfull's message is that when feelings are not expressed, they have a stifling, immobilizing effect on our bodies, minds, and spirits. I would often walk into a workshop with these little feeling dolls stuffed under my shirt, just to start the conversation.

Creative Block
Barb Kobe

Making your own doll can provide insight about how stuffing feelings impacts your body, mind, and spirit. It's a reminder that stuffing these feelings is a choice. I made the doll *Creative Block* (left) to explore what it might look like inside my body when I try to stuff a feeling. She looks stressed to me, holding her breath to keep the feeling inside. At the same time, her insides are in turmoil, agitated by all the energy of the repressed feelings. I want to say to her, "Take a deep breath and let go—you will feel better."

78

Creative Action

Practice making feeling faces. If you are a beginner, you might first practice making your doll faces using face molds from a craft store. Play with the molds in order to build confidence with the clay and with facial features. I use air-dry clays such as Crayola Model Magic and Creative Paperclay. There are other kinds of air-dry clays available. You may also polymer clay, if that's what you prefer. Next, try making faces without the molds.

Most of us have no experience with feeling identification and emotional communication. For inspiration, see the "Feeling Face Paper Doll" section in the appendix (page 224) to identify the feelings and what an entire body would look like when expressing a feeling.

Also check out the "Feelings Research" tool in the appendix (page 223). It guides you through a series of questions to explore emotions. It may provide insights that allow you to express your feelings in your dolls and deepen the healing experience. This is a fun activity to do with family and friends. It can open your eyes—and heart.

Fear Doll in Her Own Bag
Maureen Carlson

Pain, Grief, and Suffering

Rue

Lugeo

Kathryn Hall, Colorado

In late October, my nephew died after a car wreck. He was only thirty-two. I can't even allow myself to fully imagine the depths of grief that his mother finds herself in. I help as much as I'm able, but there's not a lot of help for these circumstances except to continue to be there, listen, comfort. While I was consumed with helping his mother (who is my dear friend and former sister-in-law), I wasn't doing anything to honor or acknowledge my own grief. It didn't seem important at first because hers was so overwhelming, but I began to realize that I needed to do something for myself. Ignoring it didn't mean it wasn't there, chewing on my heart.

For the three weeks following Peter's death, I didn't do anything creative at all. Normally, I do some kind of creative work daily because I must. But it just wasn't in me, I didn't think. It seemed that all joy had been sucked out of me, and with it, creativity. To even think about doing something "fun" just didn't seem right.

Eventually, I realized that I needed to create a grief doll. I needed somewhere to put this emotion. I needed to honor my feelings, and the best way, I have learned, is to do so creatively. I needed to see my grief concretely and let it ooze out of my fingers into clay. So I pulled out a ball of clay and began to make faces. In the space of just over a week, two dolls were created. I cannot even express how much it helped me to make them. It doesn't mean that the grief is gone, but it has been partially transformed. It's been honored and given a place. I don't even have the words to explain the change. It is just changed and not so heavy.

The first one I made is more abstract and symbolic, with a huge heart-shaped hole in her middle and a dangling prism of tears and light. She cradles the hole, trying to comfort herself. Her name is *Rue*. The second one represents the head-in-hands pain and a stone-heavy heart, which her body cannot even hold. It has fallen to her lap. She is *Lugeo*—Latin for "grief and mourning."

I just want to share that, in my experience, even if we have other creative endeavors waiting or in process, when something BIG comes up in our lives, we need to stop and give THE BIG THING its due time and attention. Acknowledge it. Honor it. Different people will do that in different ways. But for us dollmakers, chances are very good that making a doll is the thing to do; at least, it was for me. Once I made *Rue* and *Lugeo*, I was released to create whatever else caught my fancy and the projects that had been waiting at the time Peter died. I've been busy with sewing and painting projects since then, but the grief dolls had to come first.

The Doll Body: Inner and Outer

You have chosen a doll as the art form you will use to create healing. This kind of creative, expressive art is rooted in the mind-body connection. Working with a body form is a wonderful way to explore, play with, and express your creative self. During and after the dollmaking process, you have the opportunity to get "in touch" with yourself, your body, your essence. As you view, touch, and hold your doll, it will mirror back your body's feelings and stories, becoming a physical representation of you, your emotions, your body, and more.

Embodiment is the representation of a tangible or visible form of an idea, quality, or feeling. Your healing dolls will embody your creative process, thoughts, beliefs, feelings, symptoms, and pain. They will help you make meaning from these things.

I first heard the term *interoception* from Lisa Wimberger in her book *Neurosculpting*. The system of interoception as a whole constitutes "the material me" and relates to how we perceive feelings from our bodies that determine our mood, sense of well-being, and emotions. This system is controlled by a part of the brain called the insula, which seems to provide the basis for your personal emotional awareness.

Your dolls will embody your creative process, thoughts, beliefs, feelings, symptoms, and pain. They will help you make meaning from these things.

Making healing dolls will be expressive art that increases your sense of interoception, that is, your signaling and perception of your internal bodily sensations. Playing with and creating body images offers you a structure to express what it means to let go of fear, disease, and concepts of pain. This kind of artmaking can energize your mind-body connection. As you make your healing dolls, you will notice there is a definite feel to a doll when you hold her body in one or both of your hands. It will also be interesting to notice how it feels when you hold a part of your own body. What feels the same? What feels different?

These dolls will become safe containers and boundaries in which to explore all manners of things you may have previously feared, avoided, hidden, and secretly believed. Your thoughts and feelings about your body image—how you feel about how you look—will influence the look of your dolls and the stories they tell you about your body. Making healings dolls will help you live peacefully and confidently in your body and experience it as a vibrant, creative force. In essence, it will help you be at home in your body.

Embracing Her Core
Barb Kobe

"Art became a way of knowing myself through the experience of the personal pain. In seeing the image of the pain, I could step away. I became the artist, and the series of paintings remained as the physical creation of pain. They were now my art, completely separate from me. I became free."

Mary Rockwood Lane
Creative Healing

Your Power Lies Within
Erika Cleveland

81

Inner and Outer Body Parts and Feelings

Consider these questions when making your healing doll: Will your doll have arms and hands, legs and feet? What size will they be? How will you make her torso? What will you use to make her head and face? What body parts—such as eyes, nose, mouth, and ears—will you use in unexpected places to express a message or emotion? Will her heart be on the outside of her body?

Art therapist Erika Cleveland says, "Children often exaggerate the parts of the body that they are becoming aware of in their life at the time—heads, hands, and feet are often hugely out of proportion to the rest of the body. And parts of bodies are used to artistic and practical effect in the art of regions such as Mexico, where *milagros* (meaning 'miracles'), or metal reproductions of body parts, are placed onto altars for healing."

Shame on Me
Barb Kobe

"One participant, whose image, for me, speaks to the whole theme of the workshop created a body with a mouth in her belly, allowing the body to tell its own message, to speak its own truth."

Erika Cleveland
Art therapist, Medicine Doll participant

Making healing dolls will help you live
peacefully and confidently in your body and experience your body as a vibrant, creative force. In essence, it will help you be at home in your body.

In order to make my doll *Shame On Me* (left), I thought about the colors that remind me of feeling shame in my body—black and dark, blood red. I got in touch with what it feels like in my body to feel shame. I felt the weight of it in my arms and legs, so I put small plastic pellets in the doll's arms and legs to weigh them down. My head hangs down when I'm trying to hide, so I found a way to make the doll's head droop over the torso and hang down, looking at the ground. Finally, I created an image of a broken, cracked heart leaking love, because when I feel shame, I don't feel love from anyone, including myself. I then put her up on my wall as a reminder that I don't have to hold shame in my body.

When I was having panic attacks, I decided to create a doll that embodied what I believed panic looked like inside and outside my body (left). My thoughts seemed jagged and confused, as if they were roots coming out of my head. The expression on her face is one of trying to hold fear in, wanting to numb it. My hands and arms feel tied to my body at my center, making me feel powerless. The doll was ungrounded with no feet, only assorted sticks going many directions. The dark-red heart symbolized palpitations, as if her heart was coming out of her chest.

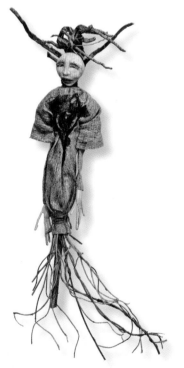

Panic Attack
Barb Kobe

Symptoms

Body symptoms can be doorways into the bodymind. They can speak "organ jargon" that furnishes you with creative inspiration to decipher and express your personal pain or challenge. Symptoms may reveal where issues of possible healing and transformation can be focused. Making healing dolls allow you to connect with your body and your symptoms. You become a detective in following your body's clues.

In his book *Listening to Pain*, David Biro says, "Metaphors of pain have structure, form and purpose; the experience becomes a story that has several characters and a plot with a beginning, middle and end." He also says, "Metaphor promises us control over experiences by supplying it with meaning."

I think this is key. A healing doll becomes a symbol of a story—whether an outward expression of a personal story or a character that lives in your body as a symptom. The doll becomes part of an internal dialogue. You may want to play with meanings of symptoms and affirmations by exploring Louise Hay's books and other offerings.

Your inner and outer symptoms may be the part of you trying to grow and develop. It's your wise signaler. When it signals to you through your body, it's called a symptom. When it signals to you through a dream, it's called a symbol. If you pay attention to these signals, talk to them, and express them through a doll, the healing process may begin in one way or another. Making art through a doll image offers ways to play with so many inner and outer parts of yourself.

Energy Healing

Energy healing is a broad term for any therapy that stimulates the energy flow in or around the human body, otherwise known as the biofield, to restore balance on all levels. This thereby enables the physical body to heal itself. The body's energy systems are rich with symbols, maps, and diagrams that can be put on a healing doll as part of an intention or story. I suggest you research pictures of these systems so they may serve as inspiration for embellishing your healing dolls.

Chakras

The seven chakras are the centers through which energy flows in our bodies. The theory is that blocked energy in the chakras can often lead to illness. So, it's important to understand what each chakra represents and what we can do to keep this energy flowing freely.

Chakra Healing Doll
Barb Kobe

"It's been my experience that what occurs in the physical is simply a manifestation of what's taking place in the energetic realm. So, I've been curious about what's been happening back stage of this physical body—those subtle and not-so-subtle thoughts and beliefs that affect what's happening within and around me."

Anne Heck
Medicine Dolls online group

"Turning toward the symptom with an attitude of respectful inquiry rather than the usual patient stance of avoidance, resistance and rejection can give the patient access to signals from those parts of the personality that are in need of expressive development."

Ernest Rossi
Bodymind researcher

Meridians

These channels transport life energy throughout the body. This energy is called *chi* or *qi* in Chinese medicine. (Other names exist as well.) The meridian theory holds that blockages can occur somewhere in the meridians, leading to a lack of energy in certain areas of the body or a surplus of energy in other areas. The meridian system is used in acupuncture, acupressure, and many other systems of healing.

Auras

The human energy field is also called the aura or subtle bodies. It is comprised of several layers of energy commonly known as the physical (or etheric), emotional, mental, and spiritual bodies. Auras (and chakras) are associated with colors, making them a great tool for choosing colors to put into and around your healing dolls.

The Endocrine System

This system is comprised of various glands producing hormonal secretions that go directly into the bloodstream and lymphatic system, circulating to all parts of the body. These body parts can be visual symbols inside and/or outside of the body of the doll.

"I think we have an added advantage being dollmakers. We can take words that describe a symptom, research the details about the system, and turn it into a metaphor. Then, using our creative toolbox, we can engage with this knowledge through artmaking that mirrors back to us a new relationship we can have with our bodies. When done, we share the story of our lessons and learning, encouraging our group to make new connections for themselves, explore deeper, and make their own metaphors and images. All so creatively scientific!"

Barb Kobe

Creative Action

Go through a variety of magazines or books that have photographs of people in various poses. Do quick sketches of these images using pencil and paper. Play with guessing what story their body positions might be telling.

Try this exercise adapted from one called "Decoding the Messages of the Body," which appears in *Dr. Judith Orloff's Guide to Intuitive Healing: 5 Steps to Physical, Emotional, and Sexual Wellness*:

1. Choose a symptom you have felt recently.

2. Think about when it first appeared. Ask yourself what life situation, thought, dream, event, or news was happening when the symptom appeared.

3. Consider what metaphor might explain the symptom. What might the symptom mean to you and your life?

4. Ask, "What does the symptom stop me from doing? What does the symptom make me want to do?"

Create an energy system collage with color and images of each system. Then take some of the colors and images and apply them to a drawing of a body. Create feeling face and body paper dolls. (See page 224 in the appendix for paper doll patterns.)

Healing Art

Pamela Hastings, Port Angeles, Washington

Transformative doll making, I realized in 2003, is part of my life. My father was a psychiatrist, so I was familiar with the concept of art as a reflection of the workings of the soul/psyche. Looking through my soft sculptures from the seventies on, I noticed a trend of showing rage and pain in my work—Yukio Mishima ripping his guts out, the Angry Woman Mask, and more—that expressed feelings in my art that I didn't feel safe expressing in my abusive marriage. As I collected images for my first book, *Doll Making as a Transformative Process* (published in 2004 and 2015), I realized the the same negative themes seemed to resonate with other artists.

Dolls, paper dolls, writing, collage . . . are all very direct ways of expressing and thereby being able to understand and channel feelings. I divorced my husband in 1982, after making lots of angry art, demonstrating feelings that I was afraid to express to him. In 2005 I moved away from the next man who was not providing the emotional support I needed. I've been able to be mostly kind to my mother by having a safe outlet for my angry feelings about her. Interesting that I have used dollmaking mostly to express anger, but for a long time, most of my dolls didn't even have mouths.

When I was in high school, and my mother was at her craziest, the art teacher was my Good Mother, and I would make things in her class that scared both of us. Figures reaching have always been part of my visual vocabulary . . . I'm always looking for answers.

Sad Woman Hugging Herself

If frightening images show up in your work, you may not want to show them to people who don't understand Raw Art. **But it is better to have the feelings outside of you, in concrete form, than to have the stress chemicals attacking your insides.** This work can be used to positive effect, as I did in formulating my idea of being a good mother to myself. Interestingly, as I look around my studio, I still don't see nearly as many embracing dolls as angry ones.

I recently made a pietà figure inspired by a war photograph for Veterans Day, and last winter I made a depressed doll who hugs herself. I'm still learning to hug myself, and I'm working on a series about accepting the changes that come with aging.

Compassion for a Veteran

We each develop our individual vocabulary of colors, symbols, and shapes to express our feelings. In addition to the lack of a mouth on dolls when I was unhappy in relationships, I notice now that many of my dolls are missing at least one arm . . . perhaps I feel powerless . . . One has a blade as a head . . . powerless but aggressive . . . Or maybe I just don't like to make hands. I used a skull with a face behind it, at a pivotal point in my life, and now it's a talisman to remind me to persevere.

In response to feeling stomach-punched by the recent US election results, I have been making a huge effort to turn out one joyful artwork a day . . . it seems to be lifting my mood a bit. Collage and paper dolls are quicker than three-dimensional dolls as studies to work up to a more time-consuming finished piece.

My advice for making any art:

- Pursue a daily practice.

- Get everything down first before you start editing.

- Walk away . . . but be sure to come back.

- Read a lot and look at art that inspires you.

- Practice, practice, practice.

- Don't censor—you can refine and rearrange later.

- Save ideas . . . I stick rough sketches into notebooks and write my thoughts every day, then I have raw material when I'm ready to refine, refine, refine.

- Read autobiographies of writers and other artists . . . nothing is easy.

- Let work in progress sit for a while (from a day to a week) before you edit for clarity.

- Keep several projects going at once, so you can always find something to work on.

- My most energetic time is midmorning, so I try to do my most challenging creative work then.

- Always have something mindless to work on to get you back into the studio.

- Don't take criticism too seriously—you know what you want to say, but listen if viewers seem confused.

- Be your own toughest critic, but be kind.

- Keep going back to the studio . . . or computer.

- If you're trying to write about a piece you made but don't feel comfortable writing, just use phrases, like a free-form poem, and the word picture will explain what you want to say.

- Trust your instincts . . . there's a lot more going on inside you than is on the surface. Try to turn off the inner critics when starting a new piece.

Angie's Story

Barb Kobe

In 2007, I made a healing doll for my friend Angie in Minneapolis. She answered The Ten Questions I ask anyone wanting me to make a healing doll for them. Angie was diagnosed with stage 4 ovarian cancer in 2006. She passed on Thursday, June 25, 2009.

Her passing took me to my ever-questing questions: What is healing? Can making a healing doll for someone heal them? Her answers to The Ten Questions are on the next page. See if you can find ways I incorporated her responses into images on the doll.

Angie's answers to The Ten Questions:

1. What colors are you drawn to? Do you wear often? Are your favorites?

Blue and brown with a splash of red.

2. What will this doll symbolize for you? What will it remind you to think, feel, and/or do when you see it?

I am healthy and strong. I am loved and supported. Positive energy from the universe is pouring into my body.

3. What elements describe you? Earth, air, water, fire?

Air and earth. I breathe in positive energy and find hope and courage in the plants sprouting from the earth in the springtime. There is life after the winter.

4. What symbols do you like or are you drawn to? What objects do you collect or like to spend time around?

Family photos, flowers and plants, crosses, mugs (for quiet tea-drinking times with friends), smooth rocks, yin and yang, Chinese symbols, angels, colored glass, mosaics.

5. What part of your body do you feel needs healing?

Spirit, to continue to be strong and courageous; lymph nodes, to be full of healing energy; feminine side, to be restored to life.

6. Describe the symptoms and location of the pain, illness, or condition.

Stage 4 ovarian cancer that has spread to the lymph nodes. I have scars on my abdomen, neck, and chest. The discomfort I have at this time is the pain around the port in my chest. It is a constant reminder that I get chemo (even more so than the hair loss!), and I have not been able to feel comfortable with it. It still bothers me when I touch it, and I hate it when they stick my IV in.

7. If an animal with special powers were to enter your life to give you power, what would that animal be?

It would be a small white furry animal that curls up with me and gives me comfort and warmth and would able to enter my cells and keep my body healthy. It would be a wise animal— an old soul who could help me on this journey. I don't get a picture of any real animal, so you'll have to invent a new one. I certainly don't want a small rodent or a cat to enter my life! Maybe it would be a Narnia lion who is wise and protective.

8. When do you feel the most powerful?

When I concentrate on breathing. When coincidences happen. When I get hugs and notes and surprise visits. When the wind blows on my face. When I hear birds and water running. SPRING!

9. What brings you the greatest joy? Makes your heart sing? What does your heart yearn for?

Family and friends and traveling and getting to know other peoples and cultures brings me joy and energy. However, the thing that brings me my greatest joy is being with my husband, daughter, and son. My heart yearns to be with them for many, many more years. The only thing that has made me cry during these five months is the thought that I might not be able to do that.

10. What is your favorite fairy tale? Explain how this fairy tale is a metaphor for your life.

"Stone Soup" is the story that keeps coming to mind throughout these months. When everyone is concerned only for themselves, there is nothing extra and everyone feels poor. When people begin to share and work together, there is an abundance. I have felt this abundance during my illness. There has never been a lack of anything because the community has shared with me and my family. I know if I'm not here to help my children through some challenge in their lives, there will be many other loving people who they can lean on. One thing that was clear from the beginning of this journey was that it had to be a WE. It might be physically happening to me, but it was also happening to everyone around me too. By taking away my illusion of living forever (or at least until I'm eighty), cancer has given me the present.

Part 3:
Creating the Healing Dolls

"What matters most is experiencing your feelings and gaining insights."

Lucia Capachione

Healing Doll Ground Rules

You are ready to begin the creative process of making five healing dolls. Before you proceed to part 3, take a moment to contemplate the "ground rules" for this journey upon which you are about to embark. These tips will support you along the way:

- Trust your intuition.

- Stay open to possibilities.

- Be willing to be in the unknown.

- Play with your imagination.

- Be inquisitive, eager to learn; ask, "What would happen if . . . ?"

- Stand back and question your beliefs.

- Know that creativity involves a process.

- Do not prejudge or anticipate where the imagery will take you.

- Allow yourself to learn and be guided by the experience.

- Remember, you are not broken and do not need to be fixed.

- Remember to connect with your witness, with whom you can share your doll creations.

- Be present and participate—meaning do the work—in the making of your dolls and art.

"You can break rules. Two wrongs can make a right. Creative problem solving can result in some very nice, unexpected side effects. Don't Fuss, try again. Re-design it."

Susanna Oroyan
Dollmaker

The Creative Process Overview

This process is very much like conceiving, gestating, and giving birth to a child. I can always tell when I'm in "transition." I wander around the studio, whiny and crabby. I've learned it is best to name it for what it is—I am birthing something—then accept the deep swells of emotions that accompany it.

You will make five healing dolls: the Guardian, the Scapegoat, the Talisman, the Loving Kindness, and the Inner Healer. This work will take you through a creative process, toward a goal of healing an aspect of yourself and your life. Your intention will drive the process and keep you focused. Your journal will become the record keeper and will provide a place for you to dialogue with your creations.

The healing doll creative process has six steps:

1. Set a healing intention to keep you focused and to guide the process.

2. Make the Guardian, an image of protection.

3. Identify what is in the way of you getting your healing intention (or identify what you blame for the pain), then go through the process of making the Scapegoat in order to release this block.

4. Choose whether you need or want to make the Loving Kindness, an image of compassion, nurturing, and understanding.

5. Transform the painful Scapegoat image into the Talisman, a new image that represents the healing goal: a less stressful, more positive way to respond to whatever causes you pain.

6. Make the Inner Healer, an image that symbolizes lessons learned and reminds you of your body's natural ability to heal itself.

While this book presents and guides you in creating the dolls in a certain order, I fully expect most makers to adapt this process as they see fit. I recommend you read through the book before making any of the dolls. Then, after an overview (or big picture) of the process, you could engage with the Creative Actions (on pages 38, 42, 49, 57, 64, 69, 72, and 84). Or you might decide to jump into the process.

It is very, *very* important to write your healing intention as directed by the Creative Action on page 97—don't skip this step, as it is the underlying energy that leads the way through. Only once your healing intention is written should you proceed with making the Guardian (starts on page 105). I tell my students, "Never go into the deep without protection, that being your Guardian." After your Guardian is created, then decide what doll you want to create next. This will depend on how you feel, what feels right, and/or what feels safe or scary. There is nothing wrong with making the remaining dolls in *your* order.

Art Shaman
Barb Kobe

"When one of us takes a journey, it affects us all. When people see my work, they are often moved to tell me their own stories—and we all become reconnected in the myth, in the oneness we all share."

Barbara Ganim
Art and Healing

The Dolls

The Guardian

The first doll in the process must be one that represents protection, safety, compassion, hope, possibility, and encouragement. This doll stands witness and is always present while you make the other dolls. I say to my students, "Never go in without protection." This is a discovery process that invites you to be curious, take creative risks, and dive deep into unknown parts of yourself.

The Scapegoat

The Scapegoat symbolizes what is getting in the way of achieving your goal. I believe making this doll opens up the most potential for healing.

The Loving Kindness

This doll allows for more compassionate, positive, and peaceful ways of responding to the creative process and to any feelings the Scapegoat may have brought up.

The Talisman

Because the Scapegoat can bring up painful emotions from the past, the Talisman offers an opportunity to balance the story of that pain. This is a strong and powerful doll that pulls you out of the past and into the present and future.

The Inner Healer

The Inner Healer reminds you that dollmaking can give voice to your heart and your wisdom. This doll will symbolize how all your resources are within you. She will remind you that you can move through painful experiences with insight and compassion, opening up pathways to your imagination.

Bless Your Heart
Barb Kobe

Although the process is designed so that each doll is made one after another, in actual practice, this may not be the case for you. I believe the Guardian must come first, but after that, the order may vary. Trust what image comes next, and stay in communication with yourself and your witness so you are conscious of where you are in your process. You may start with one doll and transform it as you take each step in the process.

For example, Michelle made a dark-red, angry Scapegoat doll in a class. As she did the journaling work and began the Talisman, she worked with the angry doll form, adding new symbols and embellishments. The Scapegoat transformed into a powerful and positive warrior-image Talisman.

Sunflower Guardian
Barb Kobe

As you make your way through the dollmaking process, you may find some stages more challenging than others. You will get in touch with powerful emotions in this healing journey. At times, you may resist the process or find yourself unable to move forward. Below are a few ideas to keep in mind if you happen to find yourself stuck or blocked. (You will also find specific tips in the Scapegoat and Loving Kindness sections.)

- Keep making dolls or doing some kind artwork every day.
- Make a small doll every day for one week.
- Draw "feeling" doodles and journal with them.
- Using clay, sculpt an image of the block or the place where you're stuck
- Watch a funny movie.
- Be with your "stuckness" and imagine how you might "unstick" it.
- Allow yourself to make mistakes and make bad art. Even "bad" has a purpose.
- Make ugly or angry dolls.
- Move ahead and make the Loving Kindness doll.
- Make another Guardian or spend time with the Guardian you created.

How Long Will It Take Me?

You may wonder how long it will take to move through this discovery and creative process. This will depend on your healing intention and creative skill level. If you are a beginner dollmaker, it may take you more time than someone who has been making art dolls for a long time. If you use paper dolls and art journaling, your process may take less time. Most of the women who participated in the Medicine Dolls online classes completed the dolls in one year; others took two or more. I've learned that real-life events tend to disrupt the best-laid plans. I suggest you create a timeline, put it on a calendar, then see how you progress. Remember to find someone to be your believing mirror, with whom you can share your dolls, as you work toward your goal.

Now, let's begin the first step of the creative process: setting a healing intention.

Thumbs Up Girl
Amy Egenburger

Guardian Quilt
Barb Kobe

94

Setting a Healing Intention

In healing, energy follows thought. More specifically, intention allows the healing energy to follow and take root where it is needed. I encourage you to create a clear healing intention before you begin the healing doll process. Many of us tend to focus on the solution of a problem, going for a quick fix. We rarely spend time defining the problem. This is similar to taking a drug for a symptom without knowing what's causing it. Many goal-setting theories talk about writing a full description of what you want, and my process begins similarly—you must set a healing intention.

When I teach healing doll classes, some students initially want to make a healing doll for a loved one. They don't see the importance of focusing on their own healing first. I caution my students about making healing dolls for others without first being clear about their own intentions. I believe it's important to make your own healing dolls first. I also believe it's impossible to know what another person needs to heal.

I ask each participant in the healing doll classes to write a healing intention statement. Let's explore some examples of intention statements participants have made.

Andi seemed very clear about what she wanted to heal. She declared,

> **Intention:** *Healing my self-worth, to focus healing energy toward accepting that I am in the body and life that is right for me at this moment. I believe healing for me will mean letting go of old outmoded ideals of what I should be or how I should look or how I should live; letting go of looking to outside sources for approval. Letting go of comparing myself to others. Replacing negative thinking and beliefs with new caring and acceptance; learning more positive self-talk.*

Andi's intention statement asked for acceptance and letting go. At the end of the class, her feedback said she accomplished that. Reflecting on what she learned and achieved, Andi wrote, "I got relief from letting out all this baggage that has been riding around in me; the process gave me permission to make something just for me, to heal me."

Mary's intention read, "To focus healing energy toward the expression of my female power and the creation of the next phase of my life." At the end of the process she wrote,

> *I think I am much more focused on accepting my power and trusting that opportunities will continue to present themselves that will foster this. My artmaking is better, and I am more willing to take risks with it. I also have a wonderful inner healer on my bedside table.*

**Watering the Roots
of Her Wisdom**
Barb Kobe

"Native American tradition teaches that you cannot succeed if you do not ask. Jesus echoed this when he said, 'Ask and ye shall receive.' We must ask for what we want, and at the same time let go of it."
Lewis Mehl-Madrona
Coyote Medicine

95

Eventually She Saw Herself
(paper doll)
Barb Kobe

More Play Today
(paper doll)
Barb Kobe

The Power to Heal Is in Her Hands
(paper doll)
Barb Kobe

Debi started with one intention and gradually refined it as she worked through the preparation activities before starting the dollmaking process. I've seen this many times in class, as almost every student starts with one intention in mind and later realizes their intention has changed. (Read more about Debi at the end of the chapter.)

Your intention statement speaks to a life change or an opportunity to move toward a dream or goal that could shake you up in new ways. It speaks to an initiation, a healing opportunity, an invitation, or a calling to open yourself up to a new adventure. This can come in many forms:

- A message or messenger; a herald (something or someone who has issued a challenge or invitation announcing the coming of change).

- A new event.

- A stirring from within in the form of a dream, fantasy, or vision.

- A feeling of being fed up with something.

- An uncomfortable situation.

- A developmental stage of life or a life change.

- An accident or illness.

- An invitation to be creative.

- Synchronicity—an occurrence of coincidental words, ideas, or events.

- Temptation.

Sweater Doll
Barb Kobe

Creative Action

Creating an Intention

1. What has called you to this process? Tell the story that brought you to the healing doll process. Use "she" (or your preferred pronoun) instead of "I" or your name. For example, "She was living her life day-by-day when something happened to wake her up. That something was _____." Once you know what has called you, now consider your intent. What do you want to do?

- Focus on a crisis.

- Focus on illness, pain, or a wound.

- Focus on a sudden change in your life.

- Investigate something confusing.

- Find what is missing in your life.

- Acknowledge and affirm a developmental stage.

- Confront a belief that no longer serves you.

- Confront a fear.

- Work through anger or grief issues.

- Get more of something: peace, love, meaning.

- Design and develop a connection with a higher power.

- Dive in deep and explore a shadow aspect of yourself.

2. Think about what you want to heal. What is the first thing that comes to your mind when you think about this? You want to heal or change _____. Then complete the following sentences:

- Healing for me will be _____.

- Transformation for me will be _____.

- I know I am moving toward healing when _____.

- I am committed to healing _____.

- I know I have healed when _____.

Consider how you and your world are now, and how they will be different once you reach your goal. How does your present world look, sound, move, feel, smell, and taste? How will your world look, sound, move, feel, smell, and taste in the future?

Make a mind map. Put your intention at the center, then spoke out with any associations, thoughts, or images that come to you. Write your intention statement in your journal. Make it large and colorful. Write it on postcards and post them around your house and where you create the dolls.

Inner Healer
Your Healing Wisdom Keeper
Purpose: Naming your healing and
wisdom ways

Intention/Guide
Setting a Healing Intention
Purpose: To keep you focused and guide
the processwisdom ways

Talisman
Stepping into the Light
Purpose: To transform the pain; to move
toward positive outcome

Spirit
Explore Your Definition
of a Spirit Doll

Guardian
Defender, Protector, Keeper
Purpose: To protect, motivate, encourage, support

Loving Kindness
Accepting, Allowing, and Self-Compassion
Purpose: To intentionally bring the energy of love
and compassion into the healing process

Scapegoat
Going into the Dark, or Shadow Doll
Purpose: Symbolizes the pain; embraces
the struggle

Before you embark on this journey, perhaps you want a Healing Doll Way map,
a big picture, to get a sense of the dolls you will be creating and the direction you
and your creations may take. Artist Debi Knight-Kennedy participated in one of
my first Medicine Dolls online classes. I invite you to read her healing doll story
(on the next page) in hopes that you will get a sense of the nature and progres-
sion of the process as well as see the dolls she created along the way.

Debi's Healing Doll Journey

Debi Knight-Kennedy, Alaska

I, Debi, intend to make a doll focusing on healing my wounded-little-girl self, with love and compassion and acceptance.

March 31

I intend to focus healing energy on my hypervigilance. I seem to be in defense mode all the time. My life has taught me that it is very likely that someone is about to attack me at any moment. It's been ten years now since I moved to Alaska and changed my attitude, my life, and my destiny. Nobody attacks me anymore. I have stopped marrying my father, a.k.a. abusive alcoholics, and I have pulled the "kick me" sign off my back. My life is really quite lovely. But I haven't been able to lose the hypervigilance thing. The most difficult thing about this group for me so far has been that I can't see anybody's face. I always need to read for signs of danger. I have had panic attacks pretty much any time I have posted anything. It's so exhausting . . . I believe healing for me will be a huge relief. I am so ready. I think this tool is just what I need to help. I have done a lot of healing work over the years and come a long way. I now need to develop the ability to trust. To let go. To live like I make art, with reckless abandon.

March 31

I tried mind-mapping this morning. I started with a tree with the roots of my hypervigilance, added some healthy pink roots of my healing process. I had been intimidated by this tool but found it to be very useful and insightful. Not only that, but it was fun and felt really good.

April 2

I have been doing some of the journaling exercises around narrowing in and possibly restating my focus. And sure enough, I found it enlightening and helpful. So here is my new statement of intention: My focus will be on love and compassion and acceptance of myself, especially my hurt, little-girl self. I don't think I have ever given her very much kindness. I have treated her just the way my mother did—always disappointed, thinking she wasn't good enough.

Wow, how obvious—treating myself just like I was treated by my mother. I guess this process asks for an all-the-way-or-nothing kind of attitude. So I want to focus on accepting the *me* that was, is, and will be. With any and all imperfections. I open the door to change and growth and letting go. I accept my gifts. I accept my limitations. I accept my pain, my life, my death. I accept it all with love, compassion, and courage. I imagine my first doll to be some kind of loving, nurturing soul. The very aspect of me that I just declared. Imagine that.

April 8

I am working on the Talisman doll. I think of her as representing what's on the other side of the block: the pain, the fear. She is quite different than anything I have made. Sort of primitive, icon-like. Her body is a dolphin vertebra that my husband found on the beach. I carved a graceful, serene bird head and shaped a piece of amber for her neck. I found a small green heart-shaped rock and inlaid it in her chest and formed a spiral in her abdomen. Various healing hands will dangle from her "arms." She will be standing in a fossilized whale vertebrae disk. It has been so moving for me. She has totally flowed. But I will acknowledge that this process has been very physical for me.

The things, changes, that my body is experiencing are very connected to the spiritual and emotional shifts that this project brings. Even now, with the making of this doll, it's not always fun, doesn't always feel good, isn't always easy. The heart-belly connection that is expressed in my doll is proving to be somewhat challenging physically.

I thought I was carving a hand,
and to my surprise, a beautiful, benevolent monster's face appeared. I loved it right then and there.

A friend just described to me the untwisting of the heart and how it can make one physically nauseous, that it is experienced in certain native rituals. I so connected with that. I feel like I am very slowly moving through this same thing, only over a time period of months rather than the days that would be traditional. I know that to others it sometimes looks like I am always having fun; they are looking only at the finished product. The process is often so disconcerting.

April 9

This whole process has been incredible. I have been unpeeling layers and opening and learning tons. The first big thing that happened was with my doll's face. I was in my shop trying to do some work for money when his face came out. I thought I was carving a hand, and to my surprise, a beautiful, benevolent monster's face appeared. I loved it right then and there. In fact, I loved it so much that I thought I should save it for a "real" doll, that it was too cool to use for myself. I was making a HEALING doll. So a huge amount of healing took place as I began my *Guardian Monster*.

When we did the early exercise about what dolls we had when we were kids, I remembered that I didn't play with dolls, that I had a ton of stuffed animals. My protectors. So my monster is composed of several animals, with human hands, holding my baby self. We are looking at each other with love and gratitude. Both emotions seem to be coming out of both of us. I will do some nondominant-hand writing about this next. I really love this doll. I'm so happy to get to keep him. He feels very protective and loving and is now so real. I can picture his smiling face whenever I need to. It almost feels a little silly to think that it matters,

but I feel so strongly that he is real. When I look at him, I feel so emotional. The little-hurt-baby me is comforted and relieved. Relieved to be alive. Relieved to have made it into this world intact. Relieved to finally have somebody or something there for me always. I guess I am kind of babbling here, but bringing your Guardian to life is such a powerful thing to do. Even more so than I thought it would be.

April 19

My Scapegoat is pretty dark. I have always made only beautiful dolls. I have always avoided the dark side. So an image came to me pretty fast. It was so creepy that I really tried to shut it out. Of course I knew I had to go with it, so I gave myself a day or so, then sort of blurted it out in a crude drawing in my journal. It was like I had to draw it quick and dirty before I chickened out. I have started actually making it, but I seem to have to give myself a little timeout after each session. It has four mean, snarling heads. I have them shaped in Fimo but have resisted baking them. I guess I am resisting making them permanent.

Today is the day. I will bake them today. The body will be that of an octopus, sort of. It is holding on to four little girls. I went to the Salvation Army just knowing that I would find what I needed. And sure enough, just as I was about to walk out the door, I saw a little plastic foot poking out of a basket. There they were—four little-girl dolls. I couldn't even grab them at first. The cashier asked me what I was looking for, and I said, "Never mind." It was too creepy.

She really encouraged me to explain, so I did. She said, "Oh my, you have to do it. We have to get this stuff out in the open." She then went on to share her experience with being abused as a child. I grabbed those dolls, and here I am. Building the courage to let the ugly arms wrap around them, hold them tight, and let the heads scream their ugly words at them. As a child, I watched my brother and sister get hit, but I was SOOOOOO good that I only got screamed at. But it was so scary. I made sure that I got straight *A*s in school. Overachieved in everything. Tried my best to be perfect so that I wouldn't get hit. I couldn't imagine how I would survive a physical attack by such a big man. I could see what would happen to me if I ever slipped from grace. I guess my dad was a very angry guy. His is a very scary doll to make, but I feel the power in doing it.

April 22

I just finished the Scapegoat doll. My heart is still pounding, and I feel like I might throw up. But other than that, I think it went pretty well. Really. Along the way, I have been having some pretty powerful insights. I think I need to go lie down.

April 24

Fair warning: the Scapegoat is pretty creepy. I do feel much better today. Yesterday was so intense. I worked on it all day, not feeling bad until it was actually done and I really looked at what I had made. It was way worth it, though. I'll tell you some of the major revelations making this doll brought to me. Thank you, Barb, for telling me to pour some compassion into my doll as I made and worked through it. The very next session I had with the heads was profound. As I was painting them, they got uglier and meaner until they were dripping blood from their eyes and mouths. Then I really looked at them and realized what pain they were in. So . . . this means the hypervigilance thing I learned as a child to protect myself is a bunch of worthless nonsense. I can just be me. It never really saved me from anything. I know that I am free. I just have to REMEMBER! This doll has been so powerful. But I'm sure glad we made the Guardian first.

April 25

I did some nondominant-hand journaling last night that I would like to share. I asked my *Guardian Monster* a couple of questions. I don't know if you could tell in the photos, but my monster is crying. When I made the face, I gave him the tears because it just seemed right. But the way I applied them meant they were slowly rubbing off as I worked on him. So I figured that was the way that it was supposed to be, that maybe he would run out of tears or reasons to cry or something. Anyhow, when I was gluing him together, in the final stages, right at the last possible moment (my epoxy was setting up fast), I suddenly fixed him with permanent tears. I wondered at that for a while but moved on. So back to the question. I asked my monster why he was crying. With my nondominant hand, he answered, "I am crying because I feel joy. I am crying because I feel sorrow. This is the stuff of life, and it deserves our tears." That really moved me. We need to feel our feelings. Without apology. Then I asked him, "Who are you?" He said, "I am you." Okay, that's the short version of his answer, but you get the idea. I love this monster; therefore, I love me. This work is so deep, it astounds me.

The shame factor totally changes the energy of fear into a much bigger, bad thing. A nearly impossible thing to work on. Take away the shame, and it is not such a big deal after all.

May 1

I have been called a fearful person. I have always felt such shame in that. And yet I have come to know that this inner world that our group is entering so deeply, so freely, so courageously, is a land that most people, including those who have accused me, absolutely fear to tread. I have come to know that it is okay to accept some fears in myself and reject others as too restrictive. The fears that I can accept have lost a great deal of their power over me. It's not that I no longer fear bears, for example; it's that I am no longer shamed by it. The fears that I have deemed too restrictive, that interfere with my life in a way that is not okay with me, I can work on now without shame. The shame factor totally changes the energy of fear into a much bigger, bad thing. A nearly impossible thing to work on. Take away the

shame, and it is not such a big deal after all. I too seek the grace and strength to not be frozen by it, to not hold back from truth seeking because of it.

May 24

My Inner Healer is *Wiser Woman*. Hopefully, if I stay open, I will just get wiser and wiser along the way. A few years ago, I set out to do a self-portrait doll. I thought it would be somehow therapeutic to look at myself in such an intense, thorough way. After a while, after I got over the weirdness of looking at myself, I got kind of bored with the process of perfecting the clay model I was making and decided to just jump right into wood carving. So I went straight into intuitive mode and started carving. What came out was a very frightened-looking old woman's face. She looked nothing like me and was somewhat disturbing. So I put her away in a box, dropped the idea altogether, and forgot about her . . . until one day, in the middle of this project, I had the overwhelming urge to find her and alter her. It was one of those strange, manic feelings.

native visionary. She is the woman who did Reiki on me that helped shift my whole life. I believe that was the boost I needed to get out of the abusive situation I was in and take the radical plunge of moving to Haines. I was wearing an ivory earring that I had made and gave it to her for the Reiki. She then removed her earring and gave it to me. How's that for a story? It has been such a strong symbol of strength to me for all these years. I put it on my doll in such a way that I can take it off and wear it if I like.

I learned that I have the courage
to allow my true, full, authentic self out into the light of day.

The other element I forgot to mention is the wings. I had made her a lovely pair of hands, but she totally rejected them in favor of wings. So then I envisioned a magnificent pair of wings, but she rejected that idea also, and we went for a somewhat wild and goofy pair. I guess that is her way of reminding me to stay light. Don't take everything sooooo seriously!

Something I learned about myself: I learned that I have the courage to allow my true, full, authentic self out into the light of day.

When I emerged from the trancelike carving session, I knew that this was the face for my final doll. She has moved through her fear and has learned much. She knows that she will continue to learn and grow forever. Her body is a piece of wood that I picked up somewhere along the way, years ago. It looks very female to me. The figure on her side, actually being birthed out of her, is an angel of suffering. She reminds me to acknowledge the suffering of myself and others.

It is so natural to hide from and block out suffering, but all that does is prolong it. The only way past is right through the middle. She also stands as a reminder of compassion. To stay open to my compassionate heart is something I need reminding of. I wanted to mention that the earring she wears is a very special one that I was given ten years ago, on the four-day ferry ride on my way up to Haines for the first time. It was from a Scottish midwife traveling with a large group of Australians, including an aboriginal shaman who gifted me some things that are in and on the pouch. They were all on their way to a gathering to honor Black Elk, a

Do I feel as if I healed some part of my life or self? Yes, I do. For one thing, I feel a huge shift in the feelings I have toward my father. Now I have true compassion for him, and that has opened up my way to more compassion for everybody, including myself. So many things are moving again in my life. I was pretty stuck. Afraid to move, to change, to grow. I feel like this project jumpstarted me back onto the path.

The Guardian

Defender, Protector, Keeper

Purpose: To protect, motivate, encourage, support

This doll represents a witness who supports you through this process. It will reflect protection, guidance, hope, possibility, and encouragement. The Guardian will be a symbol of permission to do the work that follows. She will contain positive input and encouragement as you travel on this creative journey. Once she is completed, put her where you will be creating the other dolls, as she will be a reminder that you are moving through a healing process. Always keep her present.

Your Guardian holds all your inner healing tools:

- Your ability to love unconditionally

- Your ability to support, cherish, listen, and understand

- Your ability to forgive, be kind, be joyful, and be playful

Here's what previous students have said about the Guardian:

> *The Guardian is a constant reminder to me to look at the lighter side of life, and she stands next to my bed so I see her first thing every morning. The Guardian doll, which is my favorite one, showed me the warmth that I am. It opened a place inside of me that I didn't know existed. She is beside my bed and provides much comfort and protection.*
>
> *The Guardian doll is showing me how to love myself—my little-girl self— and that she is always present and we have a lot to give each other.*

This doll is most often in the form of a guardian angel, a grandmother, an ancestor, a spirit guide, a totem animal, or a compassionate mother earth. She is often a nurturing and loving image. As you look though this part of the book, notice that many Guardians are either holding something or their hands are in the position of embracing or holding.

Then again, Debi came up with a guardian monster (pictured to right). Read Debi's story on page 99.

The Guardian
Barb Kobe

"I never allow anybody to make a shadow doll their first time. I believe that a student first needs to evoke the help of the Compassionate Mother or a similar positive archetype."

Cassandra Light
Way of the Doll

Guardian Monster
Debi Knight-Kennedy

Erika's Guardian, *Gurudevi*, helped her through a move from Connecticut to Washington, DC. (Pictured to left.)

> *It wanted to wear crystals and to be wearable. It has the face of an eagle and chakra crystals along its spine. When I thought again about what I needed for a Guardian, I knew immediately what she was going to look like. I drew her image in pencil. She was going to have the face of a bird and was meant to be worn with the harness over the shoulders. She has crystals hanging down to hang over the wearer's head. Although there were technical challenges, the whole process of making this doll went quickly.*

Jesi, an online student living with breast cancer, wrote about creating her Guardian:

> *Well, today my Guardian doll finally decided to make an appearance. YAY!!! Quilts and wrapping up were definitely part of her as well as safety and security, so I went to my stack o' stuff and began to plunder. I'm very happy with her, and I see a lot of symbols coming forth. The outside of her robe is a piece of crazy quilted material I saved from my absolute favorite shirt that I wore until the holes were just too big. The inside of her robe is lined with a starry-sky material, for the infinite possibilities that I have in my life. Her body is a piece of wood from my family farm, back in WV. I made her face very peaceful and without hair. At the moment, hair represents something to hide behind for me, so I left it off. No hiding here. LOL. No hair either! Well, there are a few tiny baby hairs beginning to make their appearance. Inside her robe, hugged up and safe, is a green nest. Nests are safe places for fragile things and places for new beginnings. The nest is sitting on a moss-covered rock, again from the family farm, a place where I have my foundation. But new things have grown from me since leaving—hence the moss. I'm sitting in the nest, and I have room to put things that I need to call into my life or things that I need to work out. I do think this lady is something special, and I have a lot of talking/journaling to do with her.*

> *It's so nice to be feeling human again. I am thinking much more clearly, and I think there are big things ahead in the near future. I'm so happy to finally be getting immersed in the [healing] doll process. It is such a powerful way of being/doing. And when things click, watch out! It's magic! So many things came up with my Guardian doll that I didn't realize until after she was almost complete. It was just WOW! Barb, I get what you meant when you said just follow the process and it will happen. Once I stopped trying to make things work, everything just fell into place. I am so loving this!*

Gurundevi
Erika Cleveland

Guardian (Closed)
Jesi Pearce

Guardian (Open)
Jesi Pearce

106

DebAnn Newell created *Guardian of the Hidden Heart*:

She is created from a yellow cone, symbolizing the yellow sun radiating light outward. My Guardian has no feet or legs; she is grounded, anchoring and stabilizing me. Her "breast plates" are eye patches my mother, Georgette, wore when she had cataract surgery a couple of years ago. They represent the warrior-like Amazons of the ancients, who battle for me and give me strength to fight.

She is encircled and encrusted with various Czech glass beads. The Czech glass harks back to my maternal grandmother, Anna, who came from Czechoslovakia after WWI and was my closest friend and confidant as a child. I believe my grandmother is always with me, as is my mother. The doll's arms are also Czech beads, held upwards in the praying position, sending up prayers. On her front are the words Love, Live, *and* Believe— *the most important things the doll reminds me to always do. At the end of* Love *is a small heart nestled in among other beads, mostly hidden, symbolizing the hidden, buried, trapped Spirit of Self. All the beads are strung on a copper-like wire, and all the parts are connected with that wire. It connects all parts that make up the whole and hold the Guardian together, making one from many parts, reminding me that my whole self is the result of many things, not only the bad/negative.*

My favorite part of dollmaking is the face, the most expressive and freeing part—soft sculpted in cloth, painted detail. My faces don't come out "pretty" by most standards, but I think they are me, at least in a symbolic way. The face is mounted on a vintage button, giving her a sort of halo. It came from Kay, a dear, now-deceased friend, who was in many ways like a second mother to me. Kay was a very strong and self-possessed woman and watches over me. On top of the doll's head is a butterfly (almost all of my dolls have a butterfly somewhere on them, if only a stamped image on the body). Butterflies have long represented the ability of an entity to possess both strength and fragility. In the last couple of years, they have also come to represent the spirit/soul. So a small silver butterfly bead sits on top of her head—my spirit, ready, waiting to take off and soar free.

Guardian of the Hidden Heart
DebAnn Newell

I learned that these dolls
are tangible expressions and emotions, full of honesty and true intent. They are us, our core being.

Guardian Bags
Barb Kobe

Anne Whitney wrote about her Guardian:

She is made from my aunt's old worn quilt. Her face is embroidered and is old and wise, with wrinkles that show a history of more smiles and laughter than worry or anger. She is weighted with metal washers inside her base so she stands easily and feels substantial when held. She is shaped like an egg, the form of a raku "wise woman" rattle I have used as a talking stick in sacred circles, and a shape that to me signifies wholeness.

Kathryn Hall said her guardian doll *Doryn* is a "woods-dweller and is mostly about a peaceful protectiveness, but she can be fierce when the occasion calls for it."

Lori's Guardian, *Estrella*, reminded her of her best friend and grandmother:

She is wisdom. She showed me the way to listen and hear my inner wisdom. She teaches me how to trust my instincts and my innate knowledge of many things. She helps me to trust that it is okay to be myself and take daily solace in this. Her energy, love, gentleness, and kindness reach out to me like a mind map "tree." She is able to go forward without paralyzing fearfulness. She listens to my ancestors and pays homage by adopting their ways. She keeps much oral tradition alive. She teaches so much in kind, gentle, nurturing ways, by imparting wisdom and knowledge about nature, life, humans, ancients, ancestors, and all living creatures. She is calm, relaxed, and emotionally, spiritually, and physically well. She relishes being alive!

She knows who she is! She breathes deeply . . . and doesn't look back. Her fellow sun helps her to continue healing every day. She is in balance with all things. Estrella is an appreciative, grateful, and thankful Guardian for all the good and positive there is to dwell on.

Ariande's Guardian is about three feet tall and stands on her own two feet (very important). Ariande used her husband's hair, her mother's pin, and her grandmother's shawl. The face belongs to her cousin's other grandmother, so she is, in a way, in Ariande's maternal line. Her intention was to create an image showing love and comfort.

Andrea wanted her Guardian to be a personal cheerleader who would give her support and permission to take chances. Her Guardian reminds her not to take most things too seriously and that we all can use some whimsy in our life.

Marietta started making this doll after she was diagnosed with breast cancer. I loved watching how the doll evolved as Marietta progressed through her cancer treatments. She decided to name her *Don't Mess with Me, Cancer*. (By the way, Marietta is now cancer-free.)

Shekmet
Christine K. Harris

The North Guardian
Barb Kobe

**Come to me dear Spirit Angel. Cleanse my Soul of
this Fear. Guide me toward the healing light
so I may let go and live in peace.**
Barb Kobe

Bird Guardian
Barb Kobe

Heidi's Guardian: *Mother Blood*

Heidi Burrowes, Ontario, Canada

I spent about fifteen hours over Friday, Saturday, and Monday working on my Guardian doll. I did not bring her back to something simple. I was lost when working on her. On Monday night when working on her, all I could think about was that I should be figuring out who I would leave my children with if I died. And then I was worried that I was not focusing on my intention of recognizing my emotions and knowing who I am, but that I was focusing instead on my death. But then I realized that I was creating a Guardian doll, and that this doll was about protection, and that she was telling me I need to make sure the people in my life who are important to me are protected, and that it was not only about my death but about losing that stress while alive and knowing that things would be all right with my family if something happened to me.

Her name is *Mother Blood*. She has spiral hair that represents the DNA of us all, for she is the mother of all. Some of the hairs are long, and some are short. Some are brown, and some are black, indicating that we are all different and unique. Her face is round and white like the full moon that represents the cycle of womanhood. She has a red knitted cape and muffler and a crocheted red skirt, made with love. Red because it is the powerful color of motherhood, the color of lifeblood and passion and also fire. Because when I first began to make her, she looked like she would get cold, and I don't like the cold. Being clothed in handmade knitted and crocheted items is a comforting thing for me.

Her feet are crocheted (my first time doing beaded crochet!) stones from my yard, so that she remains grounded. She also has crocheted pouches all down her torso with different stones that represent the chakras. The stones peek out of the pouches, indicating that her energy centers are protected but open. For her crown chakra, I used wire and sewed the stone in place. And for her third-eye chakra, I embroidered a pattern (diamond shaped) around an opening that the stone peeks through.

Trust the Process

Barb Kobe

Trust the process. This is the doll I showed to my online group to speak about resistance. I was struggling making her for days. She wanted to be made from my inner knowing, only I kept trying to control the process. She had several costume transformations, but none of them fit her—I was trying to impress an outer audience. She wouldn't have it. She had a message for me: she wanted me to follow her guidance, and to see and hear her wisdom. It was a struggle, and I pricked my fingers several times while making her. I finally listened as she said she wanted the strange headdress with the sticks coming out of its ends.

These things don't make sense in the making. She demanded the bead necklace. And she wanted to be hung under the owl—even hanging her on the wall was a balancing act. Finally, I hang her up. I see her hands open to whatever is next, then I hear an inner voice suggesting "feet" hanging from her hands. *Soles? Soul? I get it!* All the fussing and tantrums the day before was my body begging to go to the studio and feast on all the nutritious and filling soul treats, which I sometimes forget about. Hopefully this Talisman (or maybe it's a Guardian) will be a reminder for me to trust the process. More meaning to come, only in *her* timing. (In *my* timing?) Stay tune for updates. I humbly follow the creative wisdom bread crumbs. Your turn.

Trust the Process **(Guardian)**
Barb Kobe

Creative Action

Create a mind map, writing the word *Guardian* in the center of the page. Then write words and/or draw images that come to you when you think about a Guardian figure. What qualities will your Guardian have or contain?

Draw or collect images from magazines, then collage Guardian images and symbols. Choose one that most resonates with you. Don't spend too much time on this. Usually the first image or thought is the best.

What body parts does a Guardian need to have? Look at the pictures of Guardians made by past members of online groups. What do they have in common?

What images and symbols will your Guardian be holding and wearing?

What Could Be a Guardian?

- Animals with guardian qualities

- Earth Mother or Mother Earth

- Angels

- Dragons

- Owls

- Sacred figures, such as saints or people from holy books—Buddha, Tara, Kwan Yin

- Maternal figures, perhaps grandmothers or wisdom figures

- Goddesses

- Images from nature, such as trees or rocks

- Superheroes

- Healers, shamans, doctors, or nurses

Art Forms for a Guardian:

- Three-dimensional doll

- Paper doll

- Mixed media figure

- Personally embellished sculpture

Make your Guardian doll when you're ready. As stated before, it is best to make the Guardian doll first in the healing doll process.

Wounded Healer Poster
Barb Kobe

The Scapegoat

Going into the Dark, or Shadow Doll

Purpose: Symbolizes the pain; embraces the struggle

A scapegoat is an image you associate with your pain. It is an image of whom or what you blame, or whom or what should be punished for your problem. In ancient rituals, the scapegoat was the sacrificial animal upon which people put their fears, sins, illnesses, or whatever they needed or wanted to remove from the community. When it was banished, they believed it took away the negativity ascribed to it.

The Scapegoat doll will symbolize what is getting in the way of your goal and what needs to be removed—or, in this process, what needs to be transformed. In healing, the scapegoat is an object onto which you can place things you are ready to be done with or that no longer serve you, even though they may have helped you survive in the past. This doll will be the container of the pain; she will hold it so you don't have to.

I believe engaging with the energies of the Scapegoat, or the shadow doll, ignites healing in this process. When you make an image of what you fear or what is blocking you, an internal dialogue begins with that hidden part. Healing energies open up as you apply the healing salts of compassion and love.

I've seen ugly, scary images appear as the women in my classes start making dolls. The women do not like these scary images, so they start over, only to have them appear again. I've also seen women play with the simple intention of creating ugly dolls, and then their images transform into shadow dolls. When this happens, I encourage them to accept it for what it is and apply compassion to the images. Acceptance of a lost part of self creates an opening for the possibility of healing. At this point in this process, your dollmaking asks that you embrace your quest.

The key to this doll is identifying the primary emotion you connect to your pain, wound, or problem. Think back to your healing intention statement at the beginning of the process. If you remember, we discussed how people often try solving a problem without even defining what the problem is. Now's the time to turn to your healing intention and consider the problem again, looking deep into the emotions, the feelings surrounding it.

I wrote this message to the group while they were working on the Scapegoat dolls:

> *I would suggest that you consider a feeling as the scapegoat instead of looking for a person to blame. For example, "If I weren't so angry about this situation, then I could make the doll." Anger would be the scapegoat. You may also want to consider the grief and loss around your issue, and those*

Igniting Her Creative Fire to Release Her Wound
Barb Kobe

"Emotional wounds are carried in the body and need to be released through talking, writing, and expressing emotion."
Cassandra Light
Way of the Doll

Scapegoat
Marla

115

Releasing Her Rage
Barb Kobe

"Giving birth to your past may be painful and difficult at first; a strong aversion to one stage of the process may signify that something important is being born. After that moment, there may be an opening up. I kept reminding myself, 'The only way out is through.'"

Pamela Hastings

Having a Conversation with Herself
(Paper doll)
Barb Kobe

feelings would be the scapegoat. I invite you to consider one of these feelings and simply make paper dolls that represent it. At first, they most often feel scary. To begin, just start with an angry or sad scribble (it will only take five minutes), and then use writing with the nondominant hand to have a conversation with it.

Resistance, Fear, and Anger

You will likely run into some scary, confused, unsure part of yourself while making this doll. Some call this part the shadow, the critic, a negative belief, or the wound. It could also be your inner saboteur blocking your empowerment and growth. Often, something happens once you hit the dark place, and you stop the journey. Healing can require you to confront a truth you would rather not face. Your initial response to the Scapegoat doll may be resistance—to not want to make it. It may trigger a stress response.

You might withdraw from the process because you fear it might cause you more pain. This could be very possible. However, I have found that resisting pain is more painful than actually going through the pain experience. "Going into" pain rather than trying to resist it is a skill well worth learning. It is a spiritual life skill. When you push against anything—anything at all—you are only hurting yourself. You are, in fact, resisting life-force energy that wants to flow through you.

Resistance actually makes the pain bigger. Even when you think it is justified—such as when you hate and judge others for doing bad things to you, to others, or to the earth—not facing your pain hurts only you.

The same goes for when you want relief from your aches and pains, whether they are physical or emotional. You may think addressing the pain will make you feel worse. Making a healing doll may not resolve or solve the root problem, but it will release some of the pain. It allows for a release of the tension, which then allows you to focus on working toward the healing. Research has shown that when people in pain surrender to it, the symptoms can begin to loosen or relax, or mysteriously disappear altogether. In other words, people who are with their illness or pain touch it deeply, examine it, meet with it, and engage in a relationship with it. This is what making the Scapegoat symbolizes.

For many, reaching this place with the Scapegoat doll also brings out feelings of fear. You may get scared, then you may get stuck in your fears, worries, sadness, and pain. You may get so wrapped up in fear, you won't feel the good stuff: acknowledgement, love, and acceptance. Instead, the victim part of yourself may show up, and you'll start to feel sorry for yourself, powerless, and weak.

Fear can be useful when it protects you. We *should* fear some things, such as a fire on the stove, because they can threaten our life and well-being. Fear is an opportunity to gather facts, make informed decisions, and ask, "Is this fear serving me or hindering me?" It is important to get in touch with the fear you face while making the Scapegoat.

In her book *Wisdom Walks in Circles*, Margaret Hart Lewis calls these kinds of dolls Storm Kachinas. I like the idea of making Scapegoat dolls as a way of stirring up a storm. She says, "A Storm Kachina is a manifestation of your negativity so you can give it away; that it is a process of transforming negativity into power. You release the negativity by recognizing it and naming it in the form of a doll."

I suggest you keep your Guardian doll nearby while making the Scapegoat. The Guardian's image holds your intentions and reminds you that you are not alone. Allow your Guardian's wisdom to coach you through the process of making your Scapegoat. Use your journal to write your fears as well as the loving affirmations your Guardian has for you.

Reach out to your believing mirror person and your healing support team if you feel the need. Ask for help and support.

While making the Scapegoat, many women are afraid of bumping into their anger. They struggle with messages like "good girls don't get angry." This can lead to a block as well. When several members of the online group were getting blocked by their anger and frustration over not being able to make the Scapegoat, I sent out this email:

> *Why isn't it okay for us to fuss, be angry, get that pent-up energy out of our bodies? Of the many reasons, one is that society tells women it is okay to cry but not to be angry, while men get the "big boys don't cry" story. And if women do get angry, stand up for themselves, and defend their rights, they are called the b-word, and worse.*
>
> *I did a class one time where every dollmaker made a doll about just this subject. I called it the Pissy, Whiny, Moany Doll Class, and it was great fun. I remember one woman refused to make the angry doll but rather made a listener doll that was willing to listen to her friends fuss. At the end of the class, everyone wrote three things that made them angry, told angry stories, and then released the energy through laughter.*
>
> *Jean Illsley Clarke, an important mentor and teacher of mine, told me that sometimes you just need to fuss. She created an exercise where she got into a large cardboard box called the Fuss Box. She got in it and fussed, whined, and kicked at the sides of the box until she sensed the energy changing. Fussing is what I'm encouraging you to do too. (Hey, maybe we can make Thursday "Throw a Fuss Day." Just tell everyone you care about to stand clear until Friday arrives.)*
>
> *If you've been traumatized in your life and have not released the blocked energy of that trauma, you will experience residual tension every time something like it comes into your life. You must move to release this tension: walking, running, biking, and definitely breathing—deep breathing.*
>
> *Here's to fussing!*

Story of Woe
Barb Kobe

"We hold our pain like a precious gold charm locked in the safe deposit box of our heart. Never letting it see the full light of day, it leaks out venom, pumping the poison through our arteries, into our veins and onto our lives, holding us hostage with its increasing power. You can let it kill you or you can kill it. I say go there—open that Pandora's box and set your artist free. She's dying (literally) to get out of the box. And she can't emerge unless you give her back her rightful pain. She earned it. Now let her feel it. And sob from it and sculpt from it and paint it and write it and sing it."

Nancy Slonim Aronie
Writing from the Heart

Scapegoat
Jessi

The Scapegoat, the shadow doll, represents what stands in the way of your healing. As you develop a detailed, embellished picture of your problem, you can use that information to design your Scapegoat doll. Don't try to make it something beautiful or pretty. Let it be messy and chaotic. If you connect words with the image, add them.

In making the Scapegoat, what you are saying is that you are willing to meet, express, and create a part of your being that has—for a while—been ready to die, to leave you, or to transform. I congratulate you in taking this courageous step, in bringing this dark part of your life into the light. Holding these energies inside is like trying to hold back a feeling by holding your breath. To keep holding them in, you must engage your muscles and nerves to partner with you in the containment. Do you see how this could lead to illness?

I congratulate you in taking this courageous step, in bringing this dark time of your life into the light. Holding these energies inside is like trying to hold a feeling in by holding your breath. You keep trying to hold them in and then engage your muscles and nerves to partner with you in the containment. Do you see how this could lead to illness?

Here's a message I shared with the group:

Creatrix
Barb Kobe

You're learning to be a nurturing parent to the wounded inner child—the keeper of your creative sparkles. All this stern, angry yelling and emotional battering will coax her out of hiding from long-past-inflicted wounds. Your critic-bully self has not encouraged the frightened inner child to come out and play. Creating the Scapegoat may have been, for you, a process of discovering the inner bully: a once small, useful part whose first intention was to keep you safe, but now has grown big and distorted and way beyond its usefulness.

Yet through the struggle you may have discovered that there was what is called "a gift in the wound." Some lost bit of emotional wisdom that lies hidden beneath the pain and layers of tense protective muscles.

Perhaps now is a time to consider the medicine of forgiveness—not forgiveness for those who have harmed you, but forgiveness for yourself, for perceived weakness and stupidity. Perhaps it is time to call out to those lost, wounded parts of yourself, using the energies of kindness and acceptance. Call them to you by saying your name out loud three times. Use your Guardian to stand beside you as you do this. This is the part of you that believes in your strength and invincibility. Despite everything in your past, it believes you are a shining star. Once you are through with the callings and have settled within a healing circle of these gathered parts, it will be time for reflection—to be grateful and to celebrate lessons learned.

She Stuffed Her Heart in a Bottle
Barb Kobe

Creative Action

Create a mind map, writing the word *Scapegoat* in the center of the page. Then write words or draw images that come to you when you think about a Scapegoat figure. What qualities will your Scapegoat have or contain?

Draw or collect images from magazines, then collage Scapegoat images and symbols. Choose one that most resonates with you. Don't spend too much time on this. Usually the first image that comes to you is the best.

What body parts could a Scapegoat have? Look at the pictures of Scapegoats in this chapter. What do they have in common? What images and symbols might your Scapegoat be holding and wearing? (Working on the Scapegoat can be scary for some people. Exploring others' dolls is a safe way to explore what's coming up from the shadows to the light for you too.)

Revisit making feeling faces and then identify the feeling face that should be on your Scapegoat. Write about what your Scapegoat is feeling or what you feel when thinking about or creating it. Spend some time developing a full story of the problem. Play with these ideas in your journal.

What Could Be a Scapegoat?

- Animals with scapegoat qualities

- Images that look angry, scary, very sad, creepy—emotionally strong

- Dark figures—no bright colors or light

- Figures in cages, behind bars, or in boxes

- Shapes, textures, or abstract images, perhaps with words

- Images from nature; something hit by a storm

- Villains, tricksters, witches, or shadowy figures

Art Forms for a Scapegoat:

- Three-dimensional doll

- Paper doll

- Purchased image from a store, thrift store, etc.

- Mixed-media figure

- Photograph

There are more Scapegoat creative exercises on pages 128 and 129.

Kim's Scapegoat: *Demori*

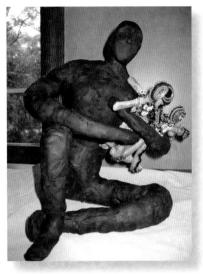

Demori (I remain) is my Scapegoat doll. He is holding my bead-embroidered fears. Their names are *But If Only*, *But What If*, and *But I Can't*. I call them the Buttlies for short. Working with the black Fimo was quite a challenge; it didn't stretch, flex, or do anything I wanted. Originally there was going to be a jar to seal the Buttlies in when they got too noisy, but I found they wanted to be held and looked at instead. They had a tendency to grow if they were stuffed away.

Ellen's Scapegoat: *Gluttony*

I've learned a lot by making my Scapegoat and owning it. Once my Talisman came to me, my life started to fall into place. I realized the food triggers I have that send me spiraling, and now I have that under control. There are no cravings or desires for stuff I really don't want to eat or drink. What have I learned through this journey so far? By treating by body with respect and by changing the way I think about the things I cannot change, I feel more grounded and at peace. I respect myself.

Kathryn Hall's First Scapegoat: *Clogg*

I so often feel two conflicting things simultaneously, which I often simply accept and move forward with, but other times it contributes to inertia—I don't know which way to go, so I do nothing. I'm still uncertain of its gender . . . a little androgynous. Maybe that's because I really miss the more feminine parts of myself, which seem to have gone into hiding. I'm feeling as unattractive as this poor creature is. I'm coming to love this rather pathetic Scapegoat. I think coming face-to-face with it is going to be a powerful and good thing after all. I've gathered together some copper plumbing elbows and have been playing with them. Design is changing again—he/she is going to be in the shape of a serpent, I think. An opening at the nether end and another nearer the head will display the "clogs." At this point, I need to keep playing with it for a while, though. Every time I think I have a "plan," it changes! Ha-ha! It's working name is simply *Clogg*, but won't know for sure if that's really it until it tells me. (Kathryn's second Scapegoat can be seen on pages 128 and 129).

Creative Action

Revisit your healing intention. In your journal, define or redefine what you want to heal. For instance, at the end of this process, what will be healed? How will you be changed? Do you want peace? To be out of pain? If you get stuck, approach it from the opposite perspective. For example, "My definition of pain, illness, struggle, suffering, is _____. I know I am not healed when _____. My healing intention is not _____.

Think about how the problem or disease expresses itself in your body. Draw an image of your body. Using words and color, answer the following questions, writing the answers around the drawing:

- What is your body trying to tell you?
- How are your thoughts expressed in symptoms?
- How does the problem/disease block your creativity?
- Where in your body do you feel sick, diseased, blocked?
- What emotions are creating problems for you?
- What is missing?

You may want to draw an image of the energy of the emotion connected to the problem. Imagine what it feels like in your body. Look for shapes and colors. When did it start? Why do you have it? What does it look like, sound like, move like, smell and taste like? How is it blocking you from getting what you want?

Here are samples of blocks, or problems that might be in the way:

- An old wound, disease, or illness
- A painful body part
- Feeling lost or confused
- Powerlessness
- An inner "yes person" who can't say no
- Feeling out of control
- Conflict between two forces
- A wall, a block, a rock
- Fear, sadness, anger
- Turmoil, war, anxiety
- A broken heart
- Guilt and shame
- Whining
- Judgment

Write down what is in your way of getting what you want. What is blocking you? Finish this statement: I can't get what I want because _____ is in my way. Write down all the things you fear, using the sentence starters below. Then write what each of them means to you.

- "I am afraid that if I _____, then _____ will happen.
- "I am afraid of _____ because _____.

Take time to think about your fears. Give yourself the opportunity to be with each one as it surfaces. Do not dismiss any as silly or inconsequential. The fears you wrote first are the ones sitting on the surface, but a deeper fear may lie at the heart of all the others. Maybe one bubbled up and made you go, "Ohhh!" If you did not write that one down—if you resisted it—do so now. Go after it. Name it. Ancient wisdom is filled with stories that teach us that naming something gives us power over it.

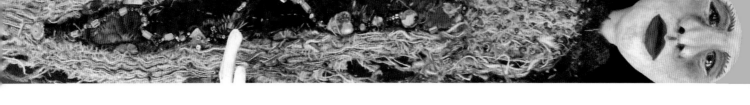

Scapegoat
Andi Stern

I Am in My Own Prison
Anne Quinby

Andi from the group described how she created her Scapegoat doll:

> *My Guardian is still in process, but the Scapegoat came out in a rush yesterday afternoon. She is a malformed, lumpy, misshapen babyesque figure, complete with fat arms thrown wide with hands open and eyes scrunched up and a piggy nose and the HUGE open mouth that screams and is never satisfied (no matter what I have or what I do, it is not enough; no one wants me because I am so needy; I am not deserving because I am never satisfied). I made her out of the basic Sculpey and baked her with aluminum foil balls under her arms to keep them from sagging. I felt a huge sense of a burden being lifted as I made her, and I also found myself loving her and having compassion for her. This process has been nothing less than amazing—one of those quiet things when you think nothing is happening until it sneaks up and there it is.*

Once you get started on the Scapegoat doll, just keep moving, even if you feel that urge to resist it. Something in you knows exactly what is supposed to happen. Don't stop and think about it too much. Let all the feelings of fear, doubt, confusion, and stuckness be part of the making. If what's taking shape does not seem right, change it and keep going until you stop and sense something within you taking a great sigh of relief. Get to the bones of it. Allow and accept what comes, and dialogue with it. The more you avoid it, the more signals you'll send to the brain that it is important to your growth. Ever have something you didn't want to think about? The more you resist it, the more it comes to visit your mind—and brings up feelings you would rather keep hidden. Move into acceptance instead of resistance, and work with the discovery of the patterns coming through.

Shena from the online research group shared this as other participants faced some resistance and uncertainty while working on the Scapegoat:

> *Sometimes the Scapegoat doll is sitting right in front of us and we don't recognize it because we're trying to focus on something bigger or think it can't possibly be that simple. Let go of making the feeling faces and consider what feelings themselves are blocking you from getting what you want, and then explore making those within the Scapegoat doll. Be easy on yourself with this one and trust the process. This image need not be large and involved to produce a change.*

If all else fails and you just don't know what to do, then hold your healing intention in your mind and make an ugly doll or a fear doll. It doesn't need to be tied to anything deeper at first. See what happens. It may just transform into the Scapegoat after all.

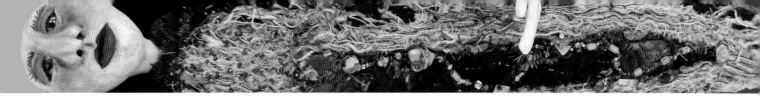

Here's my response to Erika, in the Medicine Dolls online class, about Scapegoat dolls:

The Scapegoat doll is a very powerful one to create, witness, and befriend. "Befriend? What do you mean, befriend?" you say. For me, it gets back to feelings. I've always been curious as to why most Medicine Doll participants do not attempt to complete the feeling face activitiy . . . you know, the one where you take pictures of yourself making feeling faces. What I know almost for sure is that we are afraid of our feelings. We've been told not to have them. You know, "Don't be angry!" or "Stop crying—suck it up!" or "You've got nothing to be afraid of."

I believe what happens is that we are sensitive, intuitive creatures when we arrive on the planet, and we are dependent on others to take care of us. When we see an adult having/expressing a feeling, we feel it, we connect with the energy of it, and we respond to it. Think about a time two parents were fighting and the children were either crying or huddled in a corner in fear. Maybe this happened to you as a child. Afterwards you may have asked, "Are you mad, Mommy?" or said "Dad, you look sad." Often your mother said, "I'm not angry!" when she was, or your father said, "Don't be silly—men don't get sad" when he was. So we start to doubt what we know, see, feel, and experience. We believe we are wrong for being our wonderful, creative, sensitive, intuitive selves . . . our Golden Child.

So the Scapegoat represents a big old feeling standing in the way. At least, that may be what it feels like. But what if it were just a feeling that got really big because it'd been stuffed so long that it became really angry that it hadn't been acknowledged, loved, allowed to exist and eventually change to another feeling? Our creative inner soul makes up these images so the feeling will get noticed. Other feelings get attached to it, hang around it. In my mind, all feelings are part of who we are. They are a "feeling gang," so they hang out together. Does that make sense?

So Erika, after you made the Scapegoat, you acknowledged what you were feeling. You SAW it. And that encouraged you to get IN TOUCH with your feeling self. I like to think that when you befriend your Scapegoat, it takes a big old deep breath and says, "Finally someone sees me. It's okay to have this feeling, and now I can move on." And that opens up the possibility for you to make connection with other feelings and stories and memories and more feelings.

Yes, big stuff, really big stuff . . . and important lessons to learn about feelings. Lessons we did not get growing up. Well, most of us. Now just for a moment, think about how this affected our bodies.

Thank you for doing the work and being willing to be vulnerable enough to share it.

Erika's Scapegoat: *Bruxus*

Again, the doll came to me as a fully formed image, which I drew and then had to figure out how to construct. She scared me, and it took a while to be able to make her in three dimensions. Here is what she looked like. I called her Bruxus.

I could talk in detail about what this image means, but mostly she represents the critic, the ferocious, hungry beast who can't stand feeling vulnerable. Who can't stand anything new even if it comes from within her own body. The infant she is tearing apart with her teeth and claws represents her own creative thoughts and ideas. Now I can look at her and write about her and even appreciate her to some extent, but when I created her, I felt scared and ashamed. It's difficult to face our demons and to have them out in the open. But this is an important phase in the healing journey.

Scapegoat Mind Map
Lisa Fam

Scapegoat (1)
Lisa Fam

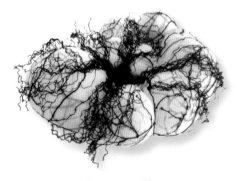

Scapegoat (2)
Lisa Fam

"Releasing Buried Wisdom: I make the Scapegoat not to get rid of negativity but to create an image of the negativity and transform it by allowing its safe expression. Creating the Scapegoat allows for a movement through suffering, an expression of anger, pain, and sadness that transmutes the pain into acceptance, joy, and connection to life."

Barb Kobe
Message to a Medicine Doll group

Lisa shared her experience of making Scapegoats:

> My Scapegoat had three mini fear Scapegoats (they were the three furies/ specters of paralysis, the beast of burden and fear of suffering), which then led on to two more Scapegoats. And there is another one lurking . . . perhaps the core of it . . . the "black dog" or inner critic. Pungent is a good word. Very smelly!
>
> The Scapegoat process is very deep and transformative, and maybe we are more conscious of (familiar with) the earlier layers that peel off as we create/ access them before we arrive at the core of the issue. It may have been too overwhelming to go straight to the core. I have a healthy respect for the protective function of the psyche.

Other authors write of creative struggles. In her book *Daring Greatly*, Brené Brown writes,

> We reckon with our emotions and get curious about what we're feeling; we rumble with our stories until we get to a place of truth; and we live this process, every day, until it becomes a practice and creates nothing short of a revolution in our lives' properties.

In her book *This Time I Dance!*, author Tama J. Kieves writes,

> We actually need some frustration, exasperation, doubt, self-criticism, desire and rage. This kind of soul-feuding hurtles us spinning out of bodies so we can't even squeeze back into our tiny, familiar selves. Our hurdles will stop us, engage us, and keep engaging us, until we summon a wild power from the bowels of the will we did not know we had. Then we can never again mask our magnificence, even to ourselves.
>
> Transformation of any kind always requires a holy tussle. The newborn butterfly struggles to open its wing so it can conjure up the strength to fly. Rise! In the fight and flight of transformation, we become pure of heart, strong of gift, and furiously alive; we meet heal, love, forgive, receive and complete ourselves.

124

She Who Has No Voice
Kathryn Hall

Creative Action

Time to start making your Scapegoat, if you haven't done so already.

Still hesitating? Make a big, bad, ugly doll or a bundle of twisted, tangled fibers, ribbons, cotton, and other found objects. See what develops.

Christine's Scapegoats

Christine K. Harris, Chesapeake, Virginia

I did the feeling faces exercise. My biggest discovery is that I have difficulty making emotional faces for the photos of myself. I don't like looking at photos of myself and have a hard time making faces unless I feel the emotion. I have become adept at hiding my emotions, although people close to me usually pick up on them.

It's not a big surprise because my survival as a child depended on my ability to conceal what I felt. As an adult, I also have to be careful and conceal emotional reactions since I am an art therapist dealing with clients. I continue to control my emotional responses within my family (with the exclusion of my husband) because I don't want to say something I regret or reveal something I want private. I am sure that I may seem to have flat affect at times.

I am able to sculpt human emotion, especially from photos. The ones I seem to sculpt most are fear, anxiety, anger, grief, and pain. I don't know if this is because I am most interested in these, surrounded by these, enjoy wallowing in these, or a combination of all. It could just be that those emotions are familiar. And although that is what appears in my artwork, I can sincerely say I am relatively content because I am pursuing art full-time.

I am with Lisa on "the more we make, the more we have coming in." I think doing something creative every day is important as a practice, even if it has to be a tiny collage or a scribble on a napkin. Even when it feels like there is nothing there, and you think it's a crappy idea, try to make something.

It helps to hear it's okay to be stuck at Scapegoat. I tend to see myself as just wallowing around in it. I have this mental image of me wallowing around in the mud, the way a pig does. It has always been hard for me to be positive and easier to be negative. Maybe it's a Gen X thing or just my thing. If I am still making Scapegoats a year from now, I will be disappointed with myself. There is a doll to make next, after all, even if I don't feel ready.

I added my second Scapegoat doll picture. I called this one *Malnourished*, referring to all the stuff we get fed that doesn't give spiritual or physical nurturance.

The part I like best: The freeing feeling after making the Scapegoat doll. The relief at letting out all this baggage that has been riding around with me. Permission to make something just for me, to heal me, instead of for the market or for a show.

http://www.christinekharris.com/

Unraveling Fear, Releasing Love

Barb Kobe

This started with me playing around with cording, wrapping it in colors I don't normally use on my dolls. After some wrapping, I started to sew a form together from the cording. I knew I wanted it to be abstract, with holes I could fill with other embellished pieces of fabric and beads. As I played with the colors, shapes, and spaces, I allowed myself to be led by my intuitive voice. Halfway through the construction, I felt drawn to open the shape up some more, to allow more air into it. It began to take on meaning, so I stepped away and started to make the doll I wanted to emerge from the cording form.

I've been dealing with anxiety attacks and fear for years. Most of the art I created to explore these feelings was dark, confined, and scary. At some point, I decided it was time to move toward the light and begin living my life, embracing all my feelings. As I looked at what I was creating, I realized that this doll was encouraging that embrace. This is a point of awareness or consciousness that I reach with most of my deep-healing dolls. In the middle of creating these dolls, there is a shift, a change in my internal energy. I then feel I can complete the doll in record time. It is as if the form begins to birth itself, and I am the midwife.

I painted and embellished a small doll and placed her within the cording form. She represents my inner child, starting to see the light and starting to be released from the bindings of fear. I placed several other small dolls amongst the wrapped cording to represent old beliefs embedded in fear. Near the end of her creation—as with most of my deep-healing dolls—I started to feel as if I were merging with the image, honoring the feeling, and releasing the energy binding me. This doll stands as a symbol of my bound-up fear and the unraveling involved in the healing process. After all, it's a process. And I trust this one.

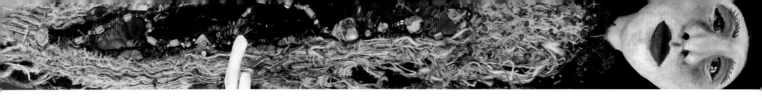

Scapegoat Collage/Painting
Cat Caracelo

What to Do If You Get Stuck

- Keep making dolls, art, crochet, etc.; collage some expressive, creative art every day.

- Make a small doll every day for a week (can be paper dolls).

- Draw feeling doodles and journal with them.

- Make an image of the block or stuck place out of clay.

- Watch a comedy or fantasy movie.

- Perform a self-forgiveness ritual.

- Make and drink a cup of tea, coffee, or water.

- Go out in nature, walk in a garden, visit a beach, or sit next to a small fire.

- Allow yourself to make mistakes and create bad art; even bad art has a purpose.

- Make a Pissy, Whinny, Moany doll.

- Have a creative temper tantrum, tear up paper, make small balls of toilet paper and throw it at a tree (ask the tree for its permission first).

- Write a letter to your stuckness.

- Messege the Facebook group or call a friend.

- Exercise—go bowling; play badminton, racket ball, or any other fast-paced activity.

Kathryn Hall's Second Scapegoat: *Esurienta*

Esurienta is naked and always hungry for something . . . She wants MORE (whether it's cake or time or space or money or talent or love or whatever). She worries and has trouble making decisions. She doesn't know what she wants and is unsure of herself. She feels empty and begs God and the Universe with her outstretched, oversized hands to fill her up, which, oddly enough, it does. But there is a ravenous snake in the great empty pit of her belly, so she is never satisfied for long. She smiles through her worry and want for her heart. She is grateful for what she does have, and she fears losing it. She knows things could be worse. MUCH worse . . . BUT. IT. IS. STILL. NEVER. ENOUGH . . .

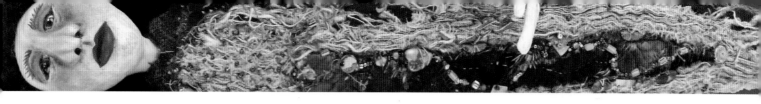

After the Scapegoat Is Complete

Once you create your Scapegoat, give it a creative, descriptive name. I've used names such as *Shame On Me*, *Brudella*, *Ruby Roja (The Wild Child)*, *Doodie Doom*, *Angerilla*, and so on.

Next, consider these questions:

1. When you look at your doll, what feeling does she seem to be expressing?

2. What do you feel when you look at your doll?

3. If your doll could speak, what feeling story would she tell you?

4. Do the doll's colors help express a certain feeling?

5. What did you feel as you were creating this doll?

6. When you think about these feelings, where do you feel them in your body? Are they old or new feelings? Did any of them surprise you?

7. How did the doll's shape, design, and symbols express her story? How did they express your thoughts and feelings?

8. Does the doll hold any special messages or meaning for you?

9. How do you feel now that you've completed the Scapegoat?

**Scapegoat
Linda**

Esurienta
Kathryn Hall

Crusher
Joyce

Carmel's Scapegoat: *Resistance*

A couple of weeks ago, a "heart problem" emerged. My heart began skipping beats frequently (very unnerving), and my blood pressure has been high (which is very unusual for me). Doctors don't seem to think it's dangerous, but I've been undergoing a number of tests. What is truly amazing is that in the weeks before my heart problem revealed itself, there were innumerable references to the heart in my dreams, in books I bought or borrowed, in things others said to me, and in books recommended by Barb (e.g., *Writing from the Heart*). In one of my dreams, I received the message that I was blocking my creativity, and if I kept this up, my body would suffer. I was very aware of how I was resisting doing my artwork, and how I was allowing other things and people to take precedence.

It is also worth reporting an astounding piece of synchronicity. Barb had picked up a book called *Golden: A Retelling of "Rapunzel"* (part of the Once Upon a Time series) by Cameron Dokey. The sorceress in the story (a wise woman) was called Melisande, the name I use for my "alter ego." Not surprisingly, this book was FULL of references to the heart.

Here are some of my musings that resulted from the course exercises:

All my life, I've wanted SOMETHING MORE! Something SPECIAL and adventurous. I've been unable to get this because all my past baggage is in my way AND I've taken on the baggage of others. (This shows up frequently in my dreams.)

My Scapegoat doll must carry all my baggage for me. But THE SCAPEGOAT ITSELF IS INNOCENT. I always felt sorry for that goat in the Bible, driven out into the desert, carrying the sins of the people. Of course, Jesus is the ultimate scapegoat—crucified for the sins of the world (I never really saw the sense in that, especially as humans continue to suffer for their sins).

Don't we do this all the time—blame someone else and make them suffer for OUR sins/shortcomings?

Although consciously I've accepted for many, many years that we are responsible for our own lives, I've nevertheless continued to feel shackled by past condi-

tioning and probably have never REALLY forgiven those who foisted their beliefs and limitations onto me.

The Scapegoat doll is a symbol—a way of unburdening myself onto something "safe" that I cannot hurt. It will carry away all the things that have been blocking me and causing distress in my body. But because IT is innocent (like the goat and like Jesus), I will feel sorry for it. I will not want it to be ugly as well as burdened. I will want to love it for what it is doing for me.

I went for a walk in the bush a month ago. At the time, I thought we were supposed to be starting the Scapegoat doll instead of the Guardian. I asked for clues to inspire me with the Scapegoat. I took a number of photos, but nothing relevant seemed to jump out at me at first. Or so it seemed at the time. I found myself admiring the lantana, which came in many colors.

Then it occurred to me that we Australians have made a scapegoat of things like lantana. We introduced lantana to this country as a garden flower, set it free to take over the bush, then called it a noxious weed and set about eradicating it (with little success). We blame the lantana for OUR sin of bringing it here in the first place. Similarly, rabbits and cats.

Note: After I finished my Scapegoat doll, I looked back at the photos I'd taken on the nature walk and was AMAZED that I had missed the "natural" scapegoat image—the "figure" wrapped in cobweb strands (left).

A fairly clear idea began to emerge of what I wanted my doll to be like. The image in my mind was of a lumpy doll with crying face, carrying a bag full of my "sins" (blocks, flaws, negative emotions, etc.), with a number of these written over her clothing. My original intention was to have a cross around her neck (to represent Scapegoat Jesus) and a bunch of lantana in her hands. In the end, these didn't seem to fit. I wanted her to be huggable but not "beautiful," at least not in the conventional sense.

I used a simple pattern from *Cloth Paper Scissors* magazine for the doll. A crying face from my "ugly doll" experiment became the face (printed onto an iron-on transfer then put onto fabric). Because of all that had happened in the interim, it was essential to attach a heart. (This has now become a personal symbol . . . I guess all my healing dolls will need to show a heart.) The heart, cut from felt, is pierced with pins, which attach it to the body. Instead of the intended crucifix around the neck, she is attached to a crude cross made of sticks. I've named her *Resistance*, inspired by comments from Barb. All those things I put in the bag are what I use as resistance to doing my creative work.

Contents of the Resistance bag: not enough time, no inspiration, not good enough, too many choices, too many things to do, people interrupting me and distracting me, unsuitable workspace, not enough room, not sure what I want to do, need to make money, hardly anyone makes money from art, too many options, other priorities, sudoku addiction, health issues, computer stuff, need more info,

need more skills, need to read books, I'm too old, I'm too tired, don't like promoting myself, nobody will buy at the price I need to sell, don't know where to sell, too many materials to choose from, too many techniques to try, too much thinking, no passion, no motivation, no energy, too much clutter, past conditioning, the good girl, the nice girl.

I also put into the bag people I've used as my scapegoat: Sister Rosary (a particularly cruel nun at primary school); members of my family, particularly my father; various bosses; artists who are particularly skilled (i.e., "I can't be as good as them"). After a while, I'll have a ritual of burning the contents of the bag. But every time I find myself resisting "doing my work," I'll pop the culprit in the bag again.

I'm not sure what to do with the doll now. I don't want it in a position where I can see it all the time . . . it needs to be sent "out into the wilderness" like the biblical scapegoat. I considered hanging it out amongst the trees, but interestingly, my husband didn't want it to be destroyed by the elements. Perhaps I could make a weatherproof shrine or something so that it's outside but not "suffering" too much. I HAVE come to love it, you see. For the moment, until I decide on its fate, I'll hang it on a little front verandah. Thus it will be nearby, but out of sight.

Of course, the Scapegoat doll is really "me," isn't it? The me I've weighed down with an impossible burden and then criticized because I've been unable to "perform." The Talisman doll, I daresay, will have to be the "me" that has shed the load.

The Emotional Midwife
Barb Kobe

Here's an email I sent to a group member:

At times, I feel like a midwife, waiting for all my pregnant creative souls to give birth to what is next for them. I am happy to hear that you consider what I say as gentle nudges. That is my intention. This delights me, fills me with appreciation for the creative process. I am blessed by the stories and dolls you and the other members create . . . it grounds me.

Thank you,

Barb

The Loving Kindness

Accepting, Allowing, and Self-Compassion

Purpose: To intentionally bring the energy of love and compassion into the healing process.

For fifteen years, I suffered with panic and anxiety attacks. I read books about fear and the healing powers of artmaking. I made feelings dolls and healing dolls on the subjects. I noticed that I felt safe and calm whenever I was making my dolls and art and when I was teaching dollmaking, yet the anxiety persisted more times than not whenever I left my house. I was starting to resent every time I felt anxious. I wondered, "What's wrong with me?"

In 2012, I met a health coach who introduced me to mindfulness, stress reduction, and loving-kindness meditation. I began to use the techniques daily and found them helpful. This changed my way of being and affected my art in new ways. My perspective shifted from focusing on what was wrong to focusing on what could possibly be right or healing. Now I'm able to act with greater balance and a sense of inner safety, especially when I experience stress, pain, and anxiety. I have a continuing meditation and mindfulness practice, and I include this wisdom in my teaching.

By 2012, the online Medicine Dolls group process hadn't changed in over ten years. There were four dolls in the sequence: the Guardian, the Scapegoat, the Talisman, and the Inner Healer. But as I read through the group members' messages, I noticed that after completing the Scapegoat, several people were struggling with how to continue on to the Talisman. I wondered if there needed to be another doll that focused on loving kindness, compassion, and self-love. And so the Loving Kindness doll was born.

Perhaps you resisted the Scapegoat at first, but then you found the courage to make it. However, you may now notice a hesitation to move forward. You feel a resistance—you may feel stuck again. Victim energy may be moving in, and you may feel powerless, empty, unworthy, depressed, unlovable, or not good enough. You're wondering what happened to you, why you can't make the next doll. You may ask, "Is there another Scapegoat?"

Starting at the Frequency of Love
Barb Kobe

"Each person confronting a crisis has his or her own special story, yet each one also embodies universal fears, hopes, angers, and realizations. Linking the uniqueness of the individual to global human concerns creates an image that touches many. Identification with the archetype, myth, or dream allows the model and the viewer to accept something too immense or difficult to otherwise grasp."

Christian Corbet
Collaborative Artist

Loving Kindness
Amelie

"A month ago, I created a beautiful nest from a book called Exuberance, *and I altered it to be called* Hatching Exuberance. *An hour ago, I realized that I, my nest, and my baby in waiting belong together—moss, paper, collage, and paint, I have planted her where she belongs! Her name is Lovey (Loving Kindness). She is newborn and has tiny wings. She is nestled in her nest, and she represents the first blush of exuberance in the form of Loving Kindness. I think she is the beginning of a series of the developmental stages of Lovey."*

Cat Caracelo
Medicine Dolls participant

An online group member commented on this feeling after completing her Scapegoat:

> When I finished the doll, I thought I'd be done with the pain and feelings she would hold. Rather, I found myself not wanting to let go of them but wanting a place to put them, so that I could see who I was, who I am, what makes me, me. I'm a bit stalled on this one, partly because I'm so busy, but partly because I want to make a forgiveness doll and I'm not all that certain what I am forgiving. Don't know if this makes any sense—it's not clear in my mind yet.

You have two ways to proceed: If you feel grounded and safe, make the Talisman. If not, make Loving Kindness.

In making the Loving Kindness doll, you can nurture and love yourself, cultivate the sensations of awareness and mercy, and embrace your pain and suffering with acceptance and tenderness.

Resistance after the Scapegoat

Making the Scapegoat allowed you to listen to and focus on feelings you thought were hidden away. Making her helped you visualize some dark parts of yourself so you could begin to shine light on your shadow self. But in this process, you may have created some armor to protect yourself. It may be difficult to move beyond that. Consider the following scenarios and see if you recognize any of them:

Making the Scapegoat exposed feelings you've been told not to have ("don't be angry" or "don't be sad"). It feels as if you've told a deep secret, as if you have betrayed a confidence. This brings up feelings of shame, rejection, and unworthiness of being yourself. You don't like this feeling, so you may be looking to find comfort or to numb the emotions . . . which means you're resisting making the next doll.

You're feeling lost and disconnected from yourself or the process. You're waiting for someone to tell you what to do and how to do it.

You don't want to feel the pain that came up while making the Scapegoat, and you want to numb yourself or run away from it.

In order to receive approval and love in your early years, you learned to suppress the feelings and expressions well-meaning adults told you were unacceptable. Over time, you no longer recognized the difference between what was internal (your real needs and feelings) and external (the needs of another). The result was that you lost touch with your true self, not knowing what you think or feel or who you really are. You surrendered your true self and needs in order to survive.

Your caregivers did not know your developmental need for authentic interaction, respect, admiration, mirroring, and unconditional positive regard. You were conditioned to meet the needs of others first. You may have believed you are not lovable and are not loved.

You're feeling grief, a deep sadness, a loss—you cannot find the energy to move on. Most of us think grief is about sadness and loss, but it can be an unfinished aspect of your life attached to fear—of loss, of the unknown, or of death. One aspect of grief is the tendency to cling and condemn and judge. It is a feeling of "not-enoughness," of being unworthy and useless, that longs to be otherwise. When you look into a symbolic mirror of your self-image, you see a distorted image, so unacceptable, so unwhole and unlovable.

You notice your inner critic's voice is loud and pestering you. You feel there is something wrong with you, that it was wrong to make the Scapegoat. Perhaps you grew up thinking that what you do must be wrong or that something is wrong with you, so your inner critic developed early. It took the form of destructive behaviors such as stress eating, substance abuse, overwork, or being in abusive relationships. You are yearning for spiritual nourishment.

You released a powerful experience or emotion by making the Scapegoat. You sense there is another to be released.

Did one or more of these scenarios bring up pain, anger, or a feeling of vulnerability for you? *Daring Greatly* author Brené Brown says, "Vulnerability is the unstable feeling we get when we step out of our comfort zone or do something that forces us to lose control." It's a sign of uncertainty, risk, and emotional exposure.

Making your Scapegoat doll could very well have exposed a vulnerable part of yourself, leaving you ready to "armor up," fearing what's next. Therefore, you may be contemplating whether or how to move forward.

Brené Brown suggests that "vulnerability is the birthplace of love, belonging, joy, courage, empathy, and creativity." So instead of feeling vulnerable, try to reframe your experience so you can see it in a positive light. For instance, see your experience of making the Scapegoat doll as something that called up great courage. So while making the healing dolls may feel uncomfortable, remember that it also allows you to open yourself up to the opportunity to make a deeper connection to yourself. You're learning news ways to be creative, express yourself, and discover more about yourself.

Here's a reflection I wrote in my heart journal in February 2014:

> *I want to heal my heart. I am convinced that my heart will be healed when I release the belief that I am doomed to have a heart attack at any time . . .*

"We think that the point is to pass the test or overcome the problem, but the truth is that things don't really get solved. They come together and they fall apart. Then they come together again and fall apart again. It's just like that. The healing comes from letting there be room for all of this to happen: room for grief, for relief, for misery, for joy."

Pema Chödrön

Loving Kindness
Anne Whitney

Loving Kindness's quilt is cut from a vintage quilt given to me by a friend who said she felt I was supposed to have it for my creative ventures. I saw each circle as representing people in my life who exemplify loving kindness, have shown it toward me, and thus, have mirrored my inner loving kindness. I embroidered their names on the insides of the circles. The doll and quilt envelop my scared and shamed Scapegoat, shielding and protecting her from the inner predator, who lies without animation or power in the background. I believe we either feed the inner predator or starve it, depending on where we place the focus of our attention, intention, and action. Looking at this doll is a good reminder for me to be mindful of where I direct my energy, both inwardly and outwardly.

135

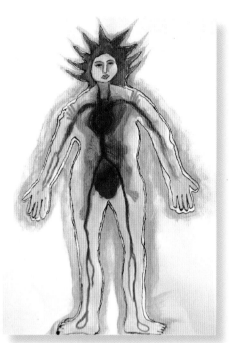

Heart of the Womb
(Watercolor)
Barb Kobe

Heart of the Womb
(Final)
Barb Kobe

I listen to meditation expert Andy Puddicombe's meditation app, Headspace, every morning. This morning I chose to begin the Heart series. Andy says this series will focus on relationships, love and kindness, and the question, "How can I generate a sense of loving kindness and be comfortable with physical sensations and focus on happiness and the well-being of myself and others?" He calls this Heart Warming. Ahhh! I like this . . . using awareness, focus, and clarity. I hear that "when you feel loved, everything always feels like it's going to work out just fine."

I know I want to embody my relationship with my heart. I've been collecting images of the heart and circulatory system. I take out the images, put them near my journal page, and begin listening to the meditation as I start with a free-flowing watercolor technique of my body. I allow the colors to run and drip. After the meditation is done, as well as the watercolor, I notice a shape in the middle of my torso in the painting . . . it looks like a baby's body clinging to my chest. This was not planned nor even noticed as I was painting. (I have to tell you this tends to happen when I approach healing this way.)

I am touched by this and curious, which takes me to the next step: exploring its meaning to me. I wonder, what does it mean when a child clings to me, and how does it relate to my heart?

I hear an answer from a voice I call my intuition: "She wants to be close to you and wants your attention." Then comes the aha: "It's difficult to share happiness, comfort, and kindness with others when you can't and won't give it to yourself."

As I look around my house and visit the photo file of previous dolls made, I realize this has been a message that has been begging my attention for quite a while.

The doll within the tall house is called Coming Home to Myself *. . . made years ago [page 56]. Her chest is filled with colorful beads, and she is wrapped in a healing shawl. Inside of the shawl I wrote, "LOVE ALIGNMENT." Some of the messages inside say, "Having learned lessons in love and trust—realizing these energies must first be given to myself before I can give them to another"; "I am enough"; and "I love who I am now and who I am becoming." These messages seem to be a manifesto of my life, my work, and they have been a focus for a very long time. It "warms" my heart to rediscover this, and it brings an awareness of the importance of doing my work around this subject.*

I used the watercolor for inspiration to create a healing doll on this subject called Heart of the Womb *[left]. Her story can be found on my website under Healing Doll Stories.*

Compassionate Mother

Anne Heck, Asheville, North Carolina

I've been working for over a year on this dear one—I pick her up and dream with her, then lay her down for a time.

She's required some inner work on my part, for which I'm very grateful. She came first in a vision. I've journaled with her and have appreciated her teachings about being gentle with myself, about knowing my truth and trusting my inner voice, and about being present with what is.

I spent hours carefully hand-beading the layers of her skirt, made of layered bright cottons with alternating layers scallop-beaded on the edge. Her scarf is hand-knitted with mohair and some glitzy art yarn. Her face is paper clay covered with cheesecloth and painted with acrylics. Her hair is wool roving. Her shoes are made from an old pair of my

Photo by Stewart Stokes

mother's leather gloves, and they too were beaded. I knit her scarf with toothpicks and gently molded her face from paper clay, incorporating the cheesecloth, and then painted it.

Even as I finished her, I already sensed another stage to her development. Her completion came just before attending my fourth level of training for Healing Touch; her presence there was powerful and deeply healing.

But it's really only a blurb. All of my medicine dolls hold meaning for me, but through this one I learned how to be compassionate with myself, which I don't feel I'd ever known how to do. Its making coincided with my sitting in a women's healing circle. The facilitator had me place a tiny statue of Kwan Yin on my altar for months and asked me to give my attention to being gentle and loving with myself. I knew this was a lesson to me, but through the making of this Loving Kindness doll, I was able to understand more of what compassion required.

She felt like she embodied every woman, all cultures, and seemed to hold features and details that indicated that. Her energy continues to be very powerful for me. I'm grateful to her for encouraging me to be patient and attentive to the details she requested so that I could learn the lesson of being truly loving, forgiving, and kind with myself.

This one I hold close to my heart, and I'm looking forward to our walk together.

www.anneheck.com

Heart Meditation
Barb Kobe

Loving Kindness Blessing

May I be at peace.
May my heart remain open.
May I realize the beauty of my own true
    nature.
May I be healed.
May I be a source of healing for this world.

Heart Energy
Barb Kobe

Here's an email I sent to an online group:

> I spent last Saturday and Sunday at a weekend dollmaking retreat with a group of five women who dealt with depression, a brain tumor, a brother who committed suicide, breast cancer, and emotional numbness, respectively. By Sunday evening, each had made a Guardian, Scapegoat, and Talisman. Working in person with dollmakers brings to focus the difficulty of moving people through this potentially powerful process by email.
>
> I am committed to offering you my best so you may receive an experience that will create some transformation in your life, despite the distance. I am reminded of the words of creativity coach Eric Maisel, author Oriah Mountain Dreamer, and dollmaker Elinor Peace Bailey. They all basically say, "You have to do the work." When feeling anxious, do the work; when doubting your skill, do the work; when feeling down and hopeless, do the work. We all have stories of pain, sorrow, and illness. And despite it all, I believe that doing creative work helps us to move through to the other side.

Still not convinced? Making healing dolls or any kind of expressive art expands your awareness. As discussed in *Spiritual Solutions* by Deepak Chopra, there are three levels of awareness: contracted, expanded, and pure.

Level one: Contracted awareness. This is the level of problems, obstacles, and struggle. You feel fear, confusion, frustration, and exhaustion. Finding a solution takes lots of effort.

Level two: Expanded awareness. This is the level where solutions begin to appear easily. You experience less conflict and more clarity. Unseen forces come to your aid. You trust your intuition, set intentions, and move toward them.

Level three: Pure awareness. This is the level where you see every challenge as a creative opportunity. You are aligned with forces of nature. Solutions arise from the level of your true self; they meet no resistance.

You may have experienced what contracted awareness felt like and looked like when you made your Scapegoat. It's not "wrong" or "bad" to see only problems and struggles. Actually, it's an opportunity!

But now, why wouldn't you want to experience what expanded awareness feels like and looks like in the dolls beyond the Scapegoat?

Creative Action

Do any of the scenarios earlier in the chapter speak to you and where you're at? Are you feeling blocked, as if you don't want to move on to the Talisman? Journal and do art about this resistance, blocked state, or feeling.

Choose one of the scenarios and consider how it might be the story you're telling yourself.

Imagine you have created armor to protect yourself. Look at your Scapegoat doll and notice whether she is wearing any form of "armor." Imagine this armor, or your Scapegoat, floating in a sea of compassion, met by softness and care that simply accepts the moment as it is. What happens when you do this? Headspace offers free introductory meditation sessions; download the Headspace app or sign up for free at www.headspace.com. You can also find other guided mindfulness meditations on YouTube.

Visit Dr. Kristin Neff's website, self-compassion.org, and explore her content with curious eyes, reading, watching videos. You can also take her self-compassion assessment at self-compassion.org/test-how-self-compassionate-you-are/. Notice what you are feeling after—or even while—taking the assessment. Draw or write it in your journal. Write down the ways you do not give yourself self-compassion.

Watch Brené Brown talk to Oprah about armors: www.youtube.com/watch?v=o7yYFHyvweE

Thinking about the three levels of awareness, what level do you think you are at in the healing doll process?

Kathryn's Loving Kindness: *Tutti*

Kathryn Hall, Colorado

Her name is *Tutti*. When I was in Colorado, I went to a restaurant by that name and learned that the word means "all the voices" or "all the instruments"—everything playing together. As soon as I heard it, I knew that would be my Loving Kindness's name. I cannot think of Loving Kindness without thinking of all the wonderful people who loved me and treated me so kindly as a child. So Tutti represents my parents and eight other women who were, in one way or another, like second mothers to me and/or who encouraged me in some kind and generous way. I was very blessed in that regard.

The problem has been in getting started on her. All of the wonderful feelings are difficult to demonstrate. So, ultimately, I chose simple symbols (one each) to represent the ways they showed their love and taught and inspired me. It was all in the doing, the hugging, the smiles, the time spent, the kind words and encouragement, and it filled me with a sense of being loved and feeling secure.

On the dress: WATER—My dad played with me outside in so many ways. APPLE PIE—My aunt Phyllis was the best pie baker ever. PAINTBRUSH—My first-grade teacher, Mrs. Beasley, let me stay after school and paint on the easels. TOMATOES—My adult cousin Jean was a wonderful gardener. FLOWERS—My mom's best friend, Marion, grew the most beautiful flower gardens. HORSE CHARM—My best friend Cindi's mom, Opaline, was like another mom for sure and sent us off on horses for great adventures. HEART—represents all of them, but most especially my parents. The heart is open at the top, and their names are all tucked inside the pocket.

In her hands: ANTIQUE BUTTON—Mrs. Ryan was an elderly woman who lived next door when I was very young. She played "hide the button" with me. SPOOL OF THREAD—Mickie, another of my mom's best friends, was a great seamstress as well as a next-door neighbor. GAME PIECES—Mom would play inside games with me, especially when I was sick. YARN DOLL—Adult cousin Connie taught me how to make these when I was very young.

Bottom line, she *is* kind of 1950s "corny," and I can't escape that fact. She *is* traditional and self-sacrificing. In some ways, I *wish* she were more wildishly *Dances With Wolves*, but she just isn't.

Loving Kindness is an important doll for me to make because I feel like I'm entering a different phase of life that I'm not sure any of my loved ones would have fully understood. I don't know what dreams they may have secretly harbored or what things they kept buttoned up inside of themselves, so maybe they would have understood. I'm confident they would support me, regardless. I had a long, deep conversation with the one of them, still living, not too long ago, and she surprised me. Point? I believe that creating this doll enables me to honor my past and these people in a way I need to acknowledge. It will remind me that their collective loving kindness is forever, and it will provide a visual "hug" from which to gather strength as I continue to move forward, no matter where I go.

Cindy's Loving Kindness

Cindy Read, Hampden, Maine

Creating my Scapegoat was an intense shadow journey. Hidden under a gray veil, she is bound with the words of my beliefs, stories, and rules of the world that negate my healing intentions. And in her center is a whole tangle of pain, fear, and confusion. As I worked on her, though, I learned that she had a luminous heart and that she was holding all this shadow for me so I could begin to release it out of my body, my mind, my heart, my spirit.

In a meditation before beginning Loving Kindness, I received the image of a being taking the stories, the pain, out of my body and transforming them with the rose-colored light of love, which became my guide in creating the next doll in the series.

Loving Kindness is deep green, the color of the heart chakra and also the color that for me represents courage. She has one hand on her heart, one cradling a golden bowl filled with rose-colored light (made from Angelina fiber). The shadow beliefs from my Scapegoat are represented by little black onyx chips in the bottom of the bowl, and around the inside of the bowl I wrote the Metta (loving kindness) Prayer that has been part of my daily practice for many years: "May I be peaceful, may I be happy, may I be well, may I be at ease in my body and spirit, may I love and be loved, may I be safe." On her gold pendant, I wrote the Tibetan syllable *Hung*, which is called the "heart essence seed syllable." She is wearing a gold shawl crocheted with the same pattern I use making baby blankets for the neonatal ICU, offering her (and therefore myself) the same comfort and love I offer those tiny vulnerable ones in the hospital.

As with my other dolls in this class, Loving Kindness spent time on my shrine before I was ready to photograph, write about, and share her. Now she sits in my study at the feet of my Guardian, with my Scapegoat behind her, and I talk with her almost every day.

Loving Kindness
Cindy Read

Scapegoat
Cindy Read

141

Discovering Loving Kindness

Make a Loving Kindness doll by focusing on the concepts of love, kindness, and one or more of the concepts below. How could a healing doll express the concepts below?

Rosarian
Barb Kobe

- Acceptance
- Compassion
- Love
- Allowance
- Forgiveness
- Peace
- Freedom
- Empowerment
- Creativity
- Security
- Sanctuary
- Joy

I love you just as you are.

I love you and I care for you willingly.

I love you when you are active and when you are quiet.

You can become separate from me and I will continue to love you.

I love who you are.

I love you even when we differ; I love growing with you.

My love is always with you. I trust you to ask for my support.

When designing your Loving Kindness doll, consider how she might embrace your Scapegoat. How will the making of the Loving Kindness doll allow you to move forward to the Talisman?

Imagine what being filled with self-compassion and caring for your body, mind, spirit—even your pain—might look like.

Read the love affirmations featured on this page (left) out loud to yourself three times. Notice which ones you take in and believe easily and which you resist. You know you're choosing self-love when you speak to yourself with care and concern rather than judgment and anger. It means you're finding pleasure in being with yourself, rather than avoiding yourself. What happens if you read the affirmations to your Scapegoat? Incorporate the affirmations you believe into Loving Kindness.

Creative Action

Consider the words and questions from "Discovering Loving Kindness" on the previous page. Make a mind map, writing the words *Loving Kindness* in the center of the page, then write words and draw images that come to you when you think about a figure that is loving and kind. What qualities will your Loving Kindness doll have on her outside and within?

Draw or collect images from magazines, then collage these Loving Kindness images and symbols. Choose one that most resonates with you. Don't spend too much time on this. Usually the first image is the best.

What images and symbols will she be holding and wearing?

Your Loving Kindness doll can be the first of several spirit guides that are walking with you on the healing dolls journey. What do you think?

What Could Be a Loving Kindness Doll?

- Animals you believe are loving and kind
- Sacred figures, such as saints or people from holy books—Buddha, Tara, Kwan Yin, etc.
- Maternal figures, perhaps grandmothers or wisdom figures
- Goddesses
- Images from nature, such as trees or rocks
- Healers, shamans, doctors, nurses

Art Forms for a Loving Kindness Doll:

- Three-dimensional doll
- Paper doll
- Purchased image from a store, thrift store, etc.
- Mixed media figure
- Photograph

Make your Loving Kindness doll.

Patty's *Blessingway*

Barb Kobe

A blessingway is a Navajo ritual performed during a Changing Woman ceremony to ensure a blessed life of good health, emotional strength, prosperity, and a positive outlook.

I created *Blessingway* for my cousin Patty, who requested a healing doll from me after she was diagnosed with stage 1 breast cancer in 2011. I asked Patty to answer The Ten Questions that I always ask someone who requests a healing doll. I use the answers to design the doll. The Ten Questions and Patty's answers are at the end of this section.

Patty was born and raised in Davenport, Iowa. She is a mother and grandmother. She and her husband lived in Arizona for a while, and she fell in love with the colors and symbols of the Southwest. I used her favorite colors as well as the colors of the elements on the doll: blue, orange, yellow, and shades of red. I also used her favorite symbols in the overall design of the doll: circles; round, curvy pottery shapes; and sand-painting figures.

The spirals on her breasts are common feminine symbols and are used in Reiki. (Reiki is a hands-on Japanese technique for stress reduction and relaxation that also promotes healing.) I used spirals on the doll's breasts because of Patty's breast cancer. Three figure symbols are around her large, female hips. They are petroglyph shapes, similar to the shapes of the female sexual organs.

Patty's response to the question about her favorite fairy tale surprised me at first. Patty's first response was "Pat-a-Cake," a very old and famous nursery rhyme. I wondered what meaning or metaphor this story contained for her and how it related to the meaning of the doll I was making for her. It wasn't until I read *Memories of Our Lost Hands: Searching for Feminine Spirituality and Creativity* by Sonoko Toyoda that I understood how women's hands express the wisdom and gifts of the body. Women's hands pick up and hold things; they are secondary eyes. Hands connect one person to another, take care of another, love and heal another. *Blessingway*'s hands connect her with the hearts and souls of her family and to life. When brought together, they pray.

In the questionnaire, Patty said the doll would be a symbol of the power of friendship and the circle of caring. At the

base of the doll's gown are pockets that hold small flat dolls that have pockets behind them. Inside those pockets are messages from Patty's loving circle of friends and family. There are extra dolls for others to share their words of support and caring. Also, there are small circles on her gown that have embroidery stitches through them with a bead in the middle. These symbolize the healthy, healing cells that are dissolving and removing the cancer cells from the body.

Blessingway wears a hat with a bandana, wrapped with a band of red roses. The hat symbolizes ongoing protection from harmful energies. Patty belongs to the Catholic Church, and within the church, the rose is seen as the queen of flowers. It is a symbol of the Virgin Mary, representing romance, religion, and healing. I felt strongly led to put roses somewhere on Patty's *Blessingway*.

Psychologist Erik Erickson identified eight stages of psychosocial human development that respectively build the virtues of hope, will, purpose, competence, fidelity, love, care, and wisdom. His wife, Joan Erikson, spotlights a ninth and final stage of life, which circles back and is similar to the first stage of life. She wisely states, "Hands, understanding, capable, talented hands . . . Conscious and attentive use of the hands would make all our lives more meaningful. Hands are essential for vital involvement in living."

Sonoko Toyoda also focuses on the importance of hands:

[We must see] hands as having their own wisdom, one truly connected to the heart and soul, as well as being necessary for the development of feminine spirituality and creativity in both women and men. Men cannot return to women what they took from them during the centuries of male domination. Women must recover it on their own.

The Ten Questions

1. **What colors are you drawn to? Do you wear often? Are your favorites?**
   Blue, orange, soft yellow, shades of red.

2. **What will this doll symbolize for you? What will it remind you to think, feel, and/or do when you see it?**
   Healing power of friendship and the circle of caring.

3. **What elements describe you? Earth, air, water, fire?**
   Earth, mountains, sky, water.

4. **What symbols do you like or are you drawn to? What objects do you collect or like to spend time around?**
   Circles. Not peace symbols or happy faces. Most of my Arizona stuff is some form of circle, pottery, figures on my sand paintings.

5. **What part of your body do you feel needs healing?**
   Right now, I would have to say my cells deep in my body that are attracted to cancer. Breast cancer usually comes back in the lungs or female organs.

6. **If an animal with special powers were to enter your life to give you power, what would that animal be?**
   Cats.

7. **When do you feel the most powerful?**
   In the company of my friends or church group mixed gender.

8. **When do you feel the least powerful?**
   When I can feel free to give up my power to someone else. It can be a good thing.

9. **What brings you the greatest joy? Makes your heart sing? What does your heart yearn for?**
   Serenity and calm, which is why I like yoga and classical music.

10. **What is your favorite fairy tale? Explain how this fairy tale is a metaphor for your life.**
    I guess I don't look on my life in a fairy tale way. I think in short spaces of time, depending on the events in my life. Right now, some of my favorites that have meaning in my life would be "Jack and Jill" and especially "Pat-a-Cake," which is the first nursery rhyme I sang with my grandkids—or my own kids, for that matter.

Moonhenge
Round-robin doll, 2012
Dollmakers involved: Kathryn, Lynn, Mary Lou, Thea, Pamela, Lori

"Moonhedge Poem" (Excerpt), by Barb Kobe

She imagines her mind as a ritual space like Stonehenge
As the full moon rises over the ancient stones
She sings a universal chant, calling her down to the earth

She stands facing the Moon
As she becomes a figure flooded in light
Accepting herself simply as she is

And affirming her choice to be a Seeker of Wisdom.

The Talisman

Stepping into the Light

Purpose: to transform the pain; to move toward positive outcome

Talismans have been used throughout history. A talisman is an object that holds meaning and purpose for the maker and the viewer. It's a visual anchor that can be protective and provide personal peace, comfort, and affirmation. It's often seen as a visual blessing that draws in abundance, love, good luck, security, and healing. A talisman can be made of almost anything and can be many sizes. They're often small so they can be worn or carried, and they're usually marked with symbols and words that are meaningful to the owner or creator.

Your Talisman doll will be a symbol of your healing intention, of what is on the other side of the wound—of the Scapegoat. This doll symbolizes the "gift in the wound," the reward you receive for doing the work and the light that shines through the pain.

You will know you are ready to create your Talisman when you feel motivated to work beyond the pain of the past or present and move into the future. Art therapist Barbara Gamin calls this stage the "re-envisioning." This is when you look at the image of your stress (the Scapegoat) and imagine how it needs to change in order to be less stress inducing and more positive, to make you feel better. Gamin states, "You can use this transformed image to serve as a guide to help you see new directions or choices."

The Talisman is your totem, a powerful symbol of recovery and of your ability to activate your healing response on many levels. For most participants in the online Medicine Dolls class, making this doll catalyzed a shift. The more involved you are in the creation of this doll, and the more you make it visible in your daily life, the more possibility you'll create for healing and reaching your goals. As you make your Talisman, the images and symbols of your healing intention will surface and unravel. Your wishes and desires will become clear and can then be placed within or upon your doll. Your feelings of pain—unearthed during the creation of the Scapegoat—will dissipate. New feelings of hope, peace, and creative celebration will emerge.

Dawning of a New Day **(Closed)**
Barb Kobe

Dawning of a New Day

Dawning of a New Day (Open)
Barb Kobe

This doll was for a man who had prostate surgery and recovered fully. He is one of the most compassionate and considerate people I know. He visits colorful, exotic places near water and lives where the sun shines almost every day.

Email to Student:

I congratulate you in taking this courageous step toward bringing this dark time of your life into the light. Holding these energies inside is like trying to hold a feeling in by holding your breathe. You keep trying to hold them in and then engage your muscles and nerves to partner with you in the containment. Do you see how this could lead to disease?

A friend of mine was diagnosed with the beginning stages of prostate cancer in late fall 2002. I asked if he would be willing to accept a healing doll from me. Once he gave me permission—a very important step in making someone a healing doll—I gave him The Ten Questions to answer.

This healing doll would be a symbol, a talisman, a thera-peutic metaphor or story that would hold the possibility for my friend's healing goal. It would remind him of the healing crisis he was moving through and the posi-tive "healed" outcome he desired. He wanted the doll to signify "the dawning of a new day" in his life and the "new compassionate and considerate person" he would become after being healed.

I looked over his answers to The Ten Questions and began the design process. He described colors and images that represented exotic places with lots of water and sunshine, so I hand-painted white muslin with tropical colors and made the face resemble a shining sun. The cloak wrapped around the doll symbolizes self-love as well as my love and care for him. The three green leaves embellishing the front represent new growth.

One of the questions was, "What is your favorite fairy tale?" His answer was "Snow White and the Seven Dwarfs." In this story, he thought the kiss from the prince represented not only a literal awakening but a symbolic one—from an afflicted, cancerous state to a new world of possibilities. I put seven little dwarf figures inside the cloak, each with a special meaning:

- **Doc:** Your inner healer, the part that loves you no matter what and has all the tools to help you heal.

- **Dopey:** Your silly, playful part. (Laughter has been proven to heal the emotions, the mind, and the body.)

- **Bashful:** The part of you that is introspective and intui-tive, allowing you to settle down and go within.

- **Grumpy:** The hard-working, rational mind, mining all the facts about the disease and the surgery.

- **Happy:** The reminder to celebrate your life and be grateful for the gifts it has provided up to this point.

- **Sleepy:** Your reminder to rest, recuperate, and recover, taking the time you need to heal and reenergize.

- **Sneezy:** How your body speaks up when your mind thinks it knows best. *Ahhhhh-CHOO!*

The body of the doll has several symbols represnting T cells—cancer-killing cells—sewn on it. A spiral, a symbol for healing energy, is sewn where the prostate is located on the male body.

My friend had treatment and recovered fully. He is now cancer-free.

Dr. Carl Simonton, an oncologist who specializes in mind-body connectedness for cancer treatment, discovered that patients who focused on what they did *not* want were less successful in reaching their healing goals. In this same vein, you want your Talisman to represent an energy or symbol capable of eliminating what is blocking you, so you can focus on what you *do* want. This doll should look very different from the Scapegoat and have very different colors.

Once complete, your Talisman will stand as a symbol of your renewed—and probably revised—healing intention. When you share your Talisman and her story to your compassionate, safe witnesses, the doll will absorb their positive energies to better help you reach your healing goals.

Generally speaking, a modern talisman can be made of just about anything, such as wood, metal, paper, stone, or natural elements. But the physical properties of a talisman are not as important as the intention(s) of its bearer. If you are grounded in your desires, your Talisman doll can act as a focal point. This concentration will help you affirm your intention and achieve your goal.

The first step is to revisit your healing intention. Does it still express your healing desire? Does it need slight changes in wording? If so, revise it until it feels right. Then play with recasting it from an intention to an affirmation.

"In being a healing mirror to others and in seeing your own reflected, changing self in others' mirrors, judgments and comparisons are replaced by forgiveness and acceptance. If you can live health consciously, live life as poetry, live from your feelings, you begin to live life as it was intended. We must remember why we are here: We are here to love and be loved."

Paul Brenner
Buddha in the Waiting Room

Holding Energy for What's Next
Barb Kobe

"The healing process is like peeling layers off an onion, and it also has a cyclical nature. The layers of coats seem to capture that idea. It also reminds me—I just thought of it as I started to write—of what happened when my Talisman wanted to shed her old skin. All similar ways of getting to a similar place."

Erika Cleveland
Medicine Dolls class

149

Summer Soltice
Barb Kobe

Blooming
Barb Kobe

Here is one of my healing intentions turned into an affirmation:

Intention: *My intention is to learn to love myself, to change and transform a little every day. I will see my body as a plant that needs to send its roots deep into earth to draw in nutrients, rise up to take in the fire of the sun, breathe in clean air, and soak in rainwater to feed and cleanse my soul.*

Affirmation: *I enjoy the gift of my own company. I walk toward balance and wholeness as I feed my body healthy, nutritious food from the earth, as I breathe in and move through fresh air, as I drink lots of water, and as I take my body outside to be with all the elements of nature.*

Here are some student healing intentions transformed into affirmations:

Intention: *It is my intention to open myself up and free the real me living inside. I want to heal or change. I want to break out of a forty-two-year pattern of pain and abuse.*

Affirmation: *I open myself up and free the real me. I no longer carry old beliefs and habits. I am saving my life. I shine a healing light on my wounds. I am whole, balanced, and free.*

Intention: *My original intention was to make the dolls, but now my intention is to connect to my true voice—to stand in my own body and be a channel for healing through my dolls, my writing, and my transformational journeys.*

Affirmation: *I am connected to my true voice. I stand in my body as a healing channel as I create my writing, dolls, and journeys.*

Intention: *My intention is to heal the critical voice that tells me I am not worthy or "good enough," and to heal the part of me that uses fear as a motivator. My intention includes learning to play in life and appreciate my creative gifts and talents—to create a wholeness and total well-being in my health.*

Affirmation: *I am worthy, whole, and healed. I release fear and use love to motivate myself. I play with life. I am grateful for my creative gifts and talents.*

You can write your affirmation before making your Talisman, or you can reverse this order if you want. If you first write the affirmation, I suggest you create a mind map with Talisman-like images and words. As with all the other healing dolls, spend some time determining your Talisman's frame or structure before determining her physical properties.

For example, perhaps she can carry a strip of paper bearing the word "love" or symbols of inner healing. Play around with enlarging or reducing body parts as you contemplate her design. Many Talisman dolls are decorated with things such as metal amulets or gemstones worn as jewelry.

For other ideas, look at your Scapegoat. Notice the symbols and colors you used, then jump across the color wheel and choose the opposite colors for your Talisman. If you want, you can transform your Scapegoat into your Talisman by giving her a mask and creating a costume that goes over her form.

In addition to creating your Talisman doll, you may already have a small object, doll, or form that can be transformed into a talisman of protection, good fortune, health, love, or serenity. You may want to wear it as a necklace, add it to a belt, or carry it in your purse or pocket. Another possibility is to take a picture of your Talisman doll, reduce its size, and print it out on ink-jet printer fabric. Then you can tack or sew it onto a small felt bag, embellish it, and call it a medicine bag.

Madisyn Taylor says this on her blog, *DailyOM*:

> *Before your object becomes a talisman, however, it must be charged. This can be done by cleansing the object with water or incense and holding a ritual of your own making. Or you can leave the object in moonlight or sunlight or bury it in the earth for a time. To preserve its effectiveness, talismans should be reconsecrated regularly. That said, it's all right if this does not fit with your way of honoring your talisman object or Talisman doll. I trust you will find your way.*

I tend to place my Talisman on my art shrine or next to me in my bedroom. And—of course—I bring her into my art studio. I think the effectiveness of her story would be well served by giving her a bag filled with special stones and affirmations.

Hemp: The Wise Woman
Barb Kobe

"Imagery is most effective when it is combined with awareness and compassion. For instance, you can use guided imagery to direct your awareness into your body and open your heart with compassion to whatever pain, frustration, and sadness may arise. You can also use imagery to bring the power of awareness to any medicine you take. Through imagery, you can empower each pill to do what you want it to do. At the same time, you can be compassionate with your fear that the medicine might not follow your direction.

"Stay open to the unexpected. Receive whatever comes, without analyzing it or judging it. Honor your initial impulses. Imagery is not right or wrong, good or bad, better than or worse than, pretty or ugly. It is about finding what is true."

Dawna Markova
No Enemies Within

Embrace the Sky Talisman
Angie Q.

Belinda's Talisman Healing Doll: *Grace*
On her chest, I put a dove pin and a scrap of lace from my mother's wedding dress. The dove pin belonged to my father. On her hip, an image of a child.

Connected to Her Roots
Barb Kobe

Belinda's Talisman: *Grace*

I am completing my Talisman. It was difficult getting started with her; embracing my shadow was a very difficult process for me. One of the things I am finding interesting is that in making the Talisman I find myself more accepting of the Scapegoat/Shadow. For some time after completing the Scapegoat/Shadow, I didn't want it in my home. I felt a need to burn or destroy it. I no longer have that need.

I resisted working on my Talisman because I didn't know where to go with it at first. Her name is *Grace*, because that is what I have learned and have gained. I feel washed in grace—my own and others'. And I am able to feel more gracious toward others. Grace, although I cannot define it in words to you, is overwhelmingly healing. It is like a soft shower—a soft, warm shower followed by a warm towel. *Grace* came out of the "doll-a-day" suggestion. After working on Scapegoat/Shadow, I was exhausted and didn't really quite know where I was going. I had a lot of conversations about her—with my witness, my husband, and my therapist. One of the questions that came out of those discussions was, "What if I could not hold/accept that part of me? Could I ever accept that in others?" WOW! Light bulb!

I let that churn while I worked on doll heads in polymer, not sure of what I was doing or where I was going. I cut felt and tried different things, and then one day *Grace* spoke to me. It was pretty darn amazing.

As I continued to work on *Grace*, I began to think quite a bit about my mother. My mother and my mother's mother were both very traditional religious women. (I am not.) This was always a source of contention for us. The Virgin Mary was a woman of great significance for both of them. I realized that my *Grace* had Madonna-like qualities. So I allowed her to take that form. I let her be.

I love that the three of us have come together in *Grace*, who so resembles their Madonna. I know that they can appreciate the irony and humor of it and that they too have been a part of this washing, this healing. So it comes to this—that my healing has to do with the three of us and our relationship. Babies really do need to be with their mothers.

I think I am much more focused on
accepting my power and trusting that opportunities to foster that acceptance will continue to present themselves. My artmaking is better, and I am more willing to take risks with it.

Patty S.
Medicine Doll Project

Linda's Talisman

I decided that the doll I wanted to make would show me being held in the arms of God. I wanted the face to show serenity, the feeling of arrival—mine. The body is made out of sunflower batik, and it is just a rough representation of a torso, head, and arms. In the arms (crossed upon the chest) is a heart with bead embroidery. The heart is me. I played around with the arms a bit. I wanted them to be firm but relaxed. Not clutching or holding (as in, "I can't escape!"), but hugging, resting. On the bottom of the torso, I hung letter beads that spelled out words I wanted to go with this picture. The first is *safe*, the next is *heard*, followed by *cherished*, *loved*, and finally *home*. I have come to see this process as my "journey" home. Not the home I grew up in, but the home I needed as a child and still need as an adult. I recognized that the story of *The Odyssey* resonates with me very strongly—I have monsters to fight and a destination to reach. My husband pointed out that the bracelet I wear has the name Athena printed on it. I wasn't aware of this, and I believe it is no coincidence that the Guardian doll I made is called *Athena* too.

Talisman
Linda

Erika's Talisman: *Rhea*

Once you make the Talisman doll, you are transformed. And so it was for me. Barb describes a talisman as "an object that is marked with symbols that have meaning for the person who creates it and is therefore considered an image of power and/or protection."

In thinking about the Talisman doll, I was reminded of an image I created twenty years ago as a conclusion to one stage of my life: ending my time in New York City, leaving my family and my job there as an art therapist in order to move to Boston with my husband. This image was a good-bye of sorts. It was of a woman sitting on a rock in the middle of the ocean—a large, full-figured woman holding a sort of graying skin in front of her. At the time, I didn't fully understand the image. I wasn't sure if she was stepping out of this gray skin or stepping into it. Gradually, I began to understand that she (*Rhea*) was stepping out of it. The gray skin was the skin of her old self, the old habits and beliefs that no longer served her. She was shedding it.

Over the last few days of completing the Talisman, I worked through barriers despite not wanting to. It was uncomfortable. I paired *Rhea* with my Scapegoat, *Bruxus [page 123]*. This allowed me to begin to accept the uncomfortable parts of myself more. *Rhea* has crystals up and down the front of her body to symbolize the seven chakras. She sits open yet vulnerable, scared yet excited about what life holds for her.

Rhea **(Drawing and Final Doll)**
Erika
Photo by James Steele

Darla's Talisman: *Race for the Cure*

Race for the Cure
Darla

Darla was diagnosed with breast cancer and created a Talisman doll to aid in her recovery of body and mind. Below is a list of the design elements and their meanings:

- Glowing cancer cell on the brown, distressed base (not shown): the cancer in my breast

- Purple face: my passion to beat cancer

- Red hands and red design behind head: the hard work and energy applied to fighting cancer and finding a cure; feelings of rage about cancer rampantly attacking so many women

- Large defined muscles: the strength and courage required to win the battle

- Christian cross around neck: the belief that I am God's child and He is with me on this journey, giving me strength, comfort, and peace

- Hard, square button over one breast: while a small part of my whole self, it is the focus of my will to continue life

- Right foot forward: spirit of hope

- Soft lock of yarn coming from top of head: the scarves I wear because of hair loss; the disastrous hit to women's pride when they feel like hiding; new growth, just like new hair, is coming at the end of the race

- Floral design on torso: the fight to still be seen as a woman, not just a cancer victim

"Dump your pictures of what you're supposed to do. Listen to your heart. Your heart is not attached to what things look like. Your heart measures what they feel like. Your heart will keep you honest and on the true path. You will find healing and wonder in unexpected places. But only if you dare to walk past those glossy one-sided expectations—and into the bright and shadowed territory of listening to your heart."

Tama J. Kieves
This Time I Dance!

Darla created this doll in 2006. In early 2017, she shared her reflections:

> *I realize how much this healing doll process contributed to my positive outlook and healing and to being a role model to others. I know it was just as instrumental to my recovery as my surgery, chemotherapy, and radiation. It certainly affects my daily life as I live and take it in. It has given me a new awareness of feelings as they are occurring. I now recognize the Guardian, Scapegoat, Talisman, and Inner Healer archetypes and energies when I encounter them.*
>
> *I think that when I took your course, I had the advantage of living life with a singular goal—getting well and overcoming the cancer—and having the time to focus, to do the work. Now that I am back in the routine of a "normal" person living her daily life, I can see how difficult it is to take time to engage in the process of healing. I really have to be disciplined to maintain time for inspiration, mediation, evaluation, and thanksgiving.*

Today I looked over the material I created with your guidance and resources. There was a whole new processing and understanding of myself—where I was, how I journeyed, where I am now, where I am going, and what I should be considering.

Lisa's Talisman

I feel this is a watershed moment for me as I share my Talisman doll, which has been two years in incubation. Of all the dolls, she has been the most challenging yet most rewarding. As Barb has said many times, the Talisman exists because you are asking for what you really want—and how many of us have done that so easily?

This doll has taught me many things: strength (how to manipulate wire, testing my mettle); persistence (it's okay not to finish a creation in one or two sittings); independence (how to stand on my own two feet—physically, emotionally, spiritually); playfulness; and the true meaning of power. She possesses original medicine—personal power that is not duplicated anywhere else on the planet. She is in her medicine and is able to bring healing to Mother Nature and all her creatures.

This prayer from Australian aboriginal elder Betty Pike was shared with me as I was creating my Talisman doll, and I would like to share it with you.

*To all who walk this land,
May you stand as tall as a tree
Be gentle as the morning mist
As strong as the earth under your feet
May the warmth of the campfire be
  in you
And may the Creator Spirit always
  watch over you.*

An Ode to the Earth Mother Goddess

*She stands as tall as a tree,
Feet firmly planted,
grounded and alert
connecting heaven with earth
she has panoramic vision
sees with the eyes of the spirit
what needs to be done to bring healing to this place.
Her gift, her medicine
is the yellow bird of creativity
held in her right hand ready to fly
and the green bird, the mindful witness
of all that is.
Clothed in soft bark
that grows and sheds
continually
her flexible, instinctual protection.
Her power is her dignity and self worth
which radiates from her centre
Heart open to the world,
she is the scapegoat transformed.*

https://lisafam.wordpress.com/

Talisman
Lisa Fam

Creative Action

Do a mind map in your journal:

1. Write the word *Talisman* in the center of the page.

2. Add words and images around the center, leaving room for more additions.

3. At the top of your page, write your original healing intention. If it has changed since you first wrote it, write the revised intention under the original one.

4. Recast your intention as an affirmation and write it at the bottom of page.

5. Find images and words that represent the affirmation and collage them onto the map.

6. Choose words and images from your mind map to use on your Talisman doll. Will she be wearing them? Holding them? Putting them inside her body?

Draw an image of your Talisman in your journal or create a Talisman paper doll and glue it into your journal. Write with both hands to dialogue with the Talisman. Your dominant hand should ask your creative self about the Talisman; your nondominant hand should responds as the Talisman. Write this dialogue in your journal.

As you look at your Talisman image, write these statements: "This is who I am becoming. This is what is possible for me. This is where I am heading." Journal about your responses to these statements.

How could a Talisman express the following? — Healing, hope, health, balance, letting go, self-love, gratitude, life, forgiveness, mercy, grace, learning, celebration.

Objects/figures that could be a Talisman:

- Animals, power animals
- Medicine people and bags
- Three-dimensional doll
- Mixed media figure
- Purchased image from a store, thrift store, etc.

- Rocks, crystals, items from nature
- Art Forms for a Talisman
- Paper doll
- Jewelry

When you are ready, make your Talisman doll.

Mary's Medicine Doll Journey

Mary is a forty-eight-year-old fiber artist who started making dolls two years ago, after taking my Medicine Dolls class online. She's been making them for herself and others ever since. Here is her intention statement from that first class:

> *I intend to focus healing energy toward the expression of my female power and the creation of the next phase of my life. I believe healing for me will be about learning to trust my intuition more each day and maintaining balance on this walk. For me, true healing is about becoming bigger than my problems, rather than nurturing them and encouraging them to grow. Creating really helps me focus on the divine that is within me, letting it expand.*

Mary is also friend of mine. Before the Medicine Dolls class began, she told me about a special she saw on public television, Christiane Northrup's *Mother-Daughter Wisdom*. She was intrigued by Northrup's description of menopause as a new birth. Mary decided to use that theme for the class project to prepare herself for a magnificent rebirth. Mary had never participated in any online groups and was generally quite introverted.

I encouraged her, telling her not to worry, that whatever she created would be good enough. I told her, "The artist in me can sometimes be a real hindrance when making my healing dolls. Just remember that you obviously have a deep well to draw from. You don't need to impress the rest of us with 'artistic talent.'"

Here are some entries from Mary's journal:

March 2005

I had a fun experience that I initially didn't think had anything to do with this project, but it ended up having everything to do with this project. I am always making dolls, and I decided over the weekend to make a spider woman (not for this project, but just for fun). Last night, I looked up the symbolism in Medicine Cards *[by Jamie Sams] and* Animal Speak *[by Ted Andrews] to help in the design process. I was blown away as I read about the spider. She is the female creative force, and she brought the written word to*

people in her web so they could record their progress on this earth journey. She also symbolizes death and rebirth, balance, gentleness, and strength. When she drops into your life, she could be encouraging you to journal (I resist the journaling exercise) and to create. One quote I thought was particularly powerful was, "Spider teaches you to use the written language with power and creativity so that your words weave a web around those who read them." So I start this particular journey with spider as my companion.

April 2005

My Guardian is a protective spirit. The doll is small and will fit into a pocket in my journal folder. Since it is a guardian spirit, I did not include personal symbols. The spider is included as a companion to this journey since she was made after the process began. Even if things aren't strictly part of the project, I have found that once I create a specific healing intention, everything in my life is part of the project. She is paper clay on a papier-mâché base. I struggled with how to make the web and ended up sewing it on a dissolvable stabilizer, and it worked great.

I may have already made my Scapegoat but will work on this more. I took a story vessel class using gourds. I made a large gourd that had photo transfers of myself, my sisters, and my mother on it. The week after, I had some powerful physical issues with my stomach—second and third chakras. I discovered that this gourd portrayed an energetic connection to the women in my family that I relied on—and that I would need to let go of in order to accept my female power and move into the next phase of my life. I decided to do a ritual and smash the gourd. It was so powerful to see the way it broke. The piece with my image stayed connected to one of my sisters, and I had to step on it again. After stepping on it again, my image still fell on a very large shard. There were a lot of other interesting things with how the images fell on the shards—one sister had her image broken in the middle, and half was attached to my mother's piece.

All I ask is that you consider

all your experiences as part of your healing process, make art, make dolls, doodle, dance, sing or scream . . . it's all energy that can shift your experience in the moment and your way of moving forward in your life.

Barb Kobe

April 2005, written in response to a group member's message:

What comes to mind when I read this candid account is the human tendency to sabotage the good things in our lives. We all do it to some extent, whether it is a diet or a marriage. In my experience with friends, this seems to be partially caused by not feeling like we deserve good things in our lives—and if something feels "too good,"

it is foreign. Then the old patterns try to bring us back to the place we are accustomed to. Obviously, doing this shadow piece has triggered events that we all need to experience in order to go on to our next step in this healing process. I had a couple of difficult nights toward the beginning of the week—very weird and unpleasant dreams. I am still trying to get a visual of the shadow. Since I am working on owning my power, it feels like it may be a whole set of beliefs that disagree with having power, and lots of nega-tive associations with power. It is very similar to women not being allowed to be angry, or how it is considered unladylike to have too much power.

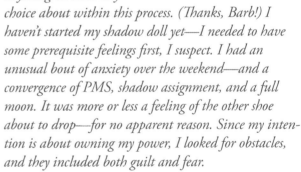

April 2005

Going into the shadow doesn't seem to be anything we have any choice about within this process. (Thanks, Barb!) I haven't started my shadow doll yet—I needed to have some prerequisite feelings first, I suspect. I had an unusual bout of anxiety over the weekend—and a convergence of PMS, shadow assignment, and a full moon. It was more or less a feeling of the other shoe about to drop—for no apparent reason. Since my inten-tion is about owning my power, I looked for obstacles, and they included both guilt and fear.

May 2005

My Scapegoat is in the shape of an egg. It reminds me of the way Don Juan, in the Carlos Castaneda books, describes the human energy field: the shamans see people as either luminous eggs or luminous spheres. So this egg represents my energy or my power. The inside is painted gold, and the eggshell has holes that represent holes in my power. It turns out that all the materials I used, even the stand, have holes. The making of this Scapegoat was accompanied by very unpleasant phys-ical symptoms, not surprisingly right in my solar plexus area. It almost felt like there was a hole there—very strange but, of course, not unexpected. I am very glad to have this piece of the project behind me.

May 2005

I have been keeping up. I started my Talisman—she is about water energy and its role in the rebirth process. I am using these works of art as an opportunity to push myself creatively in addition to the healing aspect. I continue to struggle with physical issues, especially stomach stuff, which is very unusual for me. But who said rebirth was free from physical symptoms? I think a lot of it is an awareness of the tension I have stored in my body.

May 2005

My last doll unexpectedly got created over the weekend. I had elaborate plans and even some sketches for a shrine-type piece with transparencies of images. But I sat down last Friday morning with a root I picked up on the beach of Lake Superior. After a time, I knew it was my Inner Healer. This came after a lot of work the day before with a friend and the legacies she was dealing with from her parents. I looked at my own issues with the legacy of my female power as it has been passed down, and I realized it was time to pull out and let go of the negative aspects of the legacy. I made a doll last fall called Mother, *and it has an Ojibwa beaded cord around the neck that represents the female legacy as passed down from mother to daughter. The cord is black and spiraled with yellow.*

I did a meditation while I was walking, untwisting the cord and discarding the black strands. I was left with a yellow flowing mantle—yellow is the color of the third chakra, which is our power center. The meditation was powerful, and toward the end of the walk there was a small rain shower and a rainbow. Later that evening, I saw two more rainbows.

I was ruminating about all this yesterday when I was walking and had some thoughts about the nature of personal power. It feels to me like there is a need for surrender or yielding to our power rather than a controlling attitude. The control we all try to exert over ourselves creates conflict and a loss of power. I was rereading some of Caroline Myss's work, and she says that the best way to be is to always act in accordance with our highest potential, and that most of our inner conflict is created by the struggle between the rational

and intuitive parts of ourselves. These are good things to keep in mind, since our bodies seem to become the battleground for this conflict.

Last night, I was watching a documentary about photographer Jim Brandenburg. He talked about the spiritual and personal challenge of each day looking for his "one picture." He seemed to develop a deep sense of trust and risk taking that was both brave and calculated. It was really fun to hear him talk about the difference between taking hundreds of pictures in order to pick the best one and trusting himself to take just one picture and live with that decision. The results are in a book called Chased by the Light.

I looked at my own issues with the legacy of my female power as it has been passed down, and realized it was time to pull out and let go of the negative aspects of the legacy. I made a doll last fall called "Mother" and it has an Ojibwa beaded cord around the neck that represents the female legacy as passed down from mother to daughter.

We had a big storm during the night and no power this morning, so I had a chance to look at things differently since my routine was thrown off. This morning, I had a bath by candlelight, no coffee, and came to work with wet hair. Maybe a little reminder about trusting and looking to the power within rather than that which is external—that external power that we are so habitual about.

Inner Healer
Mary

June 2005

I sat down on Tuesday and opened my notebook for this project, and there was one sheet of paper left. I knew it would be my last entry. It was fitting to end on the solstice, especially since the group started on the equinox. It was fortunate to have this particular three months to plant our intentions and see them grow. Now we have our legs and can move on out into the world—changed, enhanced, healed, empowered.

Each Medicine Dolls journey and intention is so unique. This Inner Healer brings light to my life. She is strong and full of gratitude. I am reminded, upon looking at her, about my weaknesses, strengths, disappointments, and blessings.

The Inner Healer

Your Healing Wisdom Keeper

Purpose: Naming Your Healing Ways & Wisdom

The *Healing Doll Way* process is a journey to discover your Inner Healer. At this point, you have created healing intentions, gathered information, learned new things, felt feelings, reframed experiences, unwound pain in order to see the gifts in it, processed in your journal, and created four or more healing dolls. You have released much of your armor or distraction from your own internal wisdom. The Inner Healer doll will have meaning for you as she stands as a symbol of your courage and ability to move through this creative healing process. She will share a story of wisdom, of connection with your inner rhythms and healing ways—the innate part of your bodymind that knows how to heal. You may find that making your Inner Healer will increase your sense of peacefulness, dignity, harmony, and wellness.

The Inner Healer—Health and Wellness Guide

You have an effective and powerful healing program within you. It is your innate, personal, self-regulating healing energy system. Artist and medical doctor Lissa Rankin says, "This Inner Healer holds the keys to your neurophysiology, immunology, and biochemistry, generating the self-healing response. It mobilizes your resources for wellness, restores resilience, and returns you to a passionate interest in life. It can change the body's internal state so profoundly, sometimes illness disappears."

> ## A healing doll is a tangible symbol of
> a desire, wish, prayer and through its creation it is intended to give it form and bring about an awareness of the desire for health and wellness. Intention is strengthened by the creation of a visual object that acts as a symbol of intention and that is why a doll is such a powerful tool.
>
> **Katelyn Mariah, *Empowered Health and Wellness***

Your Inner Healer is wise, loving, compassionate, patient, and forgiving. She knows your pain and your struggles. Your Inner Healer has access to your unconscious mind, your inner pharmacy; she knows the path through the wilderness of pain. The primary goal of the Inner Healer is to magnetize, appropriate, and radiate the proper flow of energy, light, and power necessary to amplify the healing process. This will ultimately bring forth inner harmony and balance. Your Inner Healer puts you in touch with your source of wisdom and clarity, which can guide you in finding answers to emotional and health problems. She has the keys to your health and wellness and can be a facilitator for your mind-body connection and how you relate to the world.

The Shaman: Her Inner Healer
(transformed from *Embracing Her Pain with Love*)
Barb Kobe

"The freedom to uncover possibilities is closely connected to one's power to act. In fact, without imagination there is no action. Imagination provides the luminous clearing in which to consider possibilities, evaluate motives and make ethical judgments on the best course of action."
Kristi McFarland
The Place of Imagination and Play in Organizational Development

161

"Unlocking the potential of your Inner Healer begins with a choice to make a connection with your inner world. Here you can get access to the keys that open the hidden places within you where healing information lives. These keys belong to you and are used to define your own journey and experience of personal power on your own terms. You don't need to be 'all better' or have your 'stuff in a pile' to have an experience of wholeness right where you are, right now. The Inner Healer is a powerful presence within you that is a consciously chosen relationship, one that can change everything about how you relate to your wounds and your worlds."

Lissa Rankin, MD

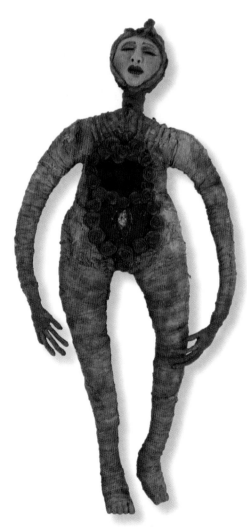

Embracing Her Pain with Love
(became *The Shaman: Her Inner Healer*)
Barb Kobe

Your Inner Healer is your body's wisdom, and she can send you messages, clues, and signs. She does so in the form of symptoms and body language such as temperature changes, pain, numbness, shivers, and trembles. It's your responsibility to develop a relationship with this important part of you and learn all the ways and languages she uses to get your attention.

Your Beliefs about Healing—What Is Your Healing Story?

Your beliefs and stories about healing have influenced how you moved through this process and the design of the dolls you created. Beliefs are powerful. They shape your perception of your world and reality. Your beliefs come from the culture you were raised in, your family, your religious and spiritual communities. They also come from your practices and experiences with pain, illness, and healing.

Your beliefs about healing stimulate your recuperative powers and put them into action. Suggestions of cures and healing arouse and focus your bodily processes. Being touched by a healing practitioner can perhaps lift your faith in the possibility of wellness and healing.

I think we have an added advantage as dollmakers. We can take words that describe a symptom, research the details about the system, and turn it into a metaphor. And then using our creative toolbox, we can engage with this knowledge through artmaking that mirrors back to us a new relationship we can have with our bodies. And when done, we share the story of our lessons and learning, which encourages our group to make new connections for themselves, explore deeper, and make their own metaphors and images. All so creatively scientific.

My message to Medicine Dolls class

Your belief in your bodymind's natural resources immediately sends powerful messages to your biological system, which supports your immune systems. When you attach healing stories and positive affirmations and messages to your beliefs, you send frequencies to your body, mind, and spirit. This encourages your body to produce what it needs for its healing.

Healing dolls can serve as placebos (medicine with no chemical value). That is, making these dolls can produce healing purely because your mind believes the stories the dolls represent. Believing that making dolls—or any art, for that matter—is healing encourages the bodymind to produce what it needs to facilitate the healing process.

Emotions, Feelings, and Healing

Physical illness has an emotional component. Psychoneuroimmunology centers on the idea that your emotions impact your physical health. Emotions are stored in the body; therefore, emotional expression and feelings help integrate the mind and the body. Dr. Candace Pert is known as "The Mother of Psychoneuroimmunology." She identified the importance of "informational substances," or biological mediators in the body that affect both physiology and emotion. It's scientific proof that your emotions and feelings are important to your healing process and can impact your health.

As you moved through the process of making your healing dolls, you might have been surprised when an emotion showed up on your doll's face, in a body expression, or as part of a story. Art therapist and healer Katelyn Mariah says, "Your Inner Physician communicates through your art." The act of making healing art, she says, is a "means for the patient to reconcile emotional conflicts, foster self-awareness, and express unspoken and frequently unconscious concerns about their disease."

Body Symptoms and Symbols

Body symptoms are your body's wisdom, its healing intelligence, sending you signals that something within or outside you needs attention and care. Your Inner Healer connects you with this source of wisdom. In fact, if you understand how your body communicates with you, then you will know your healing ways.

It's important to respect your body's wisdom and trust its signals. As the Chopra Center says, "When you override or ignore what the body is relaying, you interfere with the body's natural healing process. Sometimes the body does not want to do what you would like to do. When you honor the body's message, you honor the body's wisdom."

Sometimes the signals—the body symptoms—come as hunches or silent impulses. Other times they come through feelings of comfort, discomfort, or pain. Some are little nudges from inside. The messages may dare you, offer you hope, encourage you to reach out and open up, urge you to push toward the unknown, or invite you to bring new thinking into possibility. It's important to listen to whatever your body tells you. It never lies.

Some people call these nudges intuition. It's also sometimes called the still, small voice or your inner pilot light. Some people believe that intuition is messages from angels.

Intuition is the part of you that is connected to the source of all life. You can't limit it to physical reality—the place of time and space. It can't be rushed. It works outside of time, and it enters the space-time continuum in order to speak to you.

"Everything exists in our imagination including perfect health and the process of making intentional art will set it free. Tap into your imagination and the Inner Physician and you will be amazed at what emerges to help you become well."

Katelyn Mariah
Empowered Health and Wellness: Awakening Your Inner Physician

I Stay in the Now, I Am Present
(Paper Doll)
Barb Kobe

"Dolls represent different aspects of the emotions we are working on in our own personal healing. They can represent our most negative feelings as well as the source of our greatest power."

Barb Kobe

163

The Voice of Your Knowing

At this point in the healing doll process, your Guardian may take on the role of a healing guide or muse. Revisit your Guardian and the creative work you did while creating her. You may notice a newfound comfort or kinship or become aware of strengths and resources unknown to you at the beginning of this process. Perhaps you feel a higher level of awareness and wholeness. Or maybe you now sense a connection with all the parts of yourself that showed up in the making of your healing dolls.

INTUITION and IMAGINATION are ways to connect. The key to self-healing is learning to trust your intuition. Imagination, dreaming, and visualization are good skills.

Do you feel things in your body that you didn't notice before? Have you made friends with feelings you once feared? Do you sense communication between the areas you once guarded and the areas that hold love and compassion? There's a place deep inside you that "knows" the truth of your story. Your Inner Healer doll represents this knowing.

Eileen's Story

The story behind this: I have struggled with weight issues since I was ten. Over the years, my relationship with my body became very adversarial. I hated it. I felt ashamed of it. I blamed it for other problems in my life and used it as an excuse to not engage in life.

But then, over time, I began trying to heal the relationship. It started when the harmfulness of my hatred for my body hit me hard during a yoga class. I was trying to get into a position and just couldn't do it. I felt angry and humiliated. In my head, I directed all that rage toward my body and felt betrayed by it. At the depth of this emotion, I heard the soft voice of our teacher gently instructing us not to fight with ourselves, to be gentle and caring with our bodies. Something in me broke. I started crying as I recognized my own maliciousness toward myself. It opened me up to start changing.

This print is one in a series exploring all the systems and processes in our bodies that we take for granted. In this particular print, I wanted to see my body's larger reality, the wonderful machine that allows me to move and love and heal. That processes emotion and waste. That grows and repairs and breathes. I love how large the lungs are, taking in life.

"To me, healing is the action of being made whole, of coming into a healthy, balanced state from an unhealthy, imbalanced one. Curing is what a person or being does to heal someone completely of a sickness or disease."

Barb Kobe

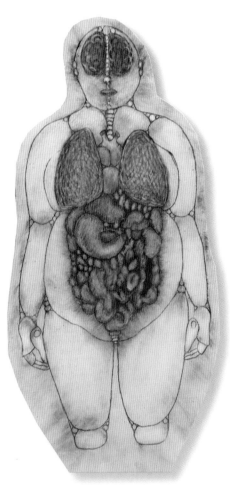

Eileen's print

"This is such a good use of listening to your inner voice. It's what I want to do now. I see that all of my most recent dolls have been representations of the Inner Healer. I have been working up to this, and I now feel almost ready to finally make the larger Inner Healer doll."

Medicine Dolls student

Gena's Inner Healer

I just finished making my Inner Healer. The idea for it came to me while making my previous doll. Originally the arms, made out of electrical wire, were intended for the Talisman. But I added another piece of material, which I was going to turn into sleeves, but it looked so beautiful hanging. Then voilà, I had created my Inner Healer. So I made arms from clay for the Talisman. It all worked out perfectly.

Inner Healer
Gena

My Inner Healer is very fluid. As you see on her face, on the right side is a small defect. I loved a little story a friend sent me one day. It went something like this: Every day a man took two pots to the well and brought them home full of water. One was slightly cracked. This pot sort of seemed to let the man down each day, as it never returned with as much water as the other pot. And when the pot confronted the man, the man told it, "I noticed that every day I lost a little water out of you when I was carrying you. But I also noticed that on the side of the road that I carried you, there are now beautiful flowers growing, so I thank you for being you." The moral of the story was that we are all cracked pots. And I like that! Each of us has what might be called a defect. While that term has a negative connotation, it gets the point across. I would be more apt to refer to it as something unique in us.

My doll opens her arms with gratitude and reaches up . . . toward the stars! I love it! Her right hand holds a star, while her left is holding the mask she once wore but no longer needs. She is healed, and in being healed, she no longer feels the need to wear a mask. A butterfly adorns her very simple frock, and on the back side is a flower with a monogrammed *G* for Gena. It is symbolic of remembering who we are . . . and always coming back to this point when feeling lost or overwhelmed.

My idea was simplicity. Healing means going back to what matters. It means leaving "things" behind and embracing life. This is what I intend to do. Remove the clutter and make room to "be."

Lastly, my Inner Healer is filled with peace, a main ingredient for healing. Underneath her frock, on the inside, invisible to the outside, is a huge heart—a symbol of love.

My journey is now complete. I set out to become my own best friend. And I feel myself becoming it. It is odd that I should lose my dad in the process. My healer will help me get through this as well, and the love and healing from my own father will too. My healer will help me learn to parent and believe in myself, the way my father/parents did. My father has given me a buoyancy. He was an artist; he was my rock.

May the joys of being alive inspire you all on your journeys!

Talisman
Gena

Shaman's Drum
Barb Kobe

Inner Healer Archetypes

Your Inner Healer holds a holistic view of your life. She sees the connections within your mind, body, emotions, soul, spirit, and nature. She may appear in many forms:

Medicine Woman / Shaman

The Inner Healer is portrayed as a Shaman in multiple ancient and indigenous cultures. Shamans collect knowledge and insight through working with the spirits of nature, such as rocks and trees and animals. This Inner Healer believes that everything is alive and carries information. The Medicine Woman archetype is similar to the Shaman in that she believes everyone is a being of wisdom, deeply connected to the phases of the moon, the tides of the sea, and the changing seasons.

Healing Ally: Inner Physician / Doctor

Your Inner Healer may represent a healing ally who held space for you as you moved through the healing doll process and created your dolls. She guided you in being responsible for your behavior and choices toward healing. You agreed to work with her to find the best solutions and healing team of care providers that work for you. You learned that you are never alone on a healing journey.

Heroine: Returning Home to Yourself

You see your Inner Healer as the Champion or Heroine of your intentional creative process. You walked the healing path one baby step at a time, and you have now returned to center and come home to yourself. You could incorporate a labyrinth or mandala symbol into your Inner Healer's design, making your journey meaningful, with the end result of finding balance and harmony.

Ancestor / Wise Elder / Crone

This Inner Healer may represent an Ancestor whose life story changed the ways you thought about yourself and whose image invited you to heal. This Inner Healer could represent a part of yourself that is older and wiser and whose image and story gave you permission to heal and step into your power.

Creatrix: Mystic / Healer / Artist

The Creatrix represents your beliefs about life mysteries, spirit, higher power, and God or Goddess as universal healing energy and love. She may represent a sacred guidance, perhaps as a Spirit Guide or Holy Life Midwife. This Inner Healer archetype will be in the form of whatever you imagine as a vision of spirit, soul, angels, light workers, intuitive guidance, or whatever fits within your belief system of the sacred.

Inner Healer Creatrix
Barb Kobe

Your Inner Healer may also come in the form of healing energies, concepts, actions, or affirmations.

Gratitude / Peace / Joyful Celebration

Your Inner Healer may represent the culmination of your healing journey. She is a symbol of celebration and gratitude. Art therapist Pat Allen says, "Gratitude at this stage helps to empty us out and brings in the support we need to tolerate the space of ending before the cycle can begin again; it ensures that the flow will return again." Joy is experienced when you have listened to your body and honored your body's needs. Vitality improves and joy awakens in your heart. You know you are in sync with the body's wisdom when the body "hums" with vitality and joy. Your Inner Healer could be an affirmation of the magic, surprise, delight, and joy that celebrate you coming back to balance.

Self-Love / Self-Trust / Self-Acceptance

When you engaged with this healing doll process and made your dolls, you began to move toward self-acceptance, self-trust, and self-love. Each time you made a healing doll, you embraced a part of your body, mind, emotion, and spirit. You learned to make friends with all your feelings, you released a part of your past, and you created visual images and metaphors to stand as symbolic proof of your growth. You feel open, healed at some level. You trust in the flow and magic of your life process. Your Inner Healer represents your connection with your authentic self.

Letting Go
Barb Kobe

Forgiveness

The healing doll process may have culminated in a visual form of self-forgiveness and making peace with yourself. Your Inner Healer may represent making amends, expressing an artful apology to yourself, or vowing a renewed commitment toward your healing intention. This Inner Healer of forgiveness could represent an awareness of your humanness, your humanity, and a move toward self-love as you accept your limits and let go of being perfect. Forgiveness is an act of courage. It is a heart-opening act that honors life and the universal human condition. It allows you the freedom to be more accepting of yourself and others.

Energy Medicine / Chakras / Meridians

Energy medicine is the practice of working with the body as a system of energies that can be used to promote health, healing, and happiness. Your Inner Healer can incorporate any number of energetic healing modalities and their symbols. Geralyn created a chakra healing doll (right). Notice the symbols she used for each chakra. The doll is wrapped in a cloak with healing affirmations written on the inside. For more information on this subject, see Donna Eden's book *Energy Medicine*.

Chakra Doll
Geralyn Sorensen

Surrender
Barb Kobe

Letting Go / Acceptance / Surrender

This Inner Healer represents how you let go of fear, disbelief, preconceived notions, and any voices that were saying, with authority, that you have this-or-that illness. Your Inner Healer invites you to approach and accept the situation with open hands, heart, and mind. She asks you to let go of the future for the moment so you can accept where you and your bodymind body are now.

Surrender is necessary for any kind of healing or transformation. Something must die if something new is to live. When we heal, we let go of old beliefs, let go of our bodies, and surrender ourselves to the power of nature to heal us in its own fashion. We even let go of the need to understand the mystery of healing and the need to control the process. The Inner Healer looks forward to the opportunity to let go and surrender on the path to wholeness and healing.

On the topic of surrender, author and counselor Jean Sullivan Finn says,

> *What does surrender feel like? From my own personal healing experience and those of my clients the point of surrender comes when the negative beliefs are literally stripped away and an image of the loving, innocent self emerges. It is so powerful an image that our hearts open up, the energy releases and we embrace and merge with that part of us we believe is flawed. Though it is most certainly an emotional experience it can happen quickly and quietly with the help of our Higher Self. The truth, our truth, cannot be denied or dismissed. We finally know the pure, perfect being that is us.*

Inner Rhythms of Wholeness

When you accept your rhythms and ways of healing, you feel an alignment with the greater rhythms around you. You feel aligned with others and the world, that we are all connected. Have you noticed these kinds of signs that you are dancing with your inner rhythms?

Serendipity: The occurrence and development of events by chance, in a happy or beneficial way.

Synchronicity: The simultaneous occurrence of events that appear significantly related but have no discernible causal connection.

The Inner Healer doll can represent coming to a place of trusting your body, mind, and spirit to integrate with your heart. She wants you to know that when you go within and ask questions, you will get answers that are perfect for you. Listening to your intuition brings self-acceptance, wisdom, and love.

Inner Rhythms
Barb Kobe

Lisa's Inner Healer: *La Lumina*

I've finished my Inner Healer doll! I call her *La Lumina*, which means "The Carrier of Light." I am really pleased with her simplicity. Something about her handmade-ness (handmaiden-ness?) brings her close to my heart. I can hold her easily in my palm. And when I look at her, I feel her light and power rising from her/my innermost being (the womb), up and out through the heart chakra.

My original intention when I began the Medicine Dolls process was to reclaim my power. Through the making of all the dolls, I have uncovered the wounded inner child and its longing for love, the wounded feminine and its wish for embodiment, the inner critic and its need for compassion, and the inner flame that needs tending.

I feel that *La Lumina* holds all these energies in her symbolism and form. Here is some of what she has said to me:

> *I am welcoming your child back to her home, the place of the heart. She is always a part of the universe, born of the celestial bodies—the moon, sky, and stars. She is part of the lineage of female ancestors—the craftswomen, home creators, and nurturers.*

> *I am here to remind you of your Inner Flame that always burns within you and the spiral of expansion and contraction that creates flow and life itself.*
>
> *Be alive! Be grateful! Rejoice in your life and the gifts you bring.*
>
> *Here in my Medicine bag, I hold the gifts of this process . . .*
>
> *Accept yourself.*
> *Nurture yourself.*
> *Be embodied.*
> *Have self-compassion.*
> *Listen to your intuition.*
> *Stay grounded.*
> *Work with the images in your body and your dreams.*
> *Trust.*
> *You are resilient.*
>
> *With much love from La Lumina*

169

Erika's Inner Healer: *Tumnus, but Not a Faun*

Tumnus, but Not a Faun, a large-scale needle-felted sculptural figure by Erika Cleveland, was created over a period of three years, spanning the artist's move from Connecticut to Washington, DC, four years ago. *Tumnus* holds magic in a myriad of ways. His many symbols and healing images show that he is a healer as well as a bringer of magic. The infinity signs on his headdress and in his hands symbolize timelessness, the ways in which time repeats itself and folds back upon itself, and the ways in which action alternates with contemplation in a full and balanced life.

Erika says that the inspiration was a piece of Y-shaped wood, which formed the legs. She then added the belly, the top body, and, finally, the embellishments. felted embellishments. He is needle-felted, with lots of other techniques integrated as well. His cape has wet-felted images that tell the story of a place where nuns collect tears in pools, where they are purified and can be used to heal people.

On his belly and chest are two trees, one in an upside-down relationship to the other, symbolizing the seasons of nature and of life. On the trees are twelve balls of light—twelve being a number to symbolize the seasons. His cloak has images of another cycle, a cycle of healing created from collected tears. On one side of the cloak, the tears are collected. The pools along his collar show the way in which the tears are purified, and on the other side of his cloak, the sick are healed from the purified tears. On the back of his cloak is an image of a figure from a previous doll created by Erika: her Talisman, *Rhea*. She, too, is a healer and represents the ways in which we shed outer skins of pain and discomfort as we go through the process of change.

You can see many more of Erika's dolls at www.transformativehealingdolls.com.

All photos on this page by James Steele

Erika's Throat Chakra Paper Doll

I want to heal my throat. I will be convinced that my throat is healed when I can speak my truth out loud as well as listen to and act on my inner voice. The throat is important to me because I once had thyroid cancer, now in remission. I will continue to take pills for it for the rest of my life. And I have to be careful to monitor the dose of the thyroid cancer hormone I take.

This doll, a paper doll, is about healing my throat. The images came to me intuitively. I have been making one paper doll each day as a way to get my creative juices flowing for a larger doll I am making—part of a series about the Inner Healer. All of the paper dolls have a healing presence in their lower bodies.

This doll, the "love courage" one, was inspired by the recent show at the Sackler Gallery here in DC called *Yoga: The Art of Transformation.* I was blown away by this show, which featured all sorts of powerful many-armed dolls. I love the idea of the many arms, each holding an element of what is healing for that particular god. My doll doesn't hold things in her hands, but her many arms make her more powerful and more able to take in what is out there for her to receive.

The image on her belly is one I found of a Tibetan goddess. The writing on her legs is about being able to speak my truth through writing—I guess to walk my talk. The orchid on her head: at first, I had it on her chest, but then it seemed to want to be on her head.

I have been reading about the chakras in Donna Eden's book *Energy Medicine.* The throat chakra is a powerful and unusual chakra. Eden says, "The throat chakra has been referred to as the Holy Grail of chakras because it holds information from all the chakras. Energies from the root, womb, solar plexus, and heart chakras move up through the throat on their way to the head; energies from the pituitary (third eye) and pineal (crown) chakras move down through the throat on their way to the trunk of the body. Within the sacred container of the throat chakra, all this energy and information is 'metabolized'—broken down and put back together into a form that becomes your unique expression in the world."

Interestingly, the throat chakra contains seven columns that carry the energy of the other chakras through the throat. The three on the left break down energy, and the three on the right synthesize energy. The seventh chamber is in the middle of an infinity pattern (one of my favorite symbols) in front of the throat chakra. It maintains a balance between all the other chambers.

Somehow the orchid seems to relate to these functions of the throat chakra. And it kind of reminds me of the chambers she describes. But there is also something very sensual about the orchid, and that related to the essence of what I want to communicate and bring more of into the world.

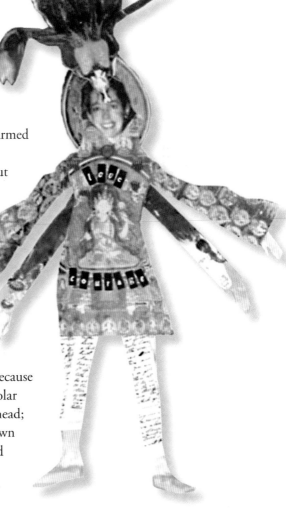

"The Inner Healer holds the possibility that I can use compassion to see and embrace my burdens, and it gives me courage to forgive myself and others."

Barb Kobe

"Yes, I like the idea of the 'possibility' of seeing and embracing our burdens and faults. Although, I wouldn't go as far as questioning that our faults are burdens. Wouldn't an Inner Healer know our faults for what they are, our own makeup, the way we are made, so that we can know our true selves, our struggles, and finally embrace them because of the lessons we learn from them?"

Line L.
Medicine Dolls student

171

Anne Heck's Inner Healer

Photo by Stewart Stokes

"The teachings of the doll are many as she and her maker relate with one another along this creative path. I've learned never to assume but to remain open and curious to what she wants to express. Once the doll feels complete, the maker can continue to receive information from her through a journaling process. This part is particularly powerful and offers insights that may not be readily apparent throughout her creation."

Anne Heck

There's a lesson about gentleness in my midst. It has a familiar face, and I'm humored I didn't recognize it sooner.

I'm not one to give in easily. It's been my nature to set a goal, hold clarity, and be consistent in my efforts towards that end. This strategy usually produces the desired result, but has had its downfalls, not the least of which is self-imposed stress.

I've worked my body consistently for nearly two years to build the strength I've been visioning. I've continued going to the gym to be able to walk with comfort, to engage in activities with family and friends. Somehow, the strength and fluidity that once inhabited this body continue to elude me.

I assumed that so much attention—all that consistent, grueling, and painful effort in the gym—would certainly produce the desired result. But as I got deeper into it, the pain became more intense. I have felt both disappointment and frustration.

It's been my experience that what occurs in the physical is simply a manifestation of what's taking place in the energetic realm. So, I've been curious about what's been happening backstage with this physical body—those subtle and not-so-subtle thoughts and beliefs that affect what's happening within and around me.

What I've learned is there are certainly benefits to being able to hold intent focus to reach a goal. There's also a wisdom that's called for to discern when to let go and simply be gentle with yourself. So, I've turned on some new lighting, some uplifting music. I'm working with small, subtle movement and am exploring this place of gentleness. So far, it feels like a good fit. Regardless of outcome, I'm quite certain I'm due this reprieve.

These past two weeks, as I sat with these musings, a new doll began to take form. She's my Inner Healer, a wisdom keeper who symbolizes a culmination of my personal healing quest. She holds a bundle of many medicinal gifts that have supported my healing. For me, she's a reminder to keep gentleness and compassion at the forefront of whatever healing path I choose.

www.anneheck.com

We each have an Inner Healer who knows us well and holds our thoughts, beliefs, and feelings about healing. And if that is so, then your Inner Healer holds your Healing Manifesto.

A traditional manifesto is a written statement declaring your intentions, opinions, dreams, and visions. A manifesto's primary goal is to infuse yourself or your reader with hope, excitement, amusement, motivation, and curiosity.

I invite you to write your Inner Healer Manifesto. Start by writing healing statements that begin with "I love . . ." "I believe . . ." and "I am committed to . . ." See where the ideas lead you. Here's an example I played with:

Inner Healer Holds onto Her Intuition
Barb Kobe

Inner Healer Manifesto by Barb Kobe

1. There is an innate part of my being that I call my bodymind. It is a self-healing, living being within me that is constantly maintaining, restoring, and bringing itself into balance.

2. My bodymind speaks to me in many ways: intuitive voices, hunches, silent impulses, feelings of comfort and discomfort, and emotional signals.

3. I listen to my bodymind's wisdom. I trust my body. I listen to my body; she never lies.

4. I love that my bodymind is an intelligent energy system that maintains my inner harmony and balance.

5. I use meditation, visualization, artmaking, movement, and engagement with nature to connect with my natural rhythms—my ways of being and healing.

6. I know I am in sync with the body's wisdom when my body "hums" with vitality and joy. When I interfere with my body's natural healing processes through poor diet, lack of exercise, or other unhealthy choices, I compromise its ability to function at optimum efficiency. When I listen to my body and honor its needs, vitality improves and joy awakens in my heart.

7. My artmaking is a form of meditation, a growth-producing, healing process that transforms my body, mind, and spirit.

8. My intuitive self is fed by images. These images provide a visual focus for directing healing energy so it will connect with my deepest, innermost self.

9. Knowing, feeling, and being with my emotions is vitally important to my healing.

10. Making healing dolls allows me to embrace myself. My artmaking takes me through a transformative process of creating images that represent my thoughts, emotions, struggles, needs, stories, and connection to spirit and my higher power.

Creative Action

Prescriptive Art – Dialogue with your Inner Healer as if speaking to an actual medical doctor. Design a Healing Prescription pad like the one to the right or just print out the sheet of four in the appendix, on page 228.

What is your ailment?

What are your symptoms?

Where do you hurt?

What are your concerns?

Add any other things you want to share with your IMD (intuitive medical doctor).

Make a list of different kinds of treatments your Inner Healer may prescribe: take a vacation, take a day off, laugh, get a hug, have a good cry, get a massage, go to an emotional rehabilitation center and tell your story using drama therapy, exercise, etc.

Have your IMD fill out the prescription and define the dosage, duration, and whether refills are available.

Post the prescription where you will see it every day.

HEALING PRESCRIPTION

FOR: _____   FROM: _____

AILMENT: _____   DATE: _____

Rx

☐ MAKE ART   ☐ MEDITATION   ☐ CALL FRIEND   ☐ JOURNAL
☐ CHILL PILL   ☐ DAY OFF   ☐ GOOD CRY   ☐ SHOPPING
☐ VACATION   ☐ LAUGHTER   ☐ MASSAGE   ☐ EXERCISE
☐ YUMMY TREAT   ☐ HUG   ☐ REHAB   ☐ OTHER

SPECIAL INSTRUCTIONS

DOSAGE: _____   ☐ PER HOUR   ☐ PER WEEK
                ☐ PER DAY   ☐ PER MONTH

DURATION: _____ ☐ HOURS   ☐ WEEKS
                 ☐ DAYS   ☐ MONTHS

REFILLS: _____   ☐ ZERO   ☐ TWO
                 ☐ ONE   ☐ THREE

_____
SIGNATURE

Tamara's Healing Doll Story

Intention: To heal areas of my body that have caused me chronic discomfort and pain, including anxiety; sinusitis; acid reflux; general muscle tension; tightness in my chest and jaw; pain in my solar plexus area; and heaviness and pain in my neck, shoulders, legs, and feet.

The Guardian: *Grandma Mable*

I was moved to create a tender, loving, supportive grandmother energy who would always have my back and who loved me unconditionally. I had created several SoulCollage cards and paper dolls with this energy and even named a "Council of Grandmothers" that included Grandma Madge, Grandma Millie, Grandma May, and Grandma Mable, each with different life stories and energies. This doll has energies from Mable and Millie.

I started with the body of a stuffed snowman I had used when I taught baby sign language. First, I cut off the snowman's head. The inside of the body was hollow with a Slinky-like spiral, so I added a plastic heart with a "diamond" and a plastic Mardi Gras–king-cake baby to the inside. This symbolized her bigheartedness and unconditional love as well as my connection to her inner child. I covered the doll's body with a doily and added a rose earring as a brooch. I sculpted the face out of clay and painted it, adding gray yarn curls, makeup, and pearl earrings. Finally, I put a doily hat on her head and wire glasses on her face.

The Guardian: *Masked Warrior*

This Guardian is a fierce masculine protector that I created out of a clay mask, a doll form, and a stand. I added a robe made out of an old shirt and an owl ring for an amulet. I also created a lance out of a stick, a flicker feather, a seashell necklace, and a piece of glass. The masked warrior is filled with mysterious medicine-man energy and is unnamed.

The Scapegoat: *Bertha*

I started with an extremely heavy rock and added a face made from a necklace. I painted a big red fake smile over the warrior's grimace and added prickly balls (from trees in Mexico) to represent her arms and hands and legs and feet—areas of chronic tension. I put a handcuff bracelet around the neck and added a prickly ball on her head to symbolize her irrational beliefs.

There is a black snakelike object at the belly area, something I found on the ground at a Rosh Hashanah celebration in the mountains years ago. I painted a red esophagus in the shape of an inverted tear, added a heart-shaped rock with red painted tears, and glued a series of yarn "cords" all over the body, mostly emanating from the head and heart. These cords are "dread locks" (notice the two-word spelling—it is intentional). Until I added them, I thought my Scapegoat was ugly and hard to look at. Once added, she looked infinitely cooler but still foreboding. I placed a green sack of heavy rocks on the doll's back, each representing a burden I have carried. I called this her "baggage" or her "S-cape." Releasing them is her only avenue of *escape*. I then placed the doll—now named *Bertha*—on a stack of dark shadow SoulCollage cards I have been creating since 2007.

The Talisman: *Sienna Ryann*

Years ago, I chose this name to represent my highest self. I found a wooden drawing mannequin, to which I added: a clay face, complete with paint and glitter; a ribbon on the head; a crystal costume-jewelry earring I inherited from my great aunt, to symbolize the heart; a feather skirt; a cape created from an orange cloth napkin; and a beaded "mantle" that used to be a necklace. I placed a metal butterfly ring around her neck so that she has butterfly wings where her neck meets her back, near her fifth chakra (the throat, where her inner voice emanates). She is holding a length of metallic orange yarn to represent the new stories she is spinning as she claims her wholeness and restores her soul essence. I then placed fifty handmade orange and purple cranes of peace (origami) at her feet. I spray painted the base copper and added glitter. Under the feather skirt, there is a small blue charm with the word "Acceptance"— my chosen word for 2014 happens to be *acceptance*, and now my Talisman has a belly filled with it!

176

The Inner Healer: *Anam Cara*

I named her *Anam Cara* ("soul friend" in Gaelic). Her base was going to be a blue vase; however, I decided to use a pillar candle to symbolize her inner light. To help her hold energy, inside I placed touchstones, including a metal charm with the word "create," a heart-shaped rock, a seashell, a crystal, a feather, a green crystal marble, a clay moon face, a metal sun, a game token, and a pink button that belonged to my great-great-aunt (to represent ancestral wisdom). I used an old curtain with a blue ribbon from my daughter's bedroom to create the robe and hood. I made the face using a clay mold, adding extra clay in which to carve spirals with an old earring (which I attached to the right side with a peacock feather). To me, this balances the right side by adding feminine energy. I painted her face metallic bronze and purple and added lime-green glitter. I found a small hand-beaded purse with small crystals inside at a thrift store, so I added that to her shoulder. Then I placed a lime-green butterfly (for vibrancy, vitality, and growth) on her forehead.

Tamara's Healing Doll Story Process

When I look back at the SoulCollage cards I have created since 2007, many embody the energies of these four dolls. I started making paper dolls some years ago and have several that depict the guardian, healer, wounding, and talisman healing energies. I have also created a lot of cards with different depictions of dolls in general. I started to create "Spirit Dolls" on July 1, 2013, and quickly birthed about twenty of them. They came from found objects—mostly natural things such as wood, shells, leaves, moss, etc. Looking back on them, I see that many fit into the four types of medicine dolls Barb encouraged us to create.

My creative process happens to involve a lot of percolating, followed by a fast and furious firestorm of chaotic creation. This time was no different. I visited Cat Caracelo in her home, and she shared her medicine dolls with me. (She has taken Barb's Medicine Dolls online class.) I came home and birthed all four dolls in four days. They were all created from objects I already owned and repurposed, except for the gray yarn used for *Grandma Mable*'s hair. I created the Scapegoat and Talisman somewhat simultaneously and then followed up with the Guardian and Inner Healer.

See more of Tamara's dolls and healing doll story at https://restoryingmylife.weebly.com/healing-dolls.html.

Creative Action

Write a healing story that includes all the dolls you have made in this process. What kept revealing itself to you throughout the journey, like a ball of yarn unraveling in front of you? What emotions have you befriended along the way? At what point did your dolls seem to have a will of their own, revealing things to you that you did not know or where not aware of?

Revisit your initial healing intention and any changes you've made to it throughout the process. Compare the first version to the final version. How is it the same and how is it different?

Make a list of the healing beliefs you gathered growing up. Then make a list of your present-day healing beliefs. Which beliefs are the same? Which are different? Which beliefs have you used in making healing dolls?

What does your Inner Healer look like? Try this visualization exercise: Sit or lie in a comfortable position and close your eyes. Fill your attention with every aspect of your breath. Imagine you are entering a temple of healing. Within this temple resides a profound source of benevolent knowledge—your Inner Healer. As you breathe in, focus more attention within. As you breathe out, surrender any attention directed elsewhere.

Be in the presence of the Inner Healer. What does she look like? What colors seem to radiate from her? What shape is she? Where is she in relation to your body? What images and symbols is she holding and wearing?

Greet her, saying your name and asking for hers.

Focus on the part of your body that you want to heal. Have your Inner Healer place her hands on that area. Notice how she performs an action that initiates healing. What does she draw your attention to? Once the healing action is performed, release what she has opened up. Then have her close the area with whatever you imagine would complete the healing process.

Your Inner Healer asks you to answer these questions:

- What was the purpose of this healing journey?

- What is the gift of the "pain"?

- How can you move forward from this point?

- What are your healing ways?

- After the visualization, make some sketches of your Inner Healer or find pictures online or in books that represent her.

Make your Inner Healer when you are ready.

The Dollmaker
Barb Kobe

Spirit of the Doll
Barb Kobe

Spirit Dolls

The inspiration for this book began with a college English paper written in 1999. After that, I continued researching and teaching the subject of dollmaking while making my own healing dolls on the side. I now feel confident in what I know about healing dolls. I may even be considered an expert in the field—a goal of mine from the beginning. And by this point in the book, I'm also confident in your newfound knowledge of healing dolls and what they can possibly look like.

End of book, right? Well, maybe not.

As I gathered information for this book, I kept coming across something called a *spirit doll*. I thought that if a healing doll, at its simplest definition, is a creative, figurative expression of a healing process, then a spirit doll, at its simplest definition, is a creative, figurative expression of spirituality. I was intrigued. I wondered, is a spirit doll a healing art doll?

Spirit dolls were a whole new dimension to explore. I realized I could spend a huge amount of time researching them, exploring concepts, and creating healing processes with other dollmakers. It occurred to me that I could even create a new series of dolls called spirit dolls or spiritual dolls. I'll leave that for another time in the near future.

In the meantime, though, it's important to briefly explore the concept here in this book. At the very least, the subject of dollmaking and healing would not be complete without a mention of spirituality and healing.

Art of the Doll Show Icon
Barb Kobe

The doll form is a tool. It does work.
It instructs, contains the sacred, represents the deep desire of the body to recreate itself, expresses every level of emotion from anger to love, pain to joy, and it embellishes space.
Elinor Peace Bailey

This chapter is an invitation to explore the definition, the meaning, and the qualities of spirit dolls. I've included photos of some of my dolls that might be spirit dolls, as they express my spirit, capture my connection to my own spirit and to a higher spirit, and reflect spiritual elements and religious and cultural influences. I've also invited other dollmakers to write about the subject and share photos of their dolls.

Acceptance Spirit Doll
Barb Kobe

181

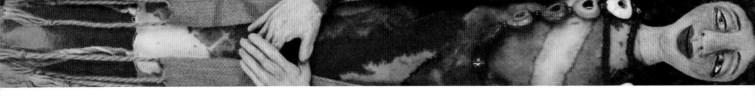

As you explore this topic, think about the following:

- What is your definition of *spirit* or *spiritual*?

- What words do dollmakers use to describe spirit dolls?

- From where does a dollmaker get her inspiration?

- What materials does she use to make spirit dolls?

- What beliefs do spirit dollmakers share?

Definition of *Spirit* and *Spirituality*

Before we attempt to define spirit dolls, we must first attempt to define the concepts of spirit and spirituality. Spirit is the nonphysical part of a person that is the seat of emotions and character. It is the immaterial, intangible aspects of ourselves: soul, intellect, will, conscience, character, energy, heart, temperament, animation, aliveness, liveliness, psyche, spark, breath, and life-force. These exist beyond the physical lifespan of the individual.

Spirituality is a sense of connection to something bigger than ourselves. It typically involves a search for meaning in life. It includes universal human experiences that offer a deep sense of aliveness and interconnectedness with the world. Terms often used to describe these states include: mystical, transcendent, divine, and metaphysical.

Spirituality is also linked to associations with organized religion. Whether through religion or personal exploration, one can activate this connection or relationship with God or a higher power through prayer, engagement with nature, life-cycle celebrations, and art.

Spirit Bird
Barb Kobe

The spiritual perspective is a way of understanding life that provides

meaning to our day-to-day experiences and the larger issues of living and dying. Spirituality sees wholes rather than parts, and patterns rather than details. When we are guided by this perspective, life seems to make sense, everything is in its place, and we feel balanced and connected. This deeper sense of self and nature is satisfying to the soul and spirit. It can have profound effects on personal attitudes, values, relationships, and unresolved conflicts, and as a consequence it can influence biochemistry and physiology.
I call these effects on the mind and body spiritual healing.

Elliott Dacher, MD

Exploring the Definition of Spirit Doll

There are so many ways to define spirit dolls because they serve many purposes for the maker, the keeper, and the collector:

A spirit doll is an art doll that acts as a vessel for "holding" spiritual things: blessings, prayers, meditation, gratitude, connection, emotion, and more. These types of dolls are often found on altars, where they are objects of devotion or reminders of life-changing experiences.

A spirit doll is an icon—a tangible, cultural image of the divine—found in world religions and used in religious ceremonies and sacred rituals. They are also used on personal altars. They might be sculptures of saints or holy figures, ancestors, angels, or gods and goddess.

A spirit doll is a three-dimensional art doll that holds prayers and longings and visually symbolizes one's connection to all there is. A spirit doll reflects what we think is meaningful at a conscious and unconscious level.

A spirit doll represents something about life that is important to you. It might be a process, journey, or lesson that affected you deeply and helped you change an aspect of your life. The act of making a spirit doll guides the maker deeper into knowing and connecting with herself and others.

A spirit doll may represent elements of nature, such as Mother Earth, a garden, or an animal. It may symbolize the four traditional elements—earth, air, fire, and water. It can be anything visible or invisible that animates the vital force that gives life to physical organisms.

A spirit doll may be used to inspire the maker to move toward dreams or visions. It may also inspire action or even activism. According to the Gaiafield Project, the making of a spirit doll is an "activity of consciousness or spirit, such as prayer, meditation, or ecstatic dance, intended to support collective healing and social change. Subtle Activism grows from the idea that there are many effective ways—some newly emerging, many as old as humanity—to positively influence social change other than overt political action."

Please Forgive Me
Barb Kobe

"In fact it is now known by neurophysiologists that art, prayer, and healing all come from the same source in the body, they all are associated with similar brain wave patterns, mind body changes and they all are deeply connected in feeling and meaning. Art, prayer, and healing connect us to our inner world, the world of imagery and emotion, of visions and feelings."

Barbara Ganim
Art and Healing

Emotional Prayer Beads
Barb Kobe

183

Spiritual Healing

The spiritual healing experience is personal in nature. There are many paths to it and different names for it: prayer, devotion, love, compassion, meditation, music, dance, art, and nature.

Spiritual healing is a way of being rather than a way of doing. It is activated when you experience a sense of wholeness within your being. You connect with a higher power or wisdom and create a persistent sense of oneness with life. The goal of spiritual healing is to reach this sense of wholeness.

To achieve this wholeness, we must rely on our intuitive knowledge, an often unused aspect of our consciousness. It is your personal intelligence, your inner wisdom and guidance, often called the small, quiet voice. It operates by speaking to us of a unifying and integrated vision of life and a sense of meaning, purpose, and coherence.

Intuitive voices come from your gut instinct, your compassionate heart, your imagination, and your creative inner visionary. Intuition may also come from a higher power or what some like to call "the universe," a term that's relatively interchangeable with "the divine."

Standing Rock Spirit Doll
Barb Kobe

The Way of the Doll **is the ultimate guide for self discovery and evaluation. In its purest artistic form it is an avenue to reveal your most hidden talents and ultimate joys. There is sorrow and growth in the course that seems to last a lifetime, but only interjects at points of pure light in the soul. It is a lifetime of revelation molded in mixed media and color . . . It will never allow you to fall back, but to bless yourself a thousand times and move onward into the next phase of growth.**

Cassandra Light

Your intuition is best communicated with and expressed through symbols, art, poetry, sacred spaces, religion, and myth. It is not unusual for the women in my healing doll classes to rediscover their intuitive voices within this process. You engage with your body, mind, and emotions as you make the dolls. At the end of the process, the dollmaker often feels a sense of peace and a deeper understanding of herself and her connection to life. This connection to life can blur the boundaries of healing and spirituality. It's just one way in which healing dolls and spirituality intersect.

Spirit Doll
Barb Kobe

184

Faith is a word often used in spiritual healing. Faith is the strong belief in God or in the doctrines of a religion, based on spiritual apprehension rather than proof. In fact, when I researched the subject of healing, many resources spoke of prayer and other religious faith practices that help people maintain a sense of peace and balance. I believe resources from any or all faith communities, along with some kind of personal creative action, can provide continuity and transcendent meaning to life.

Another definition of *faith* is a "complete trust or confidence in someone or something." This refers to initiating creative action by taking a leap of faith, usually into the unknown or into the mystery. Faith, in this case, can mean the same as believing in yourself or believing that there is a power greater than yourself. Sarah Ban Breathnach says, "Believe in yourself. And believe that there is a loving Source—A Sower of Dreams—just waiting to be asked to help you make your dreams come true."

I think either kind of definition of *faith* has a place in the discussion of spirituality and spiritual art. When art creates a shift in awareness, a change in consciousness, and a deeper connection to something greater than ourselves— that's a good thing.

I have seen women from across the globe make healing dolls and discover, or rediscover, their faith and connection to a transcendent power. I also have witnessed them discover or rediscover their faith and confidence in themselves as good, powerful, loving, creative women. Many of them reach a deeper understanding of their day-to-day lives, their place in their world, and their connection to others.

Ode to Mother Lake Superior
(Transformed from earlier doll)
Barb Kobe

There is a strong possibility that art dolls can be healing dolls and that healing dolls can be spirit dolls as well. What's important is the intention and motivation the dollmaker sets along with the beliefs, stories, emotions, and skills she blends into the creation.

Elinor Peace Bailey says her dollmaking helped her find her voice, that the making of her dolls allowed her to speak up for what she believed and to create from that place of truth. She says, "The doll form lends itself to spiritual input from the maker. The spirit does not originate with the form. The dolls I make possesses the spirit with which I make them."

My friend and colleague Cat Caracelo says it well:

> *Art as a healing practice, expressive action, and transformative process offers threshold experiences. The engagement with self and materials becomes a passageway to the inner realm, where personal and collective wisdom, and information, is held. Once known, seen, heard and recognized, this inner wisdom can be embraced, explored and expressed. Working with image, symbol and form long past the time of creating holds potency, deepens self knowledge and become one's own source material.*

Journal Page
Barb Kobe

Barb Kobe Spirit Dolls

Spirit dolls can represent an awakening to a new way of connecting and being with a woman's higher power. A few of my dolls capture this experience for me: *The Saint, Red Shrine to Upper and Lower World,* and *Ode to Tree Mother.*

The Saint

As a child, I was raised in the Catholic Church. I participated in Catechism, Communion, and Confirmation. I remembered the rich symbolism of Catholic churches: altars, relief sculptures on walls, shrines, statues of holy people and saints, decorative priests' garments, banners, chalices, and candles.

In 2002, I began reading about feminist psychology and women's spirituality. Any healing intentions at that time were to raise awareness about my beliefs as well as to learn, to grow, and to explore physical, mental, emotional, and spiritual life through my dollmaking.

I was a bit like Sue Monk Kidd, who chronicled her own exploration of spirituality in *Dance of the Dissident Daughter.* She wrote, "I was amazed to find that I had no idea how to unfold my spiritual life in a feminine way. I was surprised, and, in fact, a little terrified, when I found myself in the middle of a feminist spiritual reawakening."

Like Sue, I began to look at the messages I and other women had received from the church in the 1950s and 1960s: that I am unworthy of love, that I must take care of others first, and that I should always be a good girl—saintly.

The Saint was one of my first flat dolls. I drew the design first, knowing I wanted an arch shape at the top, a halo around the head, and three little rectangles at the bottom in which tiny dolls could rest. The doll's hands come together over her heart in a sign of self-love, and she looks inward for self-reflection. The little dolls are the "pieces of herself" that have now come home after being "spent" taking care of others. I used green to represent the heart charka, red for women's sensuality, and purple for spirit.

Red Shrine to Upper and Lower World

I made *Red Shrine to Upper and Lower World* from a form of twisted grapevine I found at a craft store. She has little indentations at her center. The Upper World has a spirit doll image connected to the sky and the tops of trees. The Lower World has a spirit doll grounded to the earth. She has a spiral at her belly, and at her feet are things made of or growing from the earth. This is one of my first spiritual dolls. Again, her creation was influenced by the shrines and tableau in the Catholic Church.

The Saint
Barb Kobe

Red Shrine to Upper and Lower World
Barb Kobe

Ode to Tree Mother

I have always been drawn to nature for inspiration. You might recall, I first began making my dolls from roots and sticks. I designed my original Medicine Dolls curriculum and classes as a four-part process based on the Native American medicine wheel and the spiritual symbols of earth, air, fire, and water. So it wasn't unusual for me to connect with earth "beings" such as trees, plants, earth, and stones.

I had a relationship with a tree in Lagoon Park in Jordan, Minnesota. I visited her (the tree) often when I would teach dollmaking at Maureen Carlson's Center for Creative Arts. I would walk to the park, sit next to her large trunk, look out at nature, and meditate. I felt embraced and nurtured by her presence.

One time when I came to Jordan to teach, Maureen told me my tree had been hit by lightning. Maureen and I went to the park, and there she stood with her center burned out. First I felt deep sadness when I saw her. Then I walked over to her and stood in the center of her burned core. I felt an even deeper connection, as if she were literally embracing me. My five-foot-ten body fit perfectly, as if she were saying, "You belong here just as you are."

The *Ode to Tree Mother* doll is a symbol of the tree in Lagoon Park. It is a Talisman and a reminder that I belong to the earth and that it's okay for me to be alive and thrive.

The next time I visited the park, she had been cut down, too fragile and dangerous to be left standing. I'm grateful for the time I had with her and that I made a Tree Mother doll to celebrate her life.

Me and the tree at Lagoon Park

Other Voices

Teaching Medicine Dolls put me on a path of discovery, one with lots of side trails, hills and valleys, and secret hiding places. But there were always bread crumbs to follow and always a quiet, gentle, and often playful voice guiding me. Mentors and allies would appear to support me and gently nudge me forward. Spirited and creative dollmakers and their dolls would appear, inspiring me and shining a light on the possibility that dollmaking could be healing and spiritual.

In the following pages, I've chosen to spotlight a few dollmakers who make spirit dolls. I've included pictures of their dolls and their stories. These women have touched my life and supported the development of this book. They are just a few of the many spirited teachers, artists, and students from all my classes who have touched my heart and soul.

Ode to Tree Mother
Barb Kobe

187

Elinor Peace Bailey: The Spirit of the Spirit Doll

I was young when I took on the word *artist* to describe myself. It was not because I was all that deft at the craft but more a matter of acknowledging that I had found my voice. I have been drawing since I could smear it on walls, and that is why my work has improved and my voice has become stronger. Initially I saw myself as a painter. As a traveling teacher, I have found that the work of many of my students and fellow teachers has been better than my own, but I have been compelled to continue. I believe there is room on this path for as many as desire to follow it, so there is no need to compete for a single spot.

I love the human figure, particularly the female form. It feels like a landscape to me and is a constant in my work, as is the face. Manipulating the proportions and the placement of the body and the face has infinite possibilities, and I delight in exploring them. Using mixed media comes from the inclination to grab whatever is at hand to create an image. I diverged from the use of a canvas when my projects were put in jeopardy by my children. Discovering fabric gave me an answer to that problem and led me to stitchery, then to quilts, and then to dolls, where I found a form that took my attention for over thirty years. Now as I move on into being an observer, I find that what compels me is telling stories, connecting with people, and connecting disparate objects to one another. Performing with the dolls provided me with an audience for those stories. They served in connecting me with people. And my garments, mixed media journals, and quilts have added to the chorus—I guess I'm not done yet.

"A doll can be a tool; it works on the artist as the artist works on it. It instructs, contains the sacred, represents the deep desire of the body to recreate itself, expresses every emotion from anger to love, pain to joy. It embellishes space. A doll allows you to see who you are."

Elinor Peace Bailey

In my work, you will find my love of the human figure; particularly, the female form is consistent in my work, as is the manipulation of proportions. My use of mixed media and three-dimensional forms stemmed from my inclination to grab whatever is at hand to create an image with my art journaling, dollmaking, quilting, and stitchery.

The Spirit of the Spirit Doll

The figures called "spirit dolls" often borrow from a primitive rendering of the human form. A fertility doll will exaggerate the sexual organs. The dolls that use outreached arms reflect Jesus on the cross, the ultimate sacrifice. Using a circular figure would mean completion. A dancing figure would represent euphoria and release. Although I cannot claim the form [spirit dolls] for myself, I am attracted to the sparse and textured minimalism and the use of found objects and mixed media, which often influences my own creative process.

I would be tempted to change the term "spirit doll" to "doll of the spirit." The doll form lends itself to spiritual input from the maker. The spirit does not originate with the form. That would imply a graven image. I avoid those. The dolls I make possess the spirit with which I make them. I give each doll a piece of myself. My experience with dolls led me to use them as performance tools—to break barriers with humor, color, and character. Bailey dolls are character dolls. That's the spirit they have.

Elinor Peace Bailey
www.epbdolls.com
www.fabric-chicks.com
elinor@epbdolls.net

Brenna Busse: Sacred Keepers

I have been on this journey called ART for many years—decades, really. It didn't come easy for me, not a gentle call. It was more like being washed up on a beach, and ART picked me up, shook me out, and set me on my path. It may sound extreme to say that art saved my life, but that is how I see it. For the last twenty years, I have created mixed media figures as my art form. Mixed media is a great, no-rules approach to artmaking. It allows me the freedom to use what I have at hand, what I find, what I love. Mostly I love clay and fiber. Each material has its special qualities: forgiving and transforming.

Sometimes I think that every piece I make is a spirit being—made of earthly materials yet having a resonance that communicates on a soul level. Here is the story of making the "Keepers" that most exemplify this elemental process.

It was January, quite a few years ago. A time of darkness, slowing down, going inside—and for me that year, depression. I knew I needed to create in order to pull myself out of this numbness.

Luckily I had many small clay heads left over from a holiday project. With those small faces of love, whimsy, and wisdom calling me, I gathered fabrics from worn clothing, sticks, thread, beads. I began. The clay head attached to stick, spine, strength—wrapped in fabric fragments, layered comfort, and protection. The thread stitch—like suture, making mark, making secure. Glass beads added precious color. Bundle, wrap, stitch. Bundle, wrap, stitch. Bundle, wrap, stitch . . . Each part of the process felt essential, like a ritual. I made forty of them and at last regained my balance!

"Keepers"

finders/keepers
finding something
to hold on to
keep fear at bay
keep faith
keep remembering purpose

Brenna Busse, Minneapolis, Minnesota
www.brennabusse.com

Photos by Petronella Ytsma

These spirit dolls embodied that inexhaustible life-force as one by one I let them go. They were held, chosen, given to those who understood, who needed them. Over the years, I have continued to create "Keepers." It's from a more joyful place, a little larger, more colorful, though with the same intention—to deeply touch and transform.

Maureen Carlson: Sacred Art

I've been making spirit dolls for more than thirty years. Perhaps one of the first intentional ones was a small wrapped figure that I made for my young friend Michelle, who was heading to Australia for a year as an exchange student. It was a pocket doll, made for her to carry as a reminder of who she was and to reassure her that she was never alone. Over the years since then, I've made many spirit dolls, though I've never before articulated just what that term means to me. But oh, how I love a good question! They are opportunities to think deeply about beliefs, actions, and motivations. Thank you, Barbara, for the question.

To me, spirit dolls are prayers. Or to phrase it differently, they are conversations with the Sacred Energy that permeates our universe. They are collaborations between that Sacred Energy and the creative energy that dwells within me. Spirit dolls belong to no specific creed or vocabulary. Each maker or recipient of a spirit doll brings her own vocabulary to the process and to its meaning.

Just as with traditional prayers, a spirit doll can be made as a meditation, a celebration, a reminder, a plea, an everyday connection, or an expression of emotion, belief, thanksgiving, or intention. I know I'm making a spirit doll when my ego lets go of perfectionism and the disabling fear of failure that is the hobgoblin of artists everywhere—at least of this one! I know I'm making a spirit doll when I become body, mind, and soul immersed in the intuitive process of joyful creation. I know I'm making a spirit doll when I implicitly trust my inner muse rather than the imagined art critic or viewer of the finished piece.

These creations speak to me almost as if they were sentient beings, though I know they are not. I don't believe we are making vessels through which spirit entities speak. Even so, there is a creative energy within them that is palpable. To me, this energy is evidence of the collaborative process between the Sacred and me. What makes me laugh with delight is that it really only matters if *I* feel it. That is enough. Once again, as with prayer, the doing is what matters. But the paradox is that if I feel it, then chances are that someone else will as well.

When I am really absorbed in the process of sacred creation, each pinch and push of the clay, each stitch or wrap of fabric, each choice of color or texture or symbol, is made as if in a

dream. As with meditation, when I'm in this sacred space, time disappears, as do hunger and thirst and my surroundings. Well, maybe the hunger doesn't disappear! But it is like I've entered a liminal space where there is a heightened awareness of now, of this moment. All that exists is what I'm doing right here, right now.

The form of a spirit doll varies depending on the intention of the maker, though there are some characteristics that allow the viewer to more easily "read" a doll as a spirit doll.

These characteristics might be a lack of realism, closed eyes, or perhaps no face at all, elimination of arms or legs, surface design rather than structured clothing, and the addition of symbolic elements.

Yet, a spirit doll doesn't have to have any of these characteristics. What is critical—to me, at least—is that it needs to be infused with a sense of wonder, with mystery. And how do I recognize that? Usually I'll know it is a spirit doll because it elicits a response that feels deeper than just an appreciation of it as a plaything, an object of beauty, or a skillful rendering of the materials. It draws me in, somewhat in the same way a beautiful sunset or a majestic tree makes me pause and breathe more slowly, more deeply. There is a stoppage of time, maybe for just a moment, but enough for me to know that this creation defies time, that it is more than just the assemblage of its materials.

I don't have just one style in which I make spirit dolls. Some are quite realistic, as are the figures in my piece *Story Box: Whistling Through the Cracks* (next page, top). Others are more symbolic, as in the small masked pendants made with polymer clay, foil, alcohol inks, and acrylic paint. A few, illustrated by the mixed-media piece *Never Alone* (next page, bottom), are reminders that I myself am part of the Sacred Mystery.

What will I create next? I don't know, but I do know that each of us can use our creativity to have a conversation not only with ourselves but also with the Sacred, by whatever name we call it.

Maureen Carlson, Jordan, Minnesota
www.maureencarlson.com
www.weefolk.com

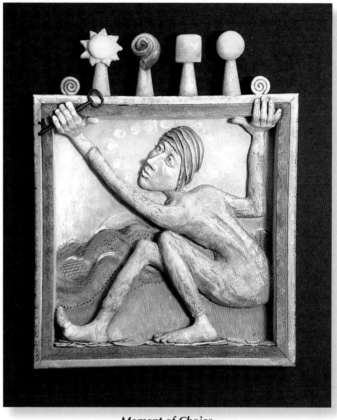

Moment of Choice
Maureen Carlson

She Who Hears the Call
Maureen Carlson

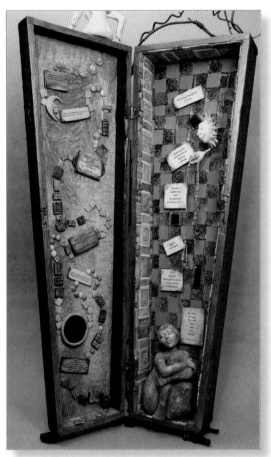

Story Box: Whistling Through the Cracks
Maureen Carlson

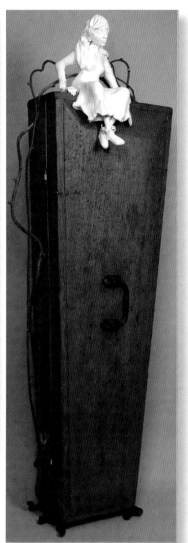

Submerged in
a dark sanctuary,
Waiting,
Listening.

she rides it
through
the crack
and
into
the
World.

© 2006 Maureen Carlson

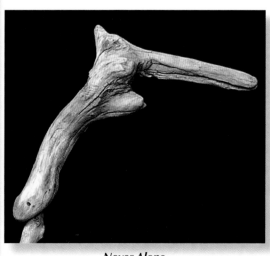

Never Alone
Maureen Carlson

Geralyn Sorensen: Spirit Dolls

When I met Barb Kobe and her dolls, I was amazed and totally drawn to them. I began taking classes in her studio once a week in 2006 and have been creating spirit dolls ever since. Creating with a small group of wise women has been life changing. We share our journeys and stories as we create. We inspire one another and offer insights into each other's work. We laugh, cry, share, grow. Barb is the catalyst, gently encouraging us on our creative journey.

Making spirit dolls takes me to a much deeper level than I've experienced before. It is cathartic. The spirit dolls represent aspects of my journey. Each one magnifies an emotion or an attribute I want to embrace or honor or work with—in myself or others. I have hidden words or messages within their bodies.

Although I find the dolls beautiful in their own ways, I have had to learn to deal with the emotions that arise when others don't feel the same way. Spirit dolls evoke raw feelings, be they positive or negative. People either get them or they don't. ("Those are scary! I don't get them." Or "I appreciate the work you put into them, but I can't say they are beautiful." Or "Not sure what to say . . . I don't understand.") It has been a good process for me, trusting my own gifts and my right to express them in a unique way. The only critic who matters is me. I am the midwife and help the dolls through their "birth."

Like an expectant parent before the advent of ultrasound, I wait to see who emerges. What is its energy? What is its message? What does it heal? Each doll guides me deeper into whatever I am. I suppose one never really knows oneself fully. Making spirit dolls is a pathway to my inner self and sometimes higher self.

When I sit with the dolls long enough, they give me their names. Sometimes life moves too fast, and it may take a year or more. Some bring comfort. Some challenge. Some bring discomfort. Some bring wisdom. Some bring incredible beauty, both inner and outer. It is a blessing to cocreate with "Spirit" and to share them with others.

I am a musician and facilitate an experience called WomanHeartSong, connecting women at the heart through music, movement, and conversation. My dolls have been incorporated into many workshops, and I have led women in making simple dolls as a part of those experiences. It is humbling to watch others create their dolls, with each one as unique as they are.

My thanks to Barb Kobe, Maureen Carlson, and the women at their art studios for inspiring my journey in dollmaking.

Shekinah: She Who Gathers

Shekinah was my first spirit doll. Although I didn't fully realize it during the process, she was about my mother and me. I was born on Mom's birthday. We had identical hands and singing voices. She was one of my best friends, but as with any mother and daughter, we had issues as well—especially once I grew into who I really was. As a younger woman, I really couldn't separate myself from her . . . especially when I heard, "You are just like your mom."

Shekinah's colors were my mom's favorites—rose and mint green. She was full-bodied, like Mom and me. I knotted her spine to make it stronger than Mom's or mine, and I grounded her with stones from Lake Superior.

One hand wanted to reach out to others. The other hand hovered over her heart. Her look was one of compassion. I struggled with why her head was so much smaller than her body. I tried to compensate with more yarn hair and a crown of stones. Still, without her shawl, her body was huge. I wrestled with it all and searched for under-

standing. Barb gently encouraged me to go deeper. Aha. Yes . . . I got it. I needed to think less and feel more! And I needed to balance my connections with others with my connection to myself.

A search on the name *Shekinah*, which came to me from a song by that name, revealed multiple meanings, which also spoke to me: "feminine aspect of God," "resting place," "divine presence," "dove," and others. When I look upon her, I see a nurturing, compassionate, full-bodied woman who gathers others and blesses them. She encourages others to pitch their tent, rest with her, and be blessed, acknowledged, and nurtured. She reaches out but also reaches within. In doing so, she nurtures herself and me . . . and honors Mom and me in our sameness. We are blessed.

Taliah

My second spirit doll was quite a surprise. As her face emerged, she definitely was a woman of color. At first I wondered if she was Asian or Native American, but as she evolved, she became Mayan. She remained barefoot with extra large feet to ground her. Her arms were reaching up to Spirit to receive strength and power. She sat on a drum and

also had one to play in front of her, recognizing the power of music, rhythm, and vibration as healing modalities.

Her hair was black wool, and she wore strong feathers in her headdress—black, white, many shades of brown, and blue-black-green, carrying the colors of the earth. Her shirt had Mayan symbols, and her medicine bag had a Mayan design on the outside and contained shells, stones, and secret healing items.

How does a woman born and raised in Iowa midwife a Mayan medicine woman spirit doll into being, one with a posture of power and strength and clarity? Who knew she was inside waiting to be born?

As I lead WomanHeartSong events, I often take *Taliah* along, hold her to my heart with her drum, and let her "play and dance" with the other wise women. I see her strength mirrored in their faces as they interact with her. We honor her as she honors us on the journey. Ho!

Geralyn Sorensen, Coon Rapids, Minnesota
geralyn@q.com
www.geralyn17.wix.com/womanheartsong

Glacial Dancer Spirit Doll

Geralyn with some of her dolls

Geralyn with some of her dolls at a WomanHeartSong gathering

197

Julia Inglis: Sacred Familiar

The spirit doll is an ancient being, familiar and beloved to many cultures around the world. And the craft of doll-making is part of our heritage as women—our healing folklore. We remember making dolls and receiving dolls as spirit companions, as guides and guardians to watch over us, and as vessels to focus on and hold when we are in need of deep healing.

To make a spirit doll is to engage in the art of healing and enchantment—to weave life and love into a creation by making something solely by hand with materials from nature. By engaging in these ancestral crafts, we weave a bridge back to our own great-grandmothers, whom I believe send blessings to us and to the doll herself before she travels on to do her work with those who need her. I am passionate about embracing and honoring these crafts of our grandmothers that have been forgotten or, worse still, have been very misunderstood.

I believe my grandmothers brought this craft back to me so that I could live in the forest, away from the city, and continue to do healing work with people without carrying the heaviness of issues they are dealing with afterward. Unfortunately, I learned this the hard way after experiencing exhaustion in my city practice. I kept seeing people receive the most beautiful visions of their spirits during healing sessions, but they were unable to hold on to this vision afterward. I saw that they needed to have something tangible and real, something physical to hold to remind them of how powerful and magical they truly are. Especially to hold through times of loss and fear.

The doll came to me in a dream thirteen years before, but it wasn't until I moved to the forest four years ago that I sat with a friend one day to be shown how to needle-felt a doll. Something huge unlocked inside me that day, and within hours I was creating dolls nonstop. It was as if my hands remembered this craft so well and were so happy! I could feel my grandmothers guiding and teaching me about fleece and fibre, how to include plants that assisted healing, and where to find them in the forest.

Bird Girl

Plant Antlers

and created dolls for the living too. I have been called to create and leave dolls at the sites of persecution of women, such as healer and witch dolls in Scotland, and I've gifted dolls to a pauper's graveyard in London known as the Cross Bones Graveyard.

The balance of dolls for the living and the dead seems to be the way that I give back for my spiritual inheritance. Another way is to leave dolls in nature, in the forest— sometimes as gifts to the trees and sometimes with a note to let people know that if they find this doll she is theirs, a free gift to them. Sometimes when someone finds a doll in nature, they ring me and ask if they can really keep her. I assure them that she is for them, and they can't believe it. Whenever I feel lacking or worried, I will create one of these "free" dolls and give her away. Not long after, I am aware of the lightening of my own load, and strange, beautiful gifts will turn up for me too.

As the years went on, I was creating a doll every day. And I began to notice a new theme turning up in my work with the spirit doll. Not only was I focusing on the person for whom I was creating, but I was also becoming aware of the stories of forgotten women and children in history, as well as the environments carrying the memories of traumatic events that had taken place. I began to create dolls for the living and the dead. The strongest stories for me were of the women and children incarcerated within the Magdalene Laundries.

I began by creating a doll and leaving it at the old site of the laundry near my home in Melbourne, Australia, to be a comfort for the spirits who may still be feeling pain there. I traveled to Ireland and left a doll for the women of the Magdalene Laundry in Dublin. I then met with survivors

Dragonfly Girl – **Scotland**

199

Banner Doll

Fern Spirit Woman

This teaching and lesson of giving for nothing is very important. You see, something very magical happens for the dollmaker. In the act of creating a spirit doll for another, we can't help but travel down that rabbit hole, like in *Alice in Wonderland*—we cannot help but dive into the depths of our own heart. I believe that this is an important process in making spirit dolls: we also get to "make" and heal ourselves. A kind of "collective shadow work." You cannot help but go inward with handmade work. There are long, long hours and much repetitive movement. Like our grand-mothers, many moons ago, caught up in the repetition of a threaded needle going into cloth or a spinning wheel forever turning, we begin to enter a kind of waking dream state. In the act of making slowly and by hand, you begin to step into a liminal space between time, and you hear the voice of your own spirit—the dreamer within the dream.

The spirit doll can be a mirror or a bridge to a powerful part of yourself that you might not be able to express. She is a friend, and the more time you spend with this friend, the more you love her. Perhaps you begin to tell the doll secrets that you hold in your heart and cannot share with others. The doll lives with you daily—through good times and bad—but is always accepting. And then a funny thing happens: you begin to feel the living spirit in this doll and how much love it has for you. You then recognize this love as part of your own spirit, and that love for the doll begins to flow back from her to you. You see that you are also a magical, beautiful, and creative being. You begin to heal yourself.

Julia Inglis
www.sacredfamiliar.com
Instagram – Sacred Familiar
Facebook – Julia Inglis

Photo by Jerry Stebbins

Barbara Bend

My art is a spiritual dialogue between my inner self and outer influences. I am compelled to respond artistically to the events that trigger the need to explore, understand, or celebrate and appreciate at a deep and personal level. The materials I use guide me; they are societal leftovers I serendipitously unearth or obtain. These materials have their own voice and purpose, whether it be utilitarian in nature or culturally generated. I do not start with a blank canvas or lump of clay. I start with things that have their own integrity, their own history, and their own place in the world. My work is responsive. I mix materials that bring different perspectives and histories together, creating a new purpose and a story that begins to respond to my artistic needs.

Creative thinking feeds on play.
Play tickles our creative energy
making it laugh out loud
Guffawing an idea to surface.

(Poem by Barbara Bend)

I have always been intrigued by the story and design of simple things—especially multiples of common or discarded items, the ordinary objects that might pass through our fingers many times, often unnoticed. I look to their intrinsic value, playing with them, creating patterns, forming rhythmic motifs. Then I search through my materials for beautiful fabrics to integrate with this pattern of

common items. I am drawn to those that have their own integrity and voice woven through their fiber content, color, design, and cultural influence. Once a fabric is found, I playfully experiment with these material concoctions and then set them aside to wait until they find their place and purpose in a piece.

Some examples of these integrations:

- Bright South American fabrics with colorful wrapped telephone wire or beaded spirals from notebooks

- Zipper pulls or snaps woven into a mesh-like material that may echo the geometric texture of another fabric

- Wrapped wire following the seams that connect two different fabrics, then branching out in a design that reflects the pattern of the textile

Archetypal shapes are spiritual connectors. Their energy bypasses our intellect, connecting directly within our genetic coding. I am drawn to the power of the arch, spiral, and circle—all of which have their ancient roots. I strive to create movement, gestures, and energy in my work while still utilizing structurally sound shapes.

The armature of my sculptural forms is made from welded metal, heavy fencing, or electrical wire. The initial forms are often simple archetypal shapes. The shapes are built up and added to by tightly wrapping strips of knit fabric, creating a solid form, and adding finer wire armatures for details. The result is a firm, self-supporting structure that can withstand the weight of the materials I choose to use. This structure allows my forms to flare out with movement, expressing the spirit of life and energy of emotions.

The Healing Power of Time (next page, top) was inspired by a recovering addict's healing story—an arch welded onto an oval and a bag of broken watchbands. I met this artist at an art fair, and we shared stories that informed and inspired our own work. She talked about her recovery and struggles with addiction and how her poetry supported her sobriety. She shared an experience about an emotional and spiritual breakthrough while walking in the Colorado mountains. She was overcome with hopelessness and, in desperation, retreated into a cave-like overhang. There she withdrew from her surroundings and retreated deep within herself to

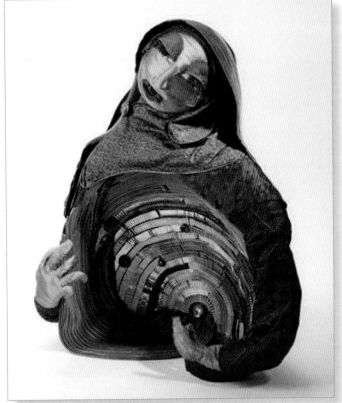

The Healing Power of Time
Photo by Jerry Stebbins

Where does spirit live in this artistic process? Spirit is fluid, like water or air. It has its own energy, rhythm, dynamics, physics. It thrives in play, quiet places, dark places. It is a place few words can touch. Artists connect to others through the discipline of returning to work again and again, sometimes full of new ideas but most often empty handed, knowing that practice and discipline keep the creative spirit alive. As artists, we tap into the intangible spirit place for inspiration, and we ruminate in an often dark inner place where ideas are born and grow. From there, something may emerge, becoming art, reaching the physical, and connecting to those around us.

Barbara Bend, Rogers, Wisconsin
brbend@gmail.com
www.barbbend.com

calm her angst and recover her emotional balance. A vision of a turtle shell enveloped her and gave her the strength to move forward under the protection of this spiritual force. The turtle had become her totem and had given her strength to move forward in her sobriety, helping heal the emptiness that her addiction had left within her.

After I heard the story, I knew the welded arch lying unused in my studio would be her shelter. Unsure how to depict the spiritual turtle energy she felt, I searched my studio. It was the bag of broken watchbands that spoke to me.

I began to play, exploring their potential, connecting them to a screen, creating an arch-like design that became the inverted turtle shell. I ran out of watchbands, so I finished the internal arch with a beautiful brass zipper shoulder wrap I had previously made, which was too heavy and not easy to wear. The arch supported a nurturing face of Mother Earth, who offered shelter and supporting hands. Turtle Spirit offered the power to move forward. The inverted shell design is a spiral, moving inward and then outward, giving strength to move forward.

The Raven
Photo by Jerry Stebbins

202

Sharon Riley: Healing Voices Dolls

Nourished by a deep and sacred connection to the Divine in all things, I draw upon the stories, rituals, traditions, and mythologies of all cultures as points of reference for the Healing Voices Dolls. These stories and mythologies speak to me of our origin, of how together we form an intricate network, a tapestry of which we are all apart. My intention is to imprint these Healing Voices with the harmonic resonance of sound and sacred geometry, the metaphysical information of stones, crystals, and other gifts from the earth.

For me, a healing spirit doll is a tangible reflection of the spirit of creation itself revealing in all things. It is both personal and universal, for it seems you cannot separate one without impacting the other. Each is irrevocably intertwined. The doll in concert with its maker. Through metaphor, intention, and the various elements used in its creation, it becomes a vehicle through which healing energies flow.

The Guardian and *The Dragon* (below) are the first of three stewards representing and supporting the element of water.

The Guardian and *The Dragon*

Sometimes the spirit doll is a personal response to a life experience or change of events that may have impacted us at a core level. The spirit doll is the vessel through which we discover lost or often deeply hidden and highly protected aspects of ourselves. The physical act of creating the spirit doll gives voice to the healing process.

Often it feels as if the voice of the Mystery of All That Is whispers in dreams, prayer, and meditation. It is a calling where we are asked to be the vehicle through which divine healing can flow into the spirit doll, thereby impacting the greater good of all. It becomes a more widely impacting instrument of healing not only for ourselves but for the entire earth—everything can be translated to energy.

Copacatchi Dream Spinner

Water Keepers

The waters of our planet and the waters within ourselves have undergone tremendous stress and pollution over time. It seems that acts of outrageous commitment and effort on our parts are required to restore and harmonize the impact to our planet and her myriad life forms. There is a sacred calling to commit to the work of cleaning, clearing, and healing the lifeblood of ourselves and our planet to restore life and balance.

203

Earth Keepers

Each carries a different instrument: a drum, a harp, a flute. Together they form a collective named "the Holographic Sound Keepers." Their single and combined tones play new harmonics into earth's hologram and all life sustained by her. They are tones of clearing, healing, and renewal. They assist in the release of trauma, pain, and memory that no longer serve the greatest good of the self and of the entire planet. They thereby facilitate a deep and abiding love for the earth and all her life-forms—a beautiful transformation.

Air Keepers

They are custodians of activation codes and emissaries for transformation. This is accomplished through revealing and returning lost "life-giving" information to all of Earth's life-forms, of which we humans are a part. They are responsible for reencrypting love, light, healing, and rebirth into the very consciousness of Mother Earth. One holds an ancient scroll, one a key and a staff, and one a shield that represents the constellation Andromeda. Each of these artifacts carry original healing—transformational codes from the beginning of time. They help the earth and all of us remember our relationship with all life sustained here and love it back into wholeness.

Sharon Riley
www.whisperofspirit.com

Sandy Wythawai Starbird: Spirit Dolls

After making fabric images for over thirty years, I still approach each new figure with the expectation that I will be taken on a journey of discovery. Any image made is a reflection of this journey. A spirit doll comes from a grand collaboration. You are working on them, but they are also working on you—shifting your perception, taking you deeper, revealing new connections and possibilities. Honor and facilitate this collaboration by being open and available and by listening to your intuition. The end result will be an illustration of the interconnectedness of all things, a true spirit doll.

My work is continually inspired by something that needs to be said—that needs a physical manifestation to speak something that someone else needs to hear (even, and especially, if we have never met and possibly never will). I think the images are always telling the truth. My input is the skill of my hands and the desire of my heart to listen carefully and translate that truth into the forms you see. It is certainly a blessing to have an invitation into that creative space where all possibilities exist (some artists call it "the zone") and to be given an opportunity to work with the possibilities that speak to you.

Coyote in Disguise as Raven

Patiently Waiting

Making of Sandy's Five Spirit Dolls

While exploring an old box of accumulated bits and pieces, I discovered the bowl of a small wooden pipe. I realized that the stem resembled a kachina mask with a blowing mouth. I cut the bowl in half and found that I had really made two masks, one expressing outward and the other inward. As I gathered fabrics to use with these two masks, I found a cache of hand-dyed and devoré (semi-transparent pattern) fabric scraps created by my good friend Melissa Arnold. I decided to patchwork them into whole cloth, creating many layers of secrets, hidden and revealed. I chose a body form that suggests a dialogue between energy that is not personi-fied as human but is willing to take on an acceptable shape to enable that dialogue.

Happy Bird

When the pair was finished, I read them to represent:

1. *Masculine Shamanic Energy*, which shows interdimen-sional knowing as an outward human experience.

2. *Feminine Shamanic Energy*, which shows interdimen-sional knowing as an inward human experience.

Each energy can be expressed by both men and women. There remained an interesting pile of scraps, so I made a third figure. This one became:

3. *Traveling Between Worlds*, the balance point and bridge between what was and what is coming into being.

There was still more lovely fabric, so I made a collage of these translucent pieces, adding a painted full moon image between the layers. This made a fourth image:

4. *Full Moon*, a balancing act between human and divine, discovering new ways to see reality, and acting on self-sourced wisdom.

With just a few tempting pieces left, I made one last collage—now much less complicated—that became a fifth image:

5. *Dark Moon*, contacting inner wisdom, a chance to be renewed, to experience unknowing, letting go of things completely.

(Dolls listed above appear on the next page, described from right to left, as viewed from the front.)

I learned that long ago we stopped using the term "dark moon" and substituted "new moon" instead. But there are two or three days before the new moon appears. It felt as though we had been avoiding the experience of unknowing and letting go. Now would be a good time to start again. Let's see what has been waiting for us to wake up from this deep sleep.

Sandy Wythawai Starbird, Eureka Springs, Arizona

Sandy's five spirit dolls (front and back)

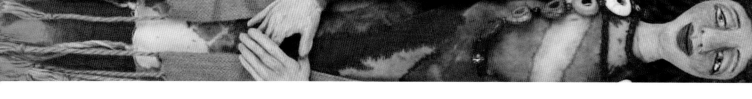

Kathryn Hall: Spirit Dolls

I look around my living room, and no less than twenty-one sets of eyes gaze back at me from all the nooks and crannies. I wonder, who here would be called a spirit doll? Would anyone *not* be? Is there anyone without a "soul"? Anyone lacking "spirit"? I pause with each and lock eyes, remembering how the sticks, wire, fabric, clay, and I partnered to create these unique beings who share my home. Some were created with a particular intention, but each also managed to surprise me, directing and demanding certain colors or embellishments that I would not have thought of.

The funny green *Frog Pond Princess* embodies a favorite childhood memory of my best friend and me on our bellies, scooting out on muddy logs in attempt to catch the big bullfrogs that shared a pond and pasture with her horses. The doll echoes our laughter and protects our young innocence for all time.

Spirit of the New Moon, for example, is infused with my directed idea of new beginnings and holiness. Her cool blues and gauzy grays cover an underlayer where these words and intentions are forever imprinted into her body. Even if, over time, I should forget, the spirit remains. She, however, is the one who asked for copper stars, brass moons, and beaded hair. I'd had a different plan in mind.

Tallula, with her extrawide hips and rounded belly, is a fertile fountain of creativity. She stands looking skyward, orange Mohawk flowing, jewels glistening, laughing with abandon, and reminding me to be fearless in pursuit of creative challenges.

Neith, the large bee goddess, converses with *Tierra*, the Earth woman, sharing a shrine in honor of the environment. Candles, stones from my sacred place, and other trinkets serve to magnify their already potent energy.

My original family of Medicine Dolls, made under the encouragement and guidance of Barb Kobe, cluster together in their own niche. Their collective wisdom wafts through the rooms of my home as they keep watch, each holding space for guardianship, honesty, healing, love, and transformation.

There are others, created perhaps with less intention at the outset but that nonetheless developed meaning during the process or later. They whisper little messages, including "I am here for joy!" or "Don't take yourself so seriously" or "I'm hopping the first train to Las Vegas—I'm a star! You be all you can be too!"

I don't pretend to fully understand how this all happens; I only recognize that it does. It's not that these dolls are magical spirits in and of themselves. There is no voodoo or hoodoo, yet the process is not without a certain sense of magic and mystery. An essence of myself is transferred, and I experience an inevitable transformation in the making. The spirit or energy of that change is lodged among the folds and the bones, somehow, as well as in my own heart. I believe it's fair to call it "spirit."

Perhaps what surprises me most of all is that I'm not the only one who can see it or hear them. They sometimes "speak" to sensitive others as well. More than one person has been transfixed and captured by a steady gaze. More than one has gasped, "She has a soul!"

Kathryn Hall
kathrynahall@aol.com
Facebook – Hilaritas Art Studios / Kathryn Hall

Rue, created to help me process grief over the death of my nephew, holds all the emotions that flowed from my heart, through my fingers, and into clay to offer me respite and comfort. I am grateful.

Creative Action

I asked Noreen Crone-Findlay—artist, dollmaker, and author of *Soul Mate Dolls*—to write a creative process for making spirit dolls.

Spirit Doll Process – by Noreen Crone-Findlay

1. **Listen** – Begin by listening to your body when there is a feeling or a voice in your mind that says or hints or nudges you to be aware that *something* needs to be celebrated or changed or acknowledged or healed. Know that Spirit is moving through this.

2. **Pause** – Contemplate these words: *What do I feel about this?*

3. **Ask** – What words, phrases, and stories rise up around this experience? What story do I tell in this moment? What story is the stepping stone that leads me forward? What is the *gift* of this? Where is the seed of compassion and wisdom hidden in this? Do I carry this forward as it is? Do I celebrate it? Do I need to change something? If so, do I change the future of this by finding a new way, a new plot, a new way of creating "yes-ness"? How do I find Spirit in this?

4. **Play** – Play with color, with texture, with size, with shape, with different things that you may never have considered as part of your dollmaking.

5. **Invite** – In your heart and hands, invite a doll to come together to be the embodiment of the healing, the wholeness, the vibrant deliciousness of owning this unique voyage of discovery that is your life.

6. **Embrace** – Embrace your dreams, your memories, your contemplations, your meditations, your prayers. If you are able, go out into nature to feel the sun, the wind, the ground, and to simply walk as you hold the gestation of this spirit doll in your heart.

7. **Open up to Receiving** – Invite the Universe to give you gifts that will become part of your spirit doll. Open yourself up to the quest for and the deliciousness of recognizing something meant to be part of your spirit doll.

8. **Trust** – Gather your dollmaking materials. Next, make a choice. Say to yourself: *I trust that this doll will come together just the way she/he/it is meant to. I am open to allowing her/him/it to show me what I need to do.* Start by putting two things together, connecting them. Then keep adding to it. And keep trusting yourself and your dollmaking process, knowing you are connecting to deep and holy places within yourself.

9. **Stick with It** – Don't let anything—whether inside your head or outside your door—stop you from making this doll, and the next, and the next, and all the other dolls singing in your soul and spirit!

10. **Honor the Process And Honor The Doll** – Hold this dollmaking process in respect and high regard. Honor your spirit doll, and don't let yourself or anyone else pass negative judgement on her/him/it. If this means keeping your spirit doll private, then do. But do visit with the doll frequently, so that you remember all the meaning and life force you experienced in the creation of her/him/it.

11. **Invite** – Invite your spirit doll to be the seed of wisdom, compassion, inspiration, and juiciness.

12. **Enjoy** – Bask in the pleasure of the making of the doll and how she/he/it has created new connections for you.

13. **Embark** – Open up to the next stage of your spirit doll journey. Bless yourself, your creations, and all that you encounter!

After the Process

What if it is not the *kinds* of dolls you create but the *process* itself, the making of them, that helps you heal, transform, and move on with life? What is your favorite kind of doll? What doll images are you drawn to? What kinds of artmaking delight you? And what beliefs about dollmaking or artmaking might be stopping you from creating? Several students from my classes commented on this:

There is huge power in showing up. The self-reflective process of creative expression is more meaningful to me than creating a beautiful product. (And I love to create things that please me visually, but it's never primary.) Art has really been my most powerful teacher and healer—and so I deeply honor the power of simply making.

As a passionate student of all things handmade, I love looking at any kind of doll, but I am most drawn to the quirky, odd, and shadowy. I love healing dolls, primitive art dolls, and feminist-style empowerment dolls.

I've always found the process—from initial sketch through to the finished piece—calming, even if it takes several tries. It doesn't really matter if I sew them, knit or crochet them, or even make them from paper; my mind is really somewhere else, and the burdens of my day-to-day head off into the background someplace. However, this process has drained the pool and exposed some not-so-pleasant feelings and issues. As I'd posted previously, my own resistance to change is partly slowing me down.

Ready for the Journey
Barb Kobe

I had some great sketches of what I was going to do for each doll, blah, blah, blah . . . But it's been too contrived and controlled. It just allowed me to keep circling the issues rather than settle in and DO. For this process, I am liking the paper doll approach. Doesn't take lots of materials (unless I want it to), and I can express, make notes, stop, make more notes, and so on. It feels more organic to me right now and is allowing some things to come to the surface that I'm deciding need a bit more attention, which is a good thing . . . I think.

In my dollmaking circle classes taught at retreats, I end with a closing ritual. Each participant brings all the dolls and art she made during the retreat to the front of the group. She talks about her dolls, names them, and says what she learned from making them. The other participants write messages of affirmation and encouragement for the person sharing. When the dollmaker is done speaking, I ask if she is ready to receive from the group. Then each participant, one at a time, approaches the dollmaker with the "gift" of affirmation and support, either spoken directly or written on little notes.

If you've done this process by yourself, rather than in a group, consider doing a similar exercise in your journal. (There are other ways to process your dolls on the next page.)

"The doll is symbolic homunculi, little life. It is the symbol of what lies buried in humans that is numinous. It is a small and glowing facsimile of the original Self. Superficially, it is just a doll. But inversely, it represents a little piece of soul that carries all the knowledge of the larger soul-Self. In the doll is the voice, in diminutive, of old La Que Sabe, The One Who Knows . . . the psyche works even when we sleep, most especially when we sleep, even when we are not fully conscious of what we are enacting. In this way the doll represents the inner spirit of us as women; the voice of inner reason, inner knowing, and inner consciousness."

Clarissa Pinkola Estés

I Will Not Die an Unlived Life
(Inspired by Dawna Markova's book)
Barb Kobe

"I Will Not Die an Unlived Life"
by Dawna Markova

I will not die an unlived life
I will not live in fear
of falling or catching fire.
I choose to inhabit my days,
to allow my living to open me,
to make me less afraid,
more accessible,
to loosen my heart
until it becomes a wing,
a torch, a promise.
I choose to risk my significance;
to live so that which came to me as seed
goes to the next as blossom
and that which came to me as blossom,
goes on as fruit.

Here is what Shena shared during her closing ritual:

> *What I do know is that this process to date has been the main reason that I know, without a shadow of a doubt, that the rest of my life will be on my terms, in my truth, and dramatically "healthier" (as in healed) than before. So much has brought me to this point. And as we know, everything has a reason; it happens as and when it is supposed to. But this project has been pivotal. And for that, I am truly grateful to you and to each and everyone who had the courage to share their stories.*

Patty S. shared this:

> *I think I am much more focused on accepting my power and trusting that opportunities will continue to present themselves that will foster this. My artmaking is better, and I am more willing to take risks with it. I also have a wonderful Inner Healer on my bedside table. (Even the cat steers clear of it, and it's in her path to getting onto the bed.)*

Processing with Your Dolls

Here are some processing assignments you can explore using your dolls, recording the experience in your journal:

Dialoguing and Journaling – Dialoguing out loud or journaling with your doll is a powerful way to understand the message she has for you. Here's one way to do this: Look at the doll. Notice your thoughts about her meaning. What is your first impression? Next, intently focus on the doll. Give her energy or send her a prayer. Let her give you energy. Journal about your experience

Dialoguing with each one of your healing dolls – This can also be done by taking a picture of each of your dolls. Print the picures, then cut them out and paste them onto designated pages in your healing journal. First, look and notice what colors, symbols, and shapes rest on different body parts in each doll. Notice similarities and differences. Journal about what you notice. Next, form a question about your healing challenge, such as "What will my healing look like, sound like, move like, feel like?" With your dominant hand, write this question on each page with a doll picture. Look at each doll's photo and imagine asking her this question. Pause and listen to her answer. Then record the answer with your nondominant hand. Also, ask (with your dominant hand) each doll her opinion about your healing journey, then have her dictate a healing prescription to you (with you nondominant hand). Take your time on this. You are doing healing research, looking for common colors, shapes, and stories. Note everything asked and shared. Remember to say thank you after each doll shares.

Activating the Energy and Intention of Your Healing Doll – Wear something that is the same color as your doll. Stand before her and take her pose. Close your eyes and see yourself as her twin sister. Feel her energy enter your body. Begin to move, dancing slowly, allowing a healing prayer to enter your mind. Keep moving until you feel a shift, then write down the prayer or record it. Repeat the process and the prayer daily for several days as a healing practice.

Become the Doll – Imagine entering the doll, taking her position, becoming her. Hold her in your lap and imagine she is telling her story. Or walk around your room as if you were the doll. How does she see the world? Give her a voice. Does she have a certain way of speaking? Have an accent? An age? Let her tell her story out loud, and record yourself (as her) telling the story. Ask her what she represents. What is her purpose? Why has she come into your life? Record this experience in your journal.

With Two Dolls – Put two in front of you. Sit and look at them. Take in the uniqueness of each. Next, do a creative action inspired by each doll. This simple action will help you implement your healing intention.

Here are some examples using the Scapegoat and the Talisman:

The Scapegoat – What would you like to do with her? What needs to happen to her? Do you need to show her to another (your witness) before she goes out into the world? Or do you need to do something with her right now (shred, tear, smash, bury, burn)? Do you need to do something to her to allow yourself to say goodbye to her, thank her, and let her go? Do you need to say goodbye and feel the sorrow of releasing an old way of being? Could it also be that you are not willing to let go of her? Do you have a curious liking for the form this piece took, even though you're ready to move on in your life? Do you have a fear you'll never be able to make such a doll again?

The Talisman – Connect with what you need to do with your Talisman. What is she asking for? Perhaps she wants to be framed and hung. Perhaps she wants you to take her to a friend or beloved so you can declare out loud, "This is who I'm becoming, this is what is possible for me, this is where I'm heading. Will you help me become this? Let me know when you see this happening and encourage me." Using your journal, write the Scapegoat's feelings about the Talisman. Write how the Talisman expresses empathy and compassion toward the Scapegoat. Using these same types of reflection questions, bring together two other dolls and have them dialogue with each other.

The Empath
Barb Kobe

Wise Sage
Barb Kobe

213

Garden Oracle
Barb Kobe

Showing and Sharing Your Healing Dolls

A Medicine Dolls student writes, "Sculpting is healing for me because it gives me distance from the heavy things in my life. I feel like I go to another place, a magical one, and when I return, my life feels more manageable. By the very process of doing that thing, I gain some balance, return to a healthier state."

If you have gained wisdom, awareness, and shifts in perception from this healing doll process, you may be excited to show your creations to others. You want to celebrate, have a ritual or party, and welcome friends and family to see what you've created. You might invite your witness or a friend to come over and see your dolls. Perhaps you'll want to host a private gathering of close friends for a viewing and discussion. Or maybe you'll want to do a entire show at a gallery.

> **Dollmaking is lots of fun and brings out the little girl in me. I work without thought, allowing my creativity to flow, moving on impulse toward whatever pleases me. The spontaneous flow of creativity engenders a sense of lightness in my creation and I don't worry in the least how the doll will appear to anyone else. There is such freedom in creating a work of art without the concern of others' approval. She is simply mine and I love her.**
>
> **Margaret Hart Lewis**
> *Wisdom Walks in Circles*

As healing artists and dollmakers, you can assume that some people will understand these emotional and creative healing dolls, but others won't. After years of making and showing my dolls, I've concluded that what I create can seem weird and ugly to some people, and it can be judged to have no value. But more importantly, I have friends, followers, and collectors who embrace my dolls and respond to them in kind and compassionate ways.

Here are some comments on the subject from Medicine Dolls students:

- "One of my closest friends, with whom I share all sorts of emotions, never comments on any of my dolls. She was uncomfortable with the whole idea. As we talked more, I realized she's not really a 'symbols person.' She has no way of accessing my symbolic realm."

- "My paper crafting and stamping group doesn't understand my dolls at all. A couple of people have been quilters, and they primarily envy my collection of fabric, which surely will outlast me. I am more interested in the reactions of my friends who do understand the art behind dolls. Not one has commented on my dolls from the first time taking this course, even though the Guardian

Drama Queen with Mask
Barb Kobe

is right next to the front door. (I keep the Scapegoat hidden.) I thought that, perhaps, most people only react to pretty, flouncy, glittery, so I wondered what would happen if I put a sparkly orange skirt on a deeper, emotional doll. Now I realize it probably wouldn't matter—most would still ignore it."

- "You are right that dolls are like our children. This is what I feel: they are a door that enables me to make contact with my inner softness and defense-less self. I suppose I should not show them to anyone outside this group, or outside my close family (who understands me), until I have finished the process, which means putting layers of protection around my tender feelings."

- "This idea of how people react to our dolls is very close to home for me too. My mother-in-law saw one of my dolls online and said, 'That's strange, isn't it?' I didn't know what to say. It was about one of my newer soft-sculpture dolls, which are a bit oddly shaped and also have to do with issues of letting darker sides be seen and accepted."

- "I've found that I have to be very discerning about whom I share my dolls with, and even then it can be a raw experience. I've been fortunate to study art therapy, and they drummed into us the importance of the person-centered approach. The therapist is always attempting to enter and understand the world of the client and the meaning of any symbology is based on the client's perspective. Of course the therapist may have ideas and perceptions about what they are seeing, and these may be offered with respect, but always with ownership: 'What I see is . . .' or 'This reminds me of . . .' or 'When I see this, I feel . . .' This takes the sting of judgment out. The client can then choose whether the additional information enlarges their sense of meaning. Ultimately, it will be helpful to discern whom you share your dolls with and whom you ask for the kind of feedback you want. For instance, ask your witness, 'What do you see/feel/etc. when you see this doll?' I share my dolls with very few and only with those whom I can trust to be open, compassionate, and kind."

Before you decide to show your doll to others, it would be useful to sit with your doll and have her speak her truth. Allow the decision to come from this relationship. She is an image of your wisdom and knowing, and in the end, that is what is most valuable.

Gaia, Centered and Grounded
Barb Kobe

Earth Dance
Barb Kobe

215

Fire Element Bowl
Barb Kobe

Making Dolls for Others

Once you've completed the *Healing Doll Way* process, you may decide you'd like to make a healing doll for someone. When someone in your life is sick or in pain, making a healing doll for that person can bring you some relief from the feeling of helplessness. Here are some guidelines and insight for creating a healing doll for another person:

- All art has the potential to produce an emotional response that will alter body chemistry, which will, in turn, affect metabolic functioning. This goes for you, the maker, as well as for the viewer and the receiver.

- A positive emotional response can activate the release of healing endorphins and boost the immune system.

- As the maker of the healing doll, you must be conscious of your intentions for making the doll for another.

- Ask yourself why you need the recipient to heal. This is vitally important. Perhaps begin by making a doll for yourself that explores your feelings about the recipient's situation.

- Art can be considered "prayer made tangible," so it is important to be sure your intentions are directed toward the highest good of the other person.

- Both you and the recipient must understand that healing dolls are not "magic" and cannot cure the healing issue for the recipient.

- Let your intentions and creativity guide you.

If you do want to make a doll for someone, please follow these guidelines:

- First, ask permission from the person for whom the doll is intended. It is a request to connect to the source of all things. Understand that this petition opens a healing presence within you and the recipient.

- Get some basic information from the recipient in order to establish an energy connection. Ask the recipient questions about his/her wound (the illness or challenge for which they need healing). What colors, shapes, stories, or fairy tales does he/she associate with the wound? Why does the recipient believe he/she has the wound? And most important, what will his/her life look like (ask for images) after he/she moves through the pain and is healed?

I highly suggest you use The Ten Questions I developed just for this purpose (page 222). Use the recipient's answers to help you design the doll.

Carrying Her Truth
Barb Kobe

Different Types of Dolls to Make for Others

Healing dolls require deep emotional exploration and contemplation, whether you make them for yourself or others. If you'd like to make a doll for someone, you may want a simpler approach. There are other kinds of "helping" dolls you can make that are simpler than healing dolls, yet they too have the potential to create some change in the recipient:

Symbolic Dolls – Symbolize what you hope or wish will happen for healing to take place. These dolls provide a nonintrusive way to focus energy and efforts. They can be given as gifts or symbolic prayers. Remember, though: what you choose as a symbol may not be meaningful for the recipient.

Caring and Comforting Dolls – Designed to give comfort, encouragement, and support. These dolls' designs and images may be similar to what you might find on a supportive greeting card. The Loving Kindness doll might be a good example.

Inspirational Dolls – Created specifically as a source of inspiration, strength, hope, joy, and love. You can begin making one of these dolls without a specific intention in mind; one may develop during creation. Many times, the dolls have stories of their own, and the doll and the story will be inspirational to others.

Collaborative or Cocreation Dolls – Dolls you make with others. You may make the dolls to give to your fellow collaborators, or you can give them to other people. This collaboration can be in the form of a cocreation or a round-robin. With cocreation, a group of dollmakers work on one doll for one specific recipient. (Be sure you set a timeline, so doll is made in a timely manner.) With the round-robin approach, each dollmaker in the group makes a blank doll body, then sends it to another member of the group. The second person adds something to the doll—costume, hair, embellishment—before sending it on to the next person. Each doll continues around the group until each member has added something. Each completed doll is then returned to the member who created the original body. Sometimes these dolls carry journals so each artist can write her thoughts as the doll travels around.

Subtle Activism Dolls – You might also want to make a subtle activism doll for yourself or others. This is an opportunity to combine dollmaking with social consciousness. Subtle activism is an activity of consciousness or spirit—such as prayer, meditation, or artmaking—intended to support collective healing and social change. The developers of the Gaiafield Project say that "Subtle Activism grows from the idea that there are many effective ways—some newly emerging, many as old as humanity—to positively influence social change other than overt political action." Making a doll focused on social change—such as peace, climate change, or environmental issues—can contribute to the healing of any global or collective concern.

Wise Woman with Basket
Barb Kobe

She Who Heals
Barb Kobe

217

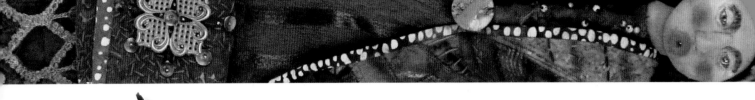

What If You Haven't Started the Process?

By the time you reach these last pages of the book, you should have completed the *Healing Doll Way* process. You have made four or five dolls, perhaps more; completed the journaling; and shared your dolls with your believing mirror or a supportive and creative healing practitioner, friend, or safe community member. You feel as if you have reached your intention, and some aspect of yourself feels healed. You are wondering what's next.

Let's be honest, though. Maybe you eagerly bought the book, loved looking at the pictures of the healing dolls, read through the whole process, and considered making a doll . . . but haven't. I confess I've done this as well. I've pored over beautiful art books with how-to, do-it-yourself instructions and then never followed through. I've also done this with online classes.

There are lots of reasons people do this. Sometimes we want to make the art but hesitate. Maybe we have questions but fear contacting the teacher or author. Sometimes we believe we lack the skills to make the art. Sometimes we tell ourselves we don't have the time, or we're just not willing to commit to the time and process. In this particular case, maybe you worry you can't make dolls that look like those in this book.

These are all challenging issues to deal with by yourself. If you want to make these kinds of healing dolls, then I suggest you sign up for the yearlong Healing Doll Way online class. The class includes information from this book and so much more. It is a deep dive into all the ways dollmaking can be healing, with the added benefit of support from others on the same journey as you. The people in my classes often make lifelong friends. Visit my website for more details.

What you'll need to feel successful in the online class:

- Some technology skills so can you message members of the private Facebook group.

- Some basic photography skills so you can share your dolls online with the group.

- Basic skills in artmaking and dollmaking, including sewing by hand or machine. However, many of these dolls can be made with paper, glue, staples, and tape. Revisit the Discovery section of this book for more tips about doll-making basics.

- A willingness to take creative risks and be vulnerable as you share feelings and thoughts with others.

Whether you enroll in the class or not, I welcome you to join the The Healing Doll Way Book Club on Facebook and share your healing art, doll photos, and stories with other makers of healing dolls around the world.

Bird Whisperer
Barb Kobe

Coming Home to Yourself

Is this the end? Do you feel healed? Transformed? Enlightened? Will you make more dolls? There is no way for me to know the answers to these questions—only you will know. What I do know is that making healing dolls can change your life. It changed mine. There may be another way to move through the *Healing Doll Way* process and that is to see it as a quest story or a heroine's journey.

Seeing the Healing Doll Way as a Quest Story

As you near the end of this process, it may be helpful and insightful to see the Healing Doll Way as a quest for healing, a journey or walking a healing path. Through this lens, the healing dolls you have created can be seen as allies, tricksters, shadowy characters, and angels that played vital roles along the path toward your healing intention.

Doll Shrine
Barb Kobe

In his book *The Wounded Storyteller*, Arthur W. Frank defined quest stories as "stories that meet suffering head on; they accept illness and seek to use it. Illness is the occasion of a journey that becomes a quest." In a quest, you—the seeker of healing—have a voice and tell your own story. I was introduced to this concept by a therapist during a time I was experiencing symptoms of perimenopause. My daughter was sixteen, and I was feeling grief and a disconnection from her. I decided to see a therapist to help me process my emotions. At the end of the first session, the therapist told me that she called this midlife time for women "Coming Home to Herself."

The researcher that I am, I searched for "Coming Home to Herself" online. I found an article called "Celebrating the Change" by Melissa West. She said most women "go through a similar period of major transition in our forties and fifties and that by honoring it as initiation into a powerful way of life, one moves into the way of wisdom." She defines the way of wisdom as seeing "the patterns that connect the pieces, the great rounds of birth and death and rebirth . . . wisdom is from the heart and soul." This initiation celebrates and supports a major life transition and changes one's relationship with the sacred and with the community, birthing a new self. I thought, "What, this isn't just normal aging and child separation? It has a bigger purpose? Then I read, "Rituals are powerful ways to honor the physical, emotional and spiritual changes. The most meaningful are those someone designs herself, trusting her own creativity." I was game!

It was during my time in therapy that I began to reframe my experience as a path or quest to find my true self as a healing artist. The dolls became players in the story I was living and telling myself.

Celebrating Winter Soltice
Barb Kobe

219

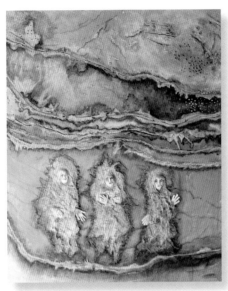

Three Muses in Journey
Barb Kobe

Books about journeys:

The Heroine's Journey
by Maureen Murdock

The Wounded Storyteller:
Body, Illness, and Ethics
by Arthur W. Frank

Wisdom Walks in Circles: The Spiraling
Journey of Your Inner Voice
by Margaret Hart Lewis

Women Who Run With Wolves
by Clarissa Pinkola Estes

Many books are available on the
Hero's Journey

Coming Home to Herself
Barb Kobe

Melissa West says these tasks of a developmental stage come in three parts:

1. Leaving Home – Leaving what is known, often feeling grief, disorientation, pain and anxiety.

2. Wilderness Time – Unknown, wrestle with old stories, shadow parts, surrendering to life cycle, etc.

3. Coming Home to Self – Birth of new self, integration of renewed or new power).

I asked myself, "You mean there's a pattern? A way to find meaning to this midlife experience." Can you see how the Healing Doll Way is a quest with three parts to the story? It begins with a departure from what is known before stepping onto a road paved with trials, tricksters, and allies, all leading you back home. By the end, you'll have discovered you are your own creative healer.

Lissa Rankin, MD, says:

> *Healing into a journey is a quest where you are the one authoring your experience. It is a destination that can last a lifetime. The context of the journey will affect your body, mind, emotions and spirit. It will influence your decisions and whether you access your Inner Healer.*

The stories you tell yourself will define the direction you travel and whether you see yourself as a victim or self-empowered. You may have guides and allies, but true healing is guided by you. When you have a relationship with yourself and see yourself on a journey, it is much more possible for the intuitive voice of the Inner Healer to reveal what needs to happen next and how it can happen.

Rankin says:

> *Your wound is like the specific object yielding to the force of your desired intention moving through the vehicle of your Inner Healer. The stored healing potential gets activated and begins to be transformed into the motion of healing. It is your decision to become a conscious co-creator with your Inner Healer.*

Learning about quests and the Hero's Journey changed the way I approached my art and my life. My dolls became game players as I moved around an invisible game board moving toward my healing intention. I invite you to play with these "Coming Home to Yourself" ideas and let me know what happens to you in the process.

Watch for a new Healing Doll Way journey map guidebook in the near future.

Cat Shaman
Barb Kobe

Appendix

The Ten Questions

If you plan to make a healing doll for someone, ask the recipient the following ten questions and get her or his responses before you begin. Use the responses to inform your making of the healing doll. You can also use these questions to assist in the design of your own healing dolls.

1. What colors are you drawn to? Do you wear often? Are your favorites?

2. What will this doll symbolize for you? What will it remind you to think, feel, and/or do when you see it?

3. What elements describe you? Earth, air, water, fire?

4. What symbols do you like or are you drawn to? What objects do you collect or like to spend time around?

5. What part of your body do you feel needs healing? Describe the symptoms and location of the pain, illness, or condition.

6. If an animal with special powers were to enter your life to give you power, what would that animal be?

7. When do you feel the most powerful? The most connected to yourself? The most comfortable in your skin? Self-loving and compassionate?

8. What makes you feel safe? Loved? Connected to self, others, universe? When do you feel the most vulnerable?

9. What brings you the greatest joy? Makes your heart sing? What does your heart yearn for?

10. What is your favorite fairy tale? Explain how this fairy tale is a metaphor for your life. (When I want to research the meaning[s] of a story, fairy tale, or myth, I do an internet search using the name of the story coupled with words like *meaning, spirit, metaphor, journey, hero* or *heroine.*)

Feeling Research

I designed this feeling research instrument while using my feelings puppets and dolls in adult workshops about emotional intelligence. You can use this list of questions to conduct feeling research with yourself, family, and friends. It may create a great dialogue and wonderful insights. The goal is to discover a variety of perceptions and beliefs about feelings. It can also build empathy skills.

Choose one feeling—such as anger, sadness, happiness, or fear—and answer the following questions as they relate to that feeling. There are no right or wrong answers.

- This feeling happens when _____.

- How is this feeling useful?

- Do you need this feeling to survive?

- Is it okay to express this feeling in a classroom? At home? At work? What would happen if you did?

- Can you learn if you are experiencing this feeling?

- Can you be honest when you are feeling this way?

- What does this feeling look like? Sound like? Feel like in the body? Smell like? Taste like?

- How do you show you are feeling this way?

Feeling Faces Exercise

Draw or paint ten feeling faces. You can follow the examples shown on page 225. Draw them first, studying the lines in the eyes, eyebrows, and mouth. Or you can look in a mirror, make your own feeling faces, and then draw what you see.

Cut the eyes, eyebrows, and mouths from the faces, then mix and match the features to create new faces. What feelings do you now see? Do they express feelings you recognize?

If you're up for a real challenge, take digital pictures of yourself making feeling faces. Hold the camera at arm's distance from your face and click away. (You can always delete the ones you don't like.) Once you get a few you like, print them out and make paper dolls with them. Position each doll's body in ways that express and exaggerate the feelings of its face. Choose colors and shapes that also help express the feeling.

Feeling Face Paper Dolls

Photocopy or print out the paper doll faces, body parts, and heads on the next three pages. Cut them all out and glue/tape a face on each head. (There are some extra blank heads on which you can draw custom faces).

Assemble the body parts (a hole punch and round-head brass fasteners from any office supply story make for an easy, posable figure). Play with putting each feeling face head on your paper doll and position its body parts to mirror the feeling on the face.

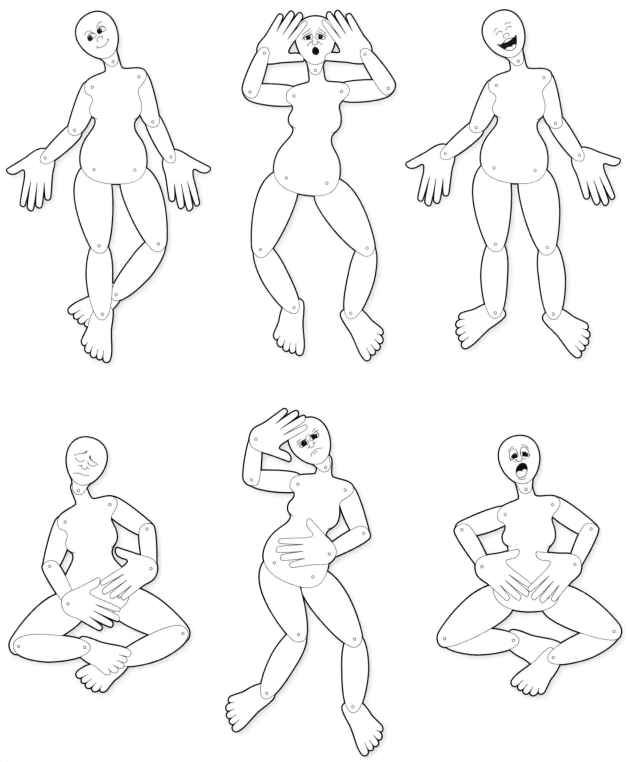

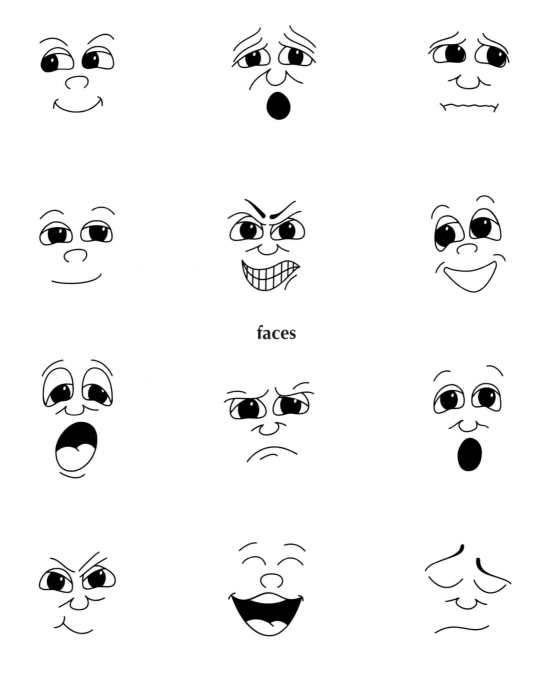

faces

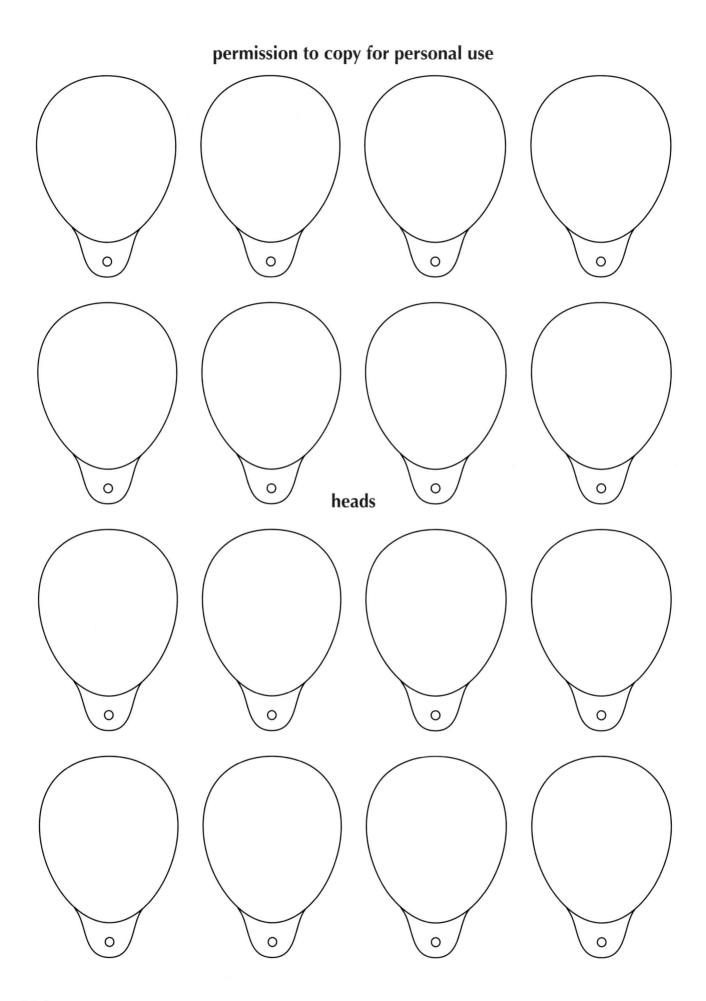

heads

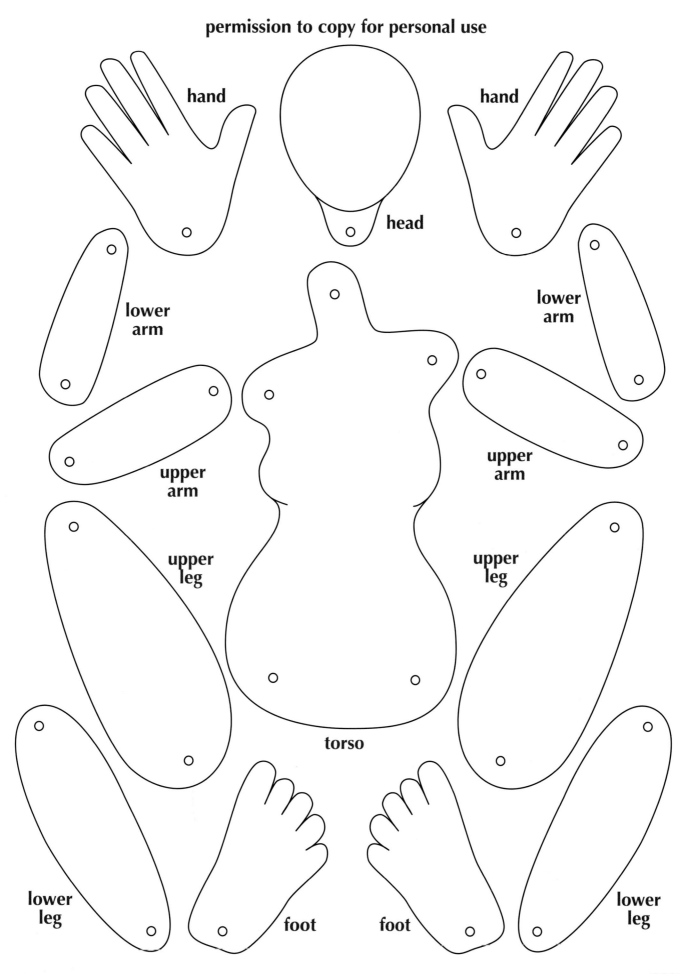

hand

head

hand

lower
arm

lower
arm

upper
arm

upper
arm

upper
leg

upper
leg

torso

lower
leg

foot

foot

lower
leg

permission to copy for personal use

HEALING PRESCRIPTION

FOR: _____   FROM: _____

AILMENT: _____   DATE: _____

Rx

- [ ] MAKE ART
- [ ] MEDITATION
- [ ] CALL FRIEND
- [ ] JOURNAL
- [ ] CHILL PILL
- [ ] DAY OFF
- [ ] GOOD CRY
- [ ] SHOPPING
- [ ] VACATION
- [ ] LAUGHTER
- [ ] MASSAGE
- [ ] EXERCISE
- [ ] YUMMY TREAT
- [ ] HUG
- [ ] REHAB
- [ ] OTHER

SPECIAL INSTRUCTIONS

DOSAGE: _____
- [ ] PER HOUR
- [ ] PER WEEK
- [ ] PER DAY
- [ ] PER MONTH

DURATION: _____
- [ ] HOURS
- [ ] WEEKS
- [ ] DAYS
- [ ] MONTHS

REFILLS: _____
- [ ] ZERO
- [ ] TWO
- [ ] ONE
- [ ] THREE

SIGNATURE _____

HEALING PRESCRIPTION

FOR: _____   FROM: _____

AILMENT: _____   DATE: _____

Rx

- [ ] MAKE ART
- [ ] MEDITATION
- [ ] CALL FRIEND
- [ ] JOURNAL
- [ ] CHILL PILL
- [ ] DAY OFF
- [ ] GOOD CRY
- [ ] SHOPPING
- [ ] VACATION
- [ ] LAUGHTER
- [ ] MASSAGE
- [ ] EXERCISE
- [ ] YUMMY TREAT
- [ ] HUG
- [ ] REHAB
- [ ] OTHER

SPECIAL INSTRUCTIONS

DOSAGE: _____
- [ ] PER HOUR
- [ ] PER WEEK
- [ ] PER DAY
- [ ] PER MONTH

DURATION: _____
- [ ] HOURS
- [ ] WEEKS
- [ ] DAYS
- [ ] MONTHS

REFILLS: _____
- [ ] ZERO
- [ ] TWO
- [ ] ONE
- [ ] THREE

SIGNATURE _____

HEALING PRESCRIPTION

FOR: _____   FROM: _____

AILMENT: _____   DATE: _____

Rx

- [ ] MAKE ART
- [ ] MEDITATION
- [ ] CALL FRIEND
- [ ] JOURNAL
- [ ] CHILL PILL
- [ ] DAY OFF
- [ ] GOOD CRY
- [ ] SHOPPING
- [ ] VACATION
- [ ] LAUGHTER
- [ ] MASSAGE
- [ ] EXERCISE
- [ ] YUMMY TREAT
- [ ] HUG
- [ ] REHAB
- [ ] OTHER

SPECIAL INSTRUCTIONS

DOSAGE: _____
- [ ] PER HOUR
- [ ] PER WEEK
- [ ] PER DAY
- [ ] PER MONTH

DURATION: _____
- [ ] HOURS
- [ ] WEEKS
- [ ] DAYS
- [ ] MONTHS

REFILLS: _____
- [ ] ZERO
- [ ] TWO
- [ ] ONE
- [ ] THREE

SIGNATURE _____

HEALING PRESCRIPTION

FOR: _____   FROM: _____

AILMENT: _____   DATE: _____

Rx

- [ ] MAKE ART
- [ ] MEDITATION
- [ ] CALL FRIEND
- [ ] JOURNAL
- [ ] CHILL PILL
- [ ] DAY OFF
- [ ] GOOD CRY
- [ ] SHOPPING
- [ ] VACATION
- [ ] LAUGHTER
- [ ] MASSAGE
- [ ] EXERCISE
- [ ] YUMMY TREAT
- [ ] HUG
- [ ] REHAB
- [ ] OTHER

SPECIAL INSTRUCTIONS

DOSAGE: _____
- [ ] PER HOUR
- [ ] PER WEEK
- [ ] PER DAY
- [ ] PER MONTH

DURATION: _____
- [ ] HOURS
- [ ] WEEKS
- [ ] DAYS
- [ ] MONTHS

REFILLS: _____
- [ ] ZERO
- [ ] TWO
- [ ] ONE
- [ ] THREE

SIGNATURE _____

Nature-Walk Ritual: Gathering Allies and Insights

The natural world is a great guide and teacher, providing a rich source of images and symbols to draw on. Native wisdom traditions teach that each part of nature holds a healing energy we can easily access by taking quiet time and asking for guidance. The nature-walk ritual is just that, an invitation for the natural world to offer guidance and wisdom. It is a request for powerful support and energy. It is an opportunity to experience an affirmation of your path.

Use the nature-walk ritual to ask for guidance on any question or about these seven key areas of life: 1) career, 2) finances, 3) health and well-being, 4) friends and family, 5) spiritual and personal growth, 6) fun and recreation, 7) home and office. Focus on one area per day, per walk, to hold the context of ritual. There is no rush. Here are some guidelines:

1. Take time before your walk to become quiet and still within. Do whatever is necessary to disengage from pressing mental activity. One way to do this is to do some deep breathing, sitting in a relaxed position with eyes closed. Another is to do a "brain dump" of all mundane "have-tos" dancing through your head. Imagine all the mental busyness floating off in a hot air balloon.

2. Drive or walk to a place where you can have pleasing contact with the natural world. Maybe it's a favorite place you've been before or somewhere new you'd like to explore. Once you arrive at your starting point, become centered once again and remind yourself of the area you have chosen to focus on. Create an intention to receive guidance and/or spiritual allies to help you with that area of focus. Then set off on your walk with a spirit of curiosity and faith that signs and symbols will be revealed to you.

3. Trust that guidance comes in many forms. You may be called to pick up an object—perhaps a rock, a colorful feather, a shell, a thistle, a shard of glass. You may see an inner image or insight triggered by a sunrise, a scent carried on the breeze, a random sighting of a fox or a bird that insists on being noticed. Be open and alert to whatever shows up. Allow your path to guide you lovingly and surely.

Time to Reflect

When your walk is complete, take some quiet time to record anything that "came to you" during the walk. If you picked up an object, spend some time with it. What message does it carry? What help does it offer? Once you are clear about the guidance you have received, determine if any action needs to be taken. How will you keep the wisdom present in your daily life?

Creative Art and Healing Theories

In my research on dollmaking and healing, I have embraced these theories that support dollmaking as a healing modality.

Art Therapy

The fundamental principal of art therapies is that they provide opportunities to make concrete objects that represent feelings and thoughts that are elusive, hidden, and mysterious. The process of the artmaking, as well as final product of the art itself, offers something to dialogue about and with. This is less threatening than talking about the difficulties directly. Artmaking can clear away emotional debris; allow you to embrace pain, wound, or illness; and reclaim your wholeness.

Expressive Arts Therapy

This emphasizes the artistic process as a means of emotional expression and release. It is similar to art therapy and may use dance, movement, narrative, and poetry to help a person open up and heal. The artwork is not used as a diagnostic tool because it is believed that only the person who created the work knows the meaning inherent in it.

Stress Reduction

Scientific studies tell us that art heals by changing a person's physiology and attitude. The body's physiology changes from one of stress to one of deep relaxation, from one of fear to one of creativity and inspiration. All the fine arts—including visual art, music, dance, and writing—put a person into a different brain wave pattern. They affect the autonomic nervous system, hormonal balance, and brain neurotransmitters.

Psychoneuroimmunology

Psychoneuroimmunology is the science of how thoughts and emotions influence health. The underlying theory of this science is that the body, mind, and spirit are interconnected; an individual cannot treat one without affecting another. It also suggests that ultimate healing must come from within the individual, that we all have a mind and a soul that influences and creates who we are—even our illness. This also means our minds have an equal capacity to make us well. Scientists endorsing this theory study the impact of emotions on the central nervous and immune systems. They have proven that painful emotions that remain unresolved and unexpressed for long periods of time have a direct and measurable effect on the immune system and the development of illness and disease. Candace Pert, author of *Molecules of Emotion*, challenged conventional science and those in the total-wellness field to reconsider how our bodies think, feel, and heal. She suggests that "where emotions are instigated is also where unexpressed emotions are stored. The catharsis of illness expresses the sudden, overwhelming release of information that has been trapped in our bodies."

Imagery and Healing

This is commonly referred to as visualization; it works with the relationship between the body and the imagination. It is used as a tool in dream work, hypnosis, trance, biofeedback, and meditation. You will see this discussed along with left- and right-brain theory. We all share and associate with universal images dependent upon the culture we were raised in. Joseph Campbell, mythologist and writer, researched and wrote about this extensively.

Narrative Psychology

Narrative psychology asserts that the stories we tell about our lives contain all the clues for what we believe, what afflicts us, and how to heal. The details of the story are more important than a diagnosis, and the storytelling allows the person to search for the answers within details of the story.

Gate Control Theory of Pain Management

Dollmaker and occupational therapist Pamela Hastings talks about this theory in *Dollmaking as a Transformative Process*. According to the gate control theory of pain, our thoughts, beliefs, and emotions may affect how much pain we feel. The fundamental basis for this theory is the belief that psychological as well as physical factors guide the brain's interpretation of painful sensations and the subsequent response. For example, many athletes do not experience pain during the intense activity of the game. After the game, when they turn their attention to their injuries, the pain suddenly appears to come from nowhere. Many pain sufferers find their pain is worst when they feel depressed and hopeless—feelings that may open the pain gate—but that it's not so bothersome when they focus on something that demands attention or is enjoyable. Although the physical cause of pain may be identical, the perception of pain is dramatically different. Pam says, and I would agree, that blocking the pain with a "buzz," such as the mental involvement of dollmaking, can block out worries and pain, leaving space for the body to relax and heal itself.

Mindfulness Meditation

Mindfulness is a mental state achieved by focusing one's awareness on the present moment while calmly acknowledging and accepting one's feelings, thoughts, and bodily sensations. Whenever you bring awareness to what you're directly experiencing via your senses, or to your state of mind via your thoughts and emotions, you're being mindful. Growing research shows that when you train your brain to be mindful, you're actually remodeling the physical structure of your brain. This state of mind is accessed through meditation.

Resources

Books, Patterns, and Face Push Molds

Maureen Carlson
www.maureencarlson.com
> *Family and Friends in Polymer Clay*
> *Fairies, Gnomes & Trolls*
Online and in-person classes
Push molds for faces, hands & feet

Pamela Hastings
www.pamelahastings.com
> *Paper Doll Inspiration*
> *Pamela's Designing a Doll and Making Faces*
>   *Inspiration Book*
> *Dollmaking as a Transformative Process*
Kindle books on Amazon:
> *Pamela's Patterns*
> *Ancestor Making*
> *Icons and Angels*

Elinor Peace Bailey
www.epbdolls.com
www.fabric-chicks.com
> *Mother Plays with Dolls...and Finds an Important*
>   *Key to Unlocking Creativity*
> *The Rag Doll: From Plain to Fancy*
Many patterns; do an internet search to find them.

Susanna Oroyan
> *Anatomy of a Doll: The Fabric Sculptor's Handbook*
> *Designing the Doll: From Concept to Construction*
> *Finishing the Figure*

Cassandra Light
> *Way of the Doll: The Art and Craft of*
>   *Personal Transformation*

Linda and Opie O'Brien
> *Mixed-Media Doll Making: Redefining the Doll with*
>   *Upcycled Materials*

Noreen Crone-Findlay
> *Soul Mate Dolls: Dollmaking as a Healing Art*

Lisa Hertzi
www.artdolladventures.com

Patti Medaris Culea
www.pmcdesigns.com
> *Creative Cloth Doll Making: New Approaches for Using*
>   *Fibers, Beads, Dyes, and Other Exciting Techniques*
> *Creative Cloth Doll Faces: Using Paints, Pastels, Fibers,*
>   *Beading, Collage, and Sculpting Techniques*

Lynne Perrella
> *Beyond Paper Dolls: Expressive Paper Personas Crafted with*
>   *Innovative Techniques and Art Mediums*

Barbara Matthiessen, Nancy Hoerner, Rick Petersen
> *The Complete Photo Guide to Dollmaking: All You Need to*
>   *Know to Make Dolls*

Jenny Doh
> *We Make Dolls!: Top Dollmakers Share Their*
>   *Secrets and Patterns*

E. J. Taylor and Ilsa Willson
> *Dollmaking*

Martha Le Van
> *Making Creative Cloth Dolls*

Terry Taylor
> *Artful Paper Dolls: New Ways to Play with*
>   *a Traditional Form*

Magazines
> *Art Doll Quarterly Magazine*
> *Soft Dolls & Animals!*
> *Prims Magazine*
> (All these magazines have been retired. Look for back issues
>   on Etsy, eBay and Pinterest)

Many more resources at www.barbkobe.com

Healing Doll Artists and Teachers Who Have Taken the Healing Dolls Class

Kathryn Hall
Longmont, Colorado

Kathryn is a retired counselor and casework supervisor with the Illinois Department of Corrections. She has a BA degree in child, family, and community services. She formerly held certifications in substance abuse counseling and elementary education. Kathryn is a longtime student of Barb Kobe and is an artist in various media, with a special emphasis in dollmaking using sticks, fabric, polymer clay, wire, found objects, and natural and other materials. She primarily works intuitively to see who and what shows up, finding that nearly all dolls have a message to share, a story to tell, and an insight to impart to the creator—all of which often result in personal healing. She is available to teach, guide, and encourage others through this process in small groups in the Boulder, Colorado, area and offers dolls and other artwork for sale. Some of her work may be seen on Facebook under HilaritasArtStudios/Kathryn Hall. She may also be reached through email.
kathrynatcrystal@aol.com

Christine K. Harris
Chesapeake, Virginia

Christine is a sculptor and art therapist. Key concepts from her art therapy training—including emphasizing process over product and using art as a vehicle for self-expression—are important in her artwork. She is inspired by mythology, nature, the animal world, scary movies, and thrift stores.
http://www.christinekharris.com

Maureen Carlson
Jordan, Minnesota

Maureen is an artist, author, storyteller, spiritual director, deep listener, and workshop facilitator. She and her husband, Dan, through their business Wee Folk Creations, have produced a series of push molds to help people get past the fear of sculpting faces and move on with the creative process of telling their own stories through their dolls. Maureen specializes in classes that help people bridge the gap between how-to and what-for. Two of her how-to books are especially helpful for dollmakers: *Family and Friends in Polymer Clay* and *Fairies, Gnomes & Trolls*, both published by North Light Books.
maureen@weefolk.com
www.maureencarlson.com

Anne Heck
Asheville, North Carolina

Anne Reeder Heck is a writer, speaker, healer, and artist who is devoted to inspiring and guiding others to trust themselves, open to their intuitive guidance, and experience the magic of life through ceremony, positive intention, and a creative, curious spirit. Her series of healing dolls has been an inspiration for much of her work, and they're highlighted in her memoir, *A Fierce Belief in Miracles: My Journey from Rape to Healing and Wholeness.* This book offers guidance and solace for those seeking healing and ready to explore paths of forgiveness and spirituality. Anne offers workshops and teachings in person and online.
www.anneheck.com/
www.facebook.com/anne.heck
www.instagram.com/anneheck1/

Lisa Fam
Melbourne, Australia

Lisa is an artist, art therapist, and healing doll maker who finds inspiration in the beauty of nature and the mysteries of the soul. She facilitates art therapy and dollmaking workshops for people from all walks of life. Her current series of Seasons of the Doll workshops focus on how understanding of the seasons and cycles of nature and applying this wisdom to our lives can be healing and transformative for ourselves and the planet. Lisa is also available to create a custom-made healing doll for you or a loved one.
www.lisafam.wordpress.com
www.seasonsofthedoll.wordpress.com
www.facebook.com/misshappinessflower

Erika Cleveland
Washington, DC

Erika is an artist, writer, and former art therapist. Through her healing dolls, her mission is to be a channel of healing for women in transition. She is at that stage of life—having recently hit fifty—where priorities shift and what once

Healing Doll Artists and Teachers Who Have Taken the Healing Dolls Class (cont.)

seemed important has changed. She says, "To be perfectly honest, change terrifies me, and so I am living the phrase, 'Teach what you most need to learn.'"
www.transformativehealingdolls.com

Rita Benson
Oshawa, Ontario, Canada
Rita is a Healing Doll Artist, Registered SoulCollage Facilitator, Registered Social Worker, and Registered Marriage & Family Therapist. While not currently taking any new therapy clients, she offers workshops and retreats that utilize art and healing processes and mindfulness meditation.
rita@willingspirits.com

Chris Hammer
New York, New York
Chris is an artist, dollmaker, teacher, somatic therapist, and poet. Her dolls range from transformative and healing to whimsical. She teaches classes that combine artmaking with personal discovery. No matter what your skill level, she can teach you techniques to make personal art dolls.
moomahamma@hotmail.com
www.bodymindmatters.com

Delphine Roch-Louvion, MA
North Brittany, France
Delphine calls herself a "practitioner of the imagination." She is an artist, teacher, and group facilitator that helps people rewrite their stories using arts, crafts, rituals, and narrative works so they can access their emotions and learn from them. Her studies and contributions to the healing doll process include art history, archeology, ethnology/ anthropology, storytelling, intuition, shamanism, fine arts, and women's studies.
brigha.poupee@gmail.com
www.poupeedemoi.com

Sharon Riley
New Brunswick, Canada
Sharon is a fiber artist and dollmaker focussing on nature and primitive art forms. She uses stitching, beading, and unique textural elements in each of her handmade creations. She created a series of Mother Earth dolls called Healing Voices to explore her own journey along with her love for the planet. In the nineties, she began creating workshops for women using dollmaking as a tool to help heal and empower them. More information about upcoming workshops can be viewed on her website.
www.whisperofspirit.com

Cat Caracelo, MA
Petaluma, California
(Details on page 235)
www.CatCaracelo.com
www.JourneyPathInstitute.com

Professional Teaching Artist, Coaches, Counselors, and Therapists

Julia Inglis
Sherbrooke Forest, Australia

Julia's work centers around ancestral folklore, dollmaking, folk magic, and the healing power of stories.
www.sacredfamiliar.com

Lani A. Gerity, PhD, DA, ATR
Ottawa, Canada

Lani is a puppet-maker, author, world traveler, and a trained art therapist with a master's degree and a doctorate from NYU. She studied with Edith Kramer and edited Edith's last book, *Art as Therapy: Collected Papers*. Lani's passions have led her to search out, explore, and teach workshops in nontraditional art forms like dollmaking, puppet-making, and bookbinding. She maintains a website, blogs, and online groups filled with encouragement and alternative arts for artists, art therapists, and art educators.
www.lanipuppetmaker.com
http://topsecretannex.blogspot.com/

Cat Caracelo, MA
Petaluma, California

Cat's education includes an BA in psychology and an MA in transformative arts and consciousness studies, with extensive training and mentoring with New York Times bestselling author and coach Debbie Ford. Cat works with cross-cultural myth, depth psychology, dream work, shamanic journeying, and creative visualization, which is woven into her work as she guides the "art and life" process. Incorporating art as a powerful intuitive and complementary practice, Cat offers guidance and support for creative inquiry and life design.
www.CatCaracelo.com
www.JourneyPathInstitute.com

Fonda Clark Haight
North Carolina

Fonda is a mixed-media artist and teacher. Her goal is to inspire those who see her work to look more carefully at the world around them, to discover beauty in unusual places, and to question the truth in themselves.
fonda@restonline.com
www.fondaclarkhaight.com

Gunhild Lorenzen
Mer, France

Gunhild is a speaker, author, intuitive energy field reader, life guide, artist, and teacher. Besides individual guidance, she does workshops and presentations on creativity, consciousness, and dreams in Europe, Asia, and Australia.
info@gunhildlorenzen.com
www.gunhildlorenzen.com

Marney Makridakis
Dallas, Texas

Marney is the founder of the online creativity community Artella Land, which since 2002 has been inspiring artists, writers, and creative spirits and supporting them in following their dreams. Her "Complete Idealist" series and ARTbundance™ Certification Training Program are examples of Marney's drive to help creative-minded people do exactly what she did: design a successful business rooted in true passion, personal joy, and creative meaning.
www.artellaland.com

Bibliography

Achterberg, Jeanne. *Imagery in Healing: Shamanism and Modern Medicine.* Boston: Shambhala Publications, 1985.

Achterberg, Jeanne and G. Frank Lawlis. *Bridges of the Bodymind: Behavioral Approaches to Health Care.* Champaign, IL: Institute for Personality and Ability Testing, Inc., 1980.

Allen, Pat B. *Art Is a Way of Knowing: A Guide to Self-Knowledge and Spiritual Fulfillment through Creativity.* New York: Shambhala Publications, 1995.

———. *Art Is a Spiritual Path: Engaging the Sacred through the Practice of Art and Writing.* New York: Shambhala Publications, 2005.

Aronie, Nancy Slonim. *Writing from the Heart: Tapping the Power of Your Inner Voice.* New York: Hyperion, 1998.

Arrien, Angeles. *The Four-Fold Way: Walking the Paths of the Warrior, Teacher, Healer, and Visionary.* San Francisco, CA: HarperSanFrancisco, 1993.

Avila, Elena. *Woman Who Glows in the Dark: A Curandera Reveals Traditional Aztec Secrets of Physical and Spiritual Health.* New York: Jeremy P. Tarcher/Putnam, 1999.

Bailey, Elinor Peace. *Mother Plays with Dolls...and Finds an Important Key to Unlocking Creativity.* McLean, Virginia: EPM Publications, Inc., 1990.

———. *The Doll as a Messenger.* Self-published, 2004.

———. *Dollmaking, A Body Language: Using the Human Form as a Pathway to Self-Expression.* Self-published booklet. Hayward, CA, 2004.

Barasch, Marc. *The Healing Path: A Soul Approach to Illness.* Los Angeles: G.P. Putnam's Sons, 1993.

Biro, David. *Listening to Pain: Finding Words, Compassion, and Relief.* New York: W.W. Norton, 2010.

Bolen, Jean Shinoda. *Close to the Bone: Life-Threatening Illness and the Search for Meaning.* New York: Shribner, 1996.

Borysenko, Joan. *Minding the Body, Mending the Mind.* Reading, MA: Addison-Wesley, 1987.

Brenner, Paul. *Buddha in the Waiting Room: Simple Truths about Health, Illness, and Healing.* Hillsboro, OR: Beyond Words Publishing, 2002.

Brown, Brené. *Daring Greatly: How the Courage to Be Vulnerable Transforms the Way We Live, Love, Parent, and Lead.* New York, NY: Gotham Books, 2012.

Cameron, Julia. *Vein of Gold: A Journey to Your Creative Heart.* New York: Putnam Books, 1996.

Capacchione, Lucia. *The Power of the Other Hand.* North Hollywood, CA: Newcastle Publishing Company, 1988.

Chopra, Deepak. *Spiritual Solutions: Answers to Life's Greatest Challenges.* New York: Harmony Books, 2012.

Cohen, Gene D. *The Creative Age: Awakening Human Potential in the Second Half of Life.* New York: Avon Books, 2000.

Craighead, Meinrad. *Crow Mother and the Dog God: A Retrospective.* San Francisco: Pomegranate Publishers, 2003.

Crone-Findley, Noreen. *Soul Mate Dolls: Dollmaking as a Healing Art.* Iola, WI: Krause Publications, 2000.

Dacher, Elliott S. *Whole Healing: A Step-by-Step Program to Reclaim Your Power to Heal.* New York, New York: Penguin Group, 1996.

Dossey, Larry. *Healing Beyond the Body: Medicine and the Infinite Reach of the Mind.* Boston: Shambhala Publications, 2001.

Eden, Donna. *Energy Medicine: Balancing Your Body's Energies for Optimal Health, Joy, and Vitality.* New York : Jeremy P. Tarcher/Penguin, 2008.

Estés, Clarissa Pinkola. *Women Who Run with the Wolves*. New York: Ballantine Books, 1995.

Ford, Debbie. *The Dark Side of the Light Chasers*. New York: Riverhead Books, 1998.

Fox, John. *Poetic Medicine: The Healing Art of Poem-Making*. New York: Penguin Putnam, 1997.

Frank, Arthur W. *The Wounded Storyteller: Body, Illness, and Ethics*. Chicago: University of Chicago Press, 1995.

Frazer, James George. *The Golden Bough*. Harmondsworth, England; New York: Penguin Books, 1996.

Ganim, Barbara. *Art and Healing: Using Expressive Art to Heal Your Body, Mind and Spirit*. New York: Three Rivers Press, 1999.

———. *Drawing from the Heart: A Seven-Week Program to Heal Emotional Pain and Loss through Expressive Art*. Wheaton, IL: Quest Books, 2004.

Ganim, Barbara and Susan Fox. *Visual Journaling: Going Deeper than Words*. Wheaton, IL: Quest Books, 1999.

Gerity, Lani A. and Edith Kramer. *Creativity and the Dissociative Patient: Puppets, Narrative and Art in the Treatment of Survivors of Childhood Trauma*. London: Jessica Kingsley, 1999.

Nhat Hanh, Thich. *No Death, No Fear: Comforting Wisdom for Life*. New York: Riverhead Books, 2002.

Hastings, Pamela. *Dollmaking as a Transformative Process*. Saugerties, NY: self-published book, 2003.

Jette, Christine. *Tarot for the Healing Heart: Using Inner Wisdom to Heal Body and Mind*. St. Paul, MN: Llewellyn Publications, 2001.

Keleman, Stanley. *Your Body Speaks Its Mind*. Berkeley, CA: Center Press, 1981.

Kidd, Sue Monk. *The Dance of the Dissident Daughter*. New York, NY: HarperOne, 2006.

Kieves, Tama J. *This Time I Dance!: Creating the Work You Love*. New York: Tarcher/Penguin, 2006.

Laskow, Leonard. *Healing with Love*. Las Vegas, NV: Jesse Krieger, 2016.

Lawlis, G. Frank. *Transpersonal Medicine: A New Approach to Healing Body-Mind-Spirit*. Boston: Shambhala Publications, 1996.

Lewis, Margaret Hart. *Wisdom Walks in Circles: Spiraling Journey of Your Inner Voice*. Bloomington, IN: Self Published, 2004.

Light, Cassandra. *Way of the Doll: The Art and Craft of Personal Transformation*. San Francisco: Chronicle Books, 1996.

Longman, Robin. "Creating Art: Your Rx for Health Part I and II." *American Artist Magazine*. May and June 1994.

Mariah, Katelyn. *Empowered Health and Wellness: Awakening the Inner Physician*. St. Paul, MN: Mystick Creek Publishing, 2014.

Maisel, Eric. *Coaching the Artist Within: Advice for Writers, Actors, Visual Artists, and Musicians from America's Foremost Creativity Coach*. Novato, CA: New World Library, 2005.

Malchiodi, Cathy A. *The Soul's Palette: Drawing on Art's Transformative Powers for Health and Well-Being*. Boston: Shambhala Publications, 2002.

Markova, Dawna. *No Enemies Within*. Berkeley, CA: Conari Press, 1994.

McLaren, Karla. *The Language of Emotions: What Your Feelings Are Trying to Tell You*. Boulder, CO: Sounds True, 2010.

McNiff, Shaun. *Art as Medicine: Creating a Therapy of the Imagination*. Boston: Shambhala Publications, 1992.

———. *Art-Based Research*. London: Jessica Kingley Publishers, 1998.

———. *Imagination in Action: Secrets for Unleashing Creative Expression*. Boston: Shambhala Publications, 2015.

———. *Art Heals: How Creativity Cures the Soul*. Boston: Shambhala Publications, 1998.

Mehl-Madrona, Lewis. *Coyote Healing: Miracles in Native Medicine*. Rochester, VT: Bear and Company, 2003.

———. *Coyote Medicine: Lessons from Native American Healing*. New York, NY: Fireside, 1997.

Miller, William. *Your Golden Shadow: Discovering and Fulfilling Your Undeveloped Self*. New York, NY: HarperCollins, 1989.

Moon, Bruce L. *Art and Soul: Reflections on an Artistic Psychology*. Springfield, IL: Charles C. Thomas Publisher, 1997.

Muller, Wayne. *Legacy of the Heart: The Spiritual Advantages of a Painful Childhood*. New York: Simon & Schuster, 1992.

Myss, Caroline. *Sacred Contracts: Awakening Your Divine Potential*. New York: Harmony Books, 2001.

Northrup, Christiane. *Women's Bodies, Women's Wisdom*. New York: Bantam Books, 2010.

Orloff, Judith. *Dr. Judith Orloff's Guide to Intuitive Healing: 5 Steps to Physical, Emotional, and Sexual Wellness*. New York: Times Books, 2000.

Oroyan, Susanna. *Anatomy of a Doll: The Fabric Sculptor's Handbook*. Lafayette, CA: C&T Publishing, 1997.

Pavlik-Malone, Lisa. *Dolls & Clowns & Things: Essays for a Symbolic Self*. Newcastle, UK: Cambridge Scholars Publishing, 2011.

Rico, Gabriele. *Pain and Possibility: Writing Your Way Through Personal Crisis*. Los Angeles: Jeremy P. Tarcher, Inc., 1991.

———. *Writing the Natural Way: Turn the Task of Writing into the Joy of Writing*. New York: Jeremy P. Tarcher/Putnam, 2000.

Rogers, Natalie. *The Creative Connection: Expressive Arts as Healing*. Palo Alto, CA: Science & Behavior Books, Inc., 1993.

Samuels, Michael and Mary Rockwood Lane. *Creative Healing: How to Heal Yourself by Tapping Your Hidden Creativity*. San Franciso: HarperSanFrancisco, 1998.

Samples, Pat. *Body Odyssey: Lessons from the Bones and Belly*. Minneapolis, MN: Syren Book Company, 2005.

Shepherd, Philip. *New Self, New World: Recovering Our Senses in the Twenty-First Century*. Berkeley, CA: North Atlantic Books, 2010.

Shepherd, Rowena. *1000 Symbols: What Shapes Mean in Art and Myth*. New York: Thames & Hudson, 2002.

Simpson, Liz. *The Book of Chakra Healing*. New York: Sterling Publishing Company, 1999.

Taylor, E. J. and Ilsa Willson. *Dollmaking*. New York: Workman Publishing, 1987.

Thornton, Shelley, editor. *NIADA Art Dolls: Rich Traditions, New Ideas*. The NIADA Foundation and the Susan Quinlan Museum, 2009.

von Boehn, Max. *Dolls*. New York: Dover Publications, Inc., 1972.

Wesselman, Hank and Jill Kuykendall. *Spirit Medicine: Healing in the Sacred Realms*. Carlsbad, CA: Hay House, Inc, 2004.

Wimberger, Lisa. *Neurosculpting: A Whole-Brain Approach to Heal Trauma, Rewrite Limiting Beliefs, and Find Wholeness*. Boulder, CO: Sounds True, 2014.

How Art Heals: Mind-Body Physiology

How does art heal? Scientific studies tell us that art heals by changing a person's physiology and attitude. The body's physiology changes from one of stress to one of deep relaxation, from one of fear to one of creativity and inspiration. Art and music put a person in a different brain wave pattern; art and music affect a person's autonomic nervous system, their hormonal balance and their brain neurotransmitters.

Art and music affect every cell in the body instantly to create a healing physiology that changes the immune system and blood flow to all the organs. Art and Music also immediately change a person's perceptions of their world. They change attitude, emotional state, and pain perception. They create hope and positivity and they help people cope with difficulties. They transform a person's outlook and way of being in the world.

In fact it is now known by neurophysiologists that art, prayer, and healing all come from the same source in the body, they all are associated with similar brain wave patterns, mind body changes and they all are deeply connected in feeling and meaning. Art, prayer, and healing all take us into our inner world, the world of imagery and emotion, of visions and feelings. This journey inward into what used to be called the spirit or soul and is now called the mind, is deeply healing. For healing comes to us from within, our own healing resources are freed to allow our immune system to operate optimally and that is always how we heal. This is the contemporary version of freeing our healing energies and is now recognized to be crucial to healing. We go inward on The Creative Spiral together through art and music.

www.artashealing.org

Professional Organizations

American Art Therapy Association
4875 Eisenhower Ave Suite 240, Alexandria, VA 22304
Look for state and country chapters
www.arttherapy.org

Americans for the Arts
1000 Vermont Avenue, NW, 6th FloorWashington, DC 20005
www.americansforthearts.org

National Coalition of Creative Arts Therapies Associations, Inc.
Check here for a list of many of the creative arts therapies
www.nccata.org

International Expressive Arts Therapy Association
www.ieata.org

Association of Teaching Artists
www.teachingartists.com

Association for Play Therapy
www.a4pt.org